earn

Access 97

Robert L. Ferrett

John Preston

Sally Preston

**que
E&T**

Learn Access 97

Library of Congress Catalog No: 97-68884

ISBN:1-57576-891-7

01 00 99 98   4 3 2 1

Screens reproduced in this book were created using Collage Plus from Inner Media, Inc., Hollis, NH.

Credits

Publisher:
Robert Linsky

Executive Editor:
Kyle Lewis

Series Editors:
Robert L. Ferrett,
John Preston, Sally Preston

Development Editor:
Custom Editorial Productions

Product Marketing Manager:
Susan L. Kindel

Managing Editor:
Caroline Roop

Team Coordinator:
Angela Denny

Designer:
Louisa Klucznik

Production Team:
Custom Editorial Productions

About the Authors

Robert L. Ferrett is the Director of the Center for Instructional Computing at Eastern Michigan University. His center provides computer training and support to faculty at the university. He has authored or co-authored nearly twenty books on Access, PowerPoint, Excel, and Word, and was the editor of the *1994 ACM SIGUCCS Conference Proceedings*. He has been designing, developing, and delivering computer workshops for more than a decade. He has a BA in Psychology, an MS in Geography, and an MS in Interdisciplinary Technology from Eastern Michigan University. He is ABD in the Ph.D. program in Instructional Technology at Wayne State University.

John Preston is an Associate Professor at Eastern Michigan University in the College of Technology where he teaches microcomputer application courses at the undergraduate and graduate levels. He has been teaching, writing, and designing computer-training courses since the advent of the personal computer, and has authored and co-authored nearly twenty books on Microsoft Word, Excel, Access, and PowerPoint. He has received grants from the Detroit Edison Institute and the Department of Energy to develop web sites for energy education and alternative fuels, respectively. He has also developed one of the first Internet-based microcomputer applications courses at an accredited university. He has a BS from the University of Michigan in Physics, Mathematics, and Education and an MS from Eastern Michigan University in Physics Education. He is ABD in the Ph.D. degree program in Instructional Technology at Wayne State University.

Sally Preston is President of Preston & Associates, a computer software-training firm. She combines her extensive business experience as a bank vice president in charge of branch operations with her skills in training people on new computer systems. She provides corporate training through Preston & Associates and through the Institute for Workforce Development at Washtenaw Community College where she also teaches computer courses part-time. She has co-authored more than a dozen books on Access, Excel, and PowerPoint. She has an MBA from Eastern Michigan University.

Trademark Acknowledgments

Preface

Que Education and Training is the educational publishing imprint of Macmillan Computer Publishing, the world's leading computer book publisher. Macmillan Computer Publishing books have taught more than 20 million people how to be productive with their computers.

This expertise in producing high-quality computer tutorial and reference books is evident in every Que Education and Training title we publish. The same tried-and-true writing and product-development process that makes Macmillan Computer Publishing books bestsellers is used to ensure that educational materials from Que Education and Training provide the most accurate and up-to-date information. Experienced and respected computer application experts write and review every manuscript to provide class-tested pedagogy. Quality-assurance editors check every keystroke and command in Que Education and Training books to ensure that instructions are clear, accurate, and precise.

Above all, Macmillan Computer Publishing and, in turn, Que Education and Training have years of experience in meeting the learning demands of students across all disciplines.

Philosophy of the Learn Series

The Learn Series has been designed for the student who wants to master the basics of a particular software quickly. The books are very visual in nature because each step is accompanied by a figure that shows the the results of the step. Visual cues are given to the student in the form of highlights and callouts to help direct the student to the location in the window that is being used in a particular step. Explanatory text is minimized in the actual steps, but is included where appropriate in additional pedagogical elements. Every lesson includes reenforcement exercises to immediately give the student a chance to practice the skills that have just been learned.

Structure of a Learn Series Book

Each of the books in the Learn series is structured the same way. The following elements comprise the series:

Introduction

Each book has an introduction. This consists of an introduction to the series (how to use this book), a brief introduction to the Windows 95 operating system, and an introduction to the software.

Lesson introduction

The introduction to each lesson includes a lesson number, title, and a brief introduction to the topics that will be covered in the lesson.

Task introduction

A listing of all tasks included in the lesson are shown on the opening page of each lesson. Each task is explained in a section at the beginning of the task.

Completed project

A screen capture or printout of the results of the lesson is included at the beginning of the lesson to provide an example of what will be accomplished in the lesson.

"Why would I do this?"

At the beginning of each task is a "Why would I do this?" section which is a short explanation of the relevance of the task. The purpose is to help show why this particular element of the software is important and how it can be used effectively.

Figures

Each step has an accompanying figure placed to the right or left of the step. Each figure provides a visual reinforcement of the task at hand, and highlights buttons, menu choices, and other screen elements used in the task.

Pedagogical Elements

Three recurring elements are found in the Preston Ferrett Learn series:

In Depth: detailed look at a topic or procedure, or another way of doing something.

Quick Tip: faster or more efficient way of doing something.

Pothole: area where trouble may be encountered, along with instructions on how to recover from and/or avoid these mistakes.

Glossary

New words or concepts are printed in italics the first time they are encountered. Definitions of these words or phrases are included in the glossary at the back of the book.

End-of-lesson material

The end-of-lesson material consists of Student and Application Exercises. The Student Exercises consist of:

True/False questions There are ten True/False questions that test the understanding of the new material in the lesson.

Visual Identification A captured screen or screens gauge the familiarity with various screen elements introduced in the lesson.

Matching Ten Matching questions are included to check familiarity with concepts and procedures introduced in the lesson.

The **Application Exercises**, included at the end of each lesson, consist of three to five exercises that provide practice in the skills introduced in the tasks.

These exercises generally follow the sequence of the tasks in the lesson. Since each exercise is usually built on the previous exercise, it is a good idea to do them in the order in which they are presented.

Data disks

The data disks contain files for the step-by-step tasks in each lesson.

Annotated Instructor's Edition

If you have adopted this text for use in a college classroom, you will receive, upon request, an Annotated Instructor's Edition (AIE) at no additional charge. The Annotated Instructor's Edition is a comprehensive teaching tool that contains the student text with margin notes and tips for instructors and students. The AIE also contains suggested curriculum guides for courses of varying lengths, answers to the end-of-chapter material, test questions and answers, and PowerPoint slides. Data files and solutions for each tutorial and exercise, along with a PowerPoint presentation, are included on disk with the AIE. Please contact your local representative or write to us on school or business letterhead at Macmillan Computer Publishing, 201 West 103rd Street, Indianapolis, IN 46290-1097, Attention: Que Education and Training Sales Support.

Managing Files with Windows Explorer

Throughout most of this book you will be working in the Microsoft Access program. At times, however, you will be asked to find, retrieve, and rename files on your data disk or a hard disk. This review will help you manage files. It will show how to do this using the Windows Explorer, although all of these procedures can also be accomplished using My Computer. Use whichever method is most comfortable for you.

Launch the Windows Explorer

There are often two or three ways of performing any operation in Windows 95 or in Microsoft applications. Many people place a Windows Explorer (not to be confused with the Internet Explorer!) icon on the Windows desktop. If this icon is available, simply double-click it and Windows Explorer will be launched.

If the icon does not exist, move to the Taskbar at the bottom of the screen. The Taskbar contains the Start button, any open applications, and the time. The Taskbar may appear at the bottom of the screen, or it may be hidden. If it is hidden, move the pointer to the bottom of the screen and it should pop up.

Click the Start button and move the pointer to the Programs option. A list of available programs is displayed. Your list of programs will be different from the one shown. Windows Explorer is at or near the end of the list. Launch the Windows Explorer by moving the pointer over it and clicking the left mouse button.

Navigate the Drives and Folders

Windows Explorer is divided into two windows. The window on the left side, labeled All Folders, displays icons for each disk drive that is accessible from your computer. There may be folders within folders to make up several layers of files. If additional folders (subfolders) are available, a plus sign is placed to the left of the icon.

The All Folders section will give you an overview of the relationship between these layers while the Contents window on the right will display the details of the selected drive or folder. You can choose to show details of the files and folder or show the files and folders as icons by clicking buttons on the toolbar. Your Windows Explorer screen will look much different than the one shown, but it will contain the same elements.

To move to another disk drive, click once on the disk drive icon, such as **3 $^1/_2$ Floppy (A:).** To open a file folder, double-click the folder icon. This will open the folder and display the contents in the right-hand window.

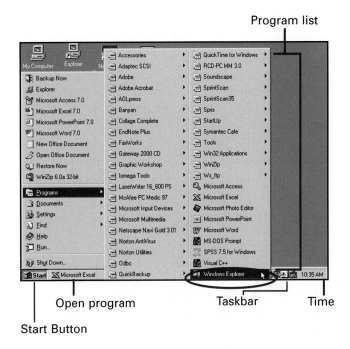

Program list

Open program

Start Button

Taskbar

Time

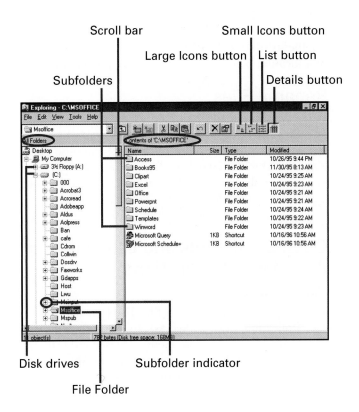

Scroll bar

Small Icons button

Large Icons button

List button

Subfolders

Details button

Disk drives

Subfolder indicator

File Folder

Find Files

Disk drives are capable of storing thousands of files. If you did not know which drive and folder a particular file was stored in, it could take a long time to open each one and read the list of its contents. Windows Explorer will find a file for you if you know at least part of its name.

The project files for this book all begin with the letters **Less** In the example shown, the student files have been moved from the data disk to the hard drive for illustration purposes.

To find all of the files that contain the letters **Less,** click on the disk drive you want to search. **Select Tools, Find, Files** or **Folders** from the menu. In the Find window type Less in the Named box, then click **Find Now.** All of the files and file folders with those letters are listed in the bottom of the **Find** window.

Once you have a list of files found, click the file you want. The location of the file is shown to the right of the file name in the **In Folder** column.

Make Copies of Existing Files

Once you have found the location of the file you need, go to the folder containing the file. Click once on the file to highlight it. Choose **Edit, Copy** from the menu, then choose **Edit, Paste.** This puts a copy of the file in the same location as the original. If you want to copy the file to another folder or disk drive, move to the new location before you perform the paste command.

Rename Files

When you have made a copy of a file and pasted it into the desired location, you will often want to rename it. To rename a file, click it, then choose **File, Rename.** The file name is highlighted. At this point you can simply type a whole new name, or you can put the cursor in the file name and edit it as you would edit text in a word processor.

Open Documents and Launch Associated Applications Automatically

There are two ways to open a file. The first is to run the application (such as **Access**), then use the **File, Open** commands from the menu. The second is to locate the file in the Windows Explorer or My Computer and double-click on the file name.

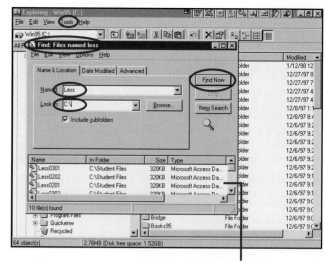

List of files found

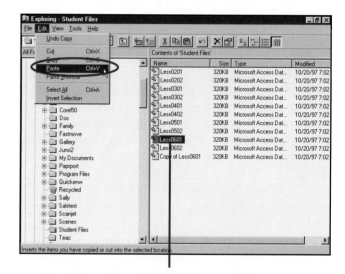

Copy of file

Introduction to Access

Access is a database management program that allows you to store, retrieve, analyze, and print information. It is a system for managing large amounts of data. A simple example of a database is an address book or a card file system listing people's names addresses and phone numbers. Access enables you to develop databases that can manage thousands of pieces of related data in an organized, efficient, and accurate manner.

How Databases Work

To begin to use Access there are a number of terms that need to be understood. An Access database consists of *Tables, Queries, Forms, Reports, Macros* and *Modules* known generally as *objects*. These objects work together to store, search, input, report, and automate the data.

Tables are the foundation of the database because they store the data in the database. Each table stores a set of related data. Tables are made up of *records* which are all the related information about one person, event or transaction. Records are displayed in *rows*. Each category of information in a record is known as a *field*. Fields are displayed in columns and the field name appears in the database table as a column heading.

Queries are used to sort, search, and limit the data to just those records that you need to see. Queries are designed to question the data that is contained in the tables. They can be based on one or more tables and can be used to create new fields that are calculated from other fields. Queries are based on the current information in a table and can be used to revise and analyze data.

Forms are generally used to input or edit data, or to view one record at a time. They can be based on a table or on a query. Forms are interactive with a table because they can be used to view the information in the table or to update the information in a table.

Reports are used to summarize information for printing and presentation of the data. Reports can be based on tables or on queries. They report information based on the current data in the tables but cannot be used to change the information in a table or a query.

Macros are used to automate existing Access commands. Macros are often a series of commands that may be attached to buttons on forms, tables or queries.

Modules are programs in the Visual Basic programming language that are used to customize the database for special needs.

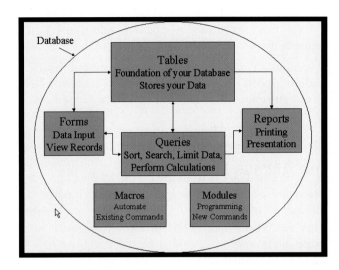

Together these six objects make up an Access database. The objects of the database are viewed from the *Database window,* which is the window that opens when you open a database.

A database is made up of columns and rows of information, similar to a spreadsheet. The columns contain fields that are types of information, such as first name, or last name. Rows contain records which represent all of the related information about a single person, event or transaction. For example, in a phone book the columns would consist of fields such as first name, last name, street address, city, state, zip code and phone number. The rows would contain all the specific information about each individual.

One of the main advantages of using an electronic database is its ability to search and sort the data and find information quickly. As a database designer, your job is to set up the tables and queries so information can be retrieved that is useful and helpful to the end user. When designing a database, it is usually best to start with the desired outcomes in order to determine the information that needs to be included in the database.

Once the database has been designed and the data entered, you will want to be able to retrieve information from the database. Queries and form filters can be used to retrieve records that meet certain conditions, such as all of your friends who live in Florida. Queries can also be used to calculate values based on other fields, or to analyze data.

Databases are also be used to print or present information. Access uses a number of wizard tools that help to design reports that can summarize data based on groups you select.

How to Identify Parts of the Access Database

There are two methods that you can use to quickly identify parts of the Access Database. They are **Screen Tips** and **What's this?**. A Screen Tip will appear if you place the pointer on a toolbar button and leave it there for a moment. The Screen Tip will display the name of the button. (If this feature does not work on your computer, you may turn it on by selecting **Tools**, **Customize** from the menu. Then click the **Options** tab and click the **Show Screen Tips on toolbars** checkbox.)

If you would like to have a more detailed description, you may choose **Help**, **What's This?** from the menu. After you select this help option the pointer will have a question mark attached to it until you click on part of the screen at which time a more detailed paragraph will appear describing the function of the object you clicked.

Parts of the Access Database Window

The main window in Access is the Database Window. This window has a tab for each of the six objects that make up an Access database. When a tab is selected it lists all of the items that have been created for that type of object. For example, when the table tab is selected, the Database Window will list all of the tables that have been created for that database. Each of the six objects in a database has at least two different ways of looking at the object. One is the view that is used when designing the object, the other is the view showing the results of the design, where the data can be seen. Each of these views has several components that you will learn how to use in this book. For a brief overview of the layout of the Database Window and its parts, see the accompanying figure.

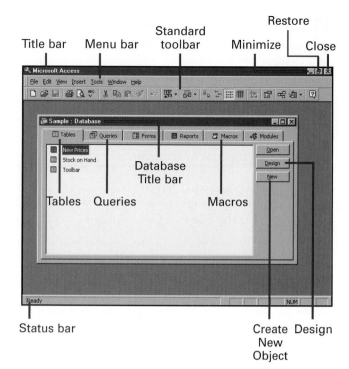

How to Launch Access

The Access program may be initiated (launched) in several ways. When the Access program was installed on your computer, its name was added to the list of programs that may be found when you click the Start button on the Windows taskbar and then click Programs. The Access program may be listed by itself or you may have to open a folder such as Microsoft Office to find the icon that represents the program. When you find it, click on it and the program will launch. There may be other shortcut methods of launching Access on your computer, but this method is the one that will work on most machines.

There are several faster ways to launch Access. It is possible to add the Access program icon to the list of commonly used programs that appears immediately when you click Start. The Access icon could be placed on the desktop or it could be part of a small toolbar at the top of the screen. In general, if you see the Access icon you can click or double-click on it to launch Access.

If you are using the Windows Explorer or My Computer program to search for files, you may notice that the Access files have a small Access icon displayed next to their names. When this is the case, you can double-click on the file name and Access will launch automatically and then open the file as well. Unlike other Office 97 programs, each time you open an Access file from the Explorer, a new version of Access will open on your computer. Be careful that you do not end up with numerous copies of Access open at the same time. If you do, simply close the extra copies of Acess that appear in your taskbar.

Exit Access

When you are done with the Access program you should close it before you turn off the computer. To do this, you may click the Close button on the Title Bar. If you have not saved your most recent changes to an object in the database, you will be asked if you wish to do so before the program closes. You may also close Access by using the **File** and **Close** options from the menu.

The Concept of this Book

This book is designed for people who are new to Access but who also need to know how to use it in real life applications. The authors have combined their many years of business experience and classroom teaching to provide a basic step-by-step approach that leads to the development of skills that are advanced enough to be useful in the workplace. We have designed the book so that you will be successful immediately and will create a useful database in the very first lesson. In the lessons that follow, you will learn how to create a database from scratch, work with large databases, use analytical tools, present information, and link your database to other applications. Finally, we recognize that few people can remember everything that they learn in class so we conclude the book by showing you how to get help from the online manuals, from the Internet, and from additional textbooks.

To the Student:

Your *Learn* textbook comes with a Learn On-Demand CD-ROM. Learn On-Demand provides you with unique ways to learn and practice the material covered in the book. This CD-ROM can help make your learning experience more enjoyable and help you pass your tests by allowing you to learn in an interactive environment.

Learn On-Demand is available to you through your campus' computer lab or you can install it on your own computer. This section shows you how to install the software on your computer and how to use Learn On-Demand.

System Requirements

The minimum system requirements that you need to install Learn On-Demand are

- An IBM-compatible PC with a minimum of 486SX CPU

- 8MB RAM (16MB recommended)

- Microsoft Windows 95®

- Microsoft Office 97®

- VGA display adapter and monitor (640×480 or better)

- Two-button mouse

- Audio sound card (optional, but recommended)

- 4x speed or faster CD-ROM

If you are taking a course that includes more than one Learn book, you will need additional hard drive space to install the software for those books. The following table will help you determine how much additional hard drive space you need.

FILE TYPES	ESTIMATED HARD DISK SPACE REQUIREMENTS
Learn On-Demand program files	2MB
Application support files	1MB per application
Content files (for example, graphics and lesson files)	3.5MB per lesson
Sound files	20–25MB (optional)

If you would like to access Learn On-Demand's audio, you can choose to run the sound directly from your CD-ROM, which will lower the memory requirements.

If you add new titles to **Learn On-Demand** at a later date, you have the option of specifying the directory\folder where the content will be installed. If you use the existing directory\folder, new content files are added to that directory\folder. If you specify a new directory\folder, the install program determines that a previous installation is present and prompts you to do one of the following: select **Yes** to install all new files and move all old files to the new specified location, select **No** to install all new files to the old location, or select **Cancel** to specify a new location.

Installing Learn On-Demand

You can install Learn On-Demand in several ways. Note the following install options:

OPTION	DESCRIPTION
Minimal install	Copies the basic program files to your computer but requires the CD for graphics and sound.
Standard install	Copies all program files to your computer but requires the CD for sound.
Full install	Copies all program and sound files to your computer.

If you accept the default directory\folder to install Learn On-Demand, all Learn On-Demand files are placed in \Learn\OnDemand\Learn Access 97. If you choose another location to install Learn On-Demand, all the files are copied to the directory\folder you specify. No files are copied to any other location during the install.

Use the following procedure to install **Learn On-Demand** from the CD-ROM to your hard drive. Place the **Learn On-Demand** CD in the CD-ROM drive.

1 From the taskbar, select the **Start** Menu.

2 Point to **Settings**.

3 Select Control Panel. The Control Panel window opens.

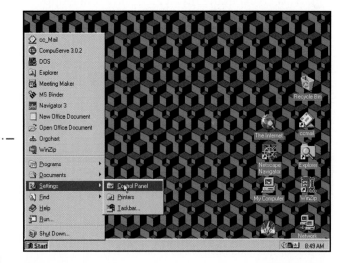

4 Double-click the **Add/Remove Programs** icon. The **Add/Remove Programs** dialog box opens.

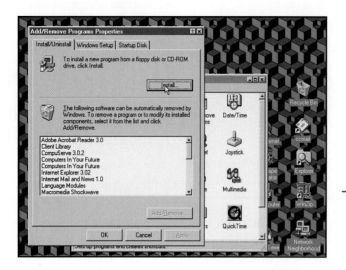

5 Select **Install**. The Install Program From Floppy Disk or CD-ROM dialog box opens.

6 Select **Next** in the Install Program From Floppy Disk or CD-ROM dialog box.

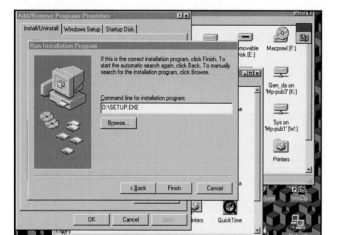

7 If necessary, type **D:\SETUP.EXE. (D:\ represents the CD-ROM drive. Your CD-ROM drive may be different.)** Please verify that the drive letter is correct. The command appears in the **Command line** text box. Select **Finish.** The **Learn On-Demand** Installation program launches.

8 Follow the directions as they appear on your screen. **Learn On-Demand** is installed with the options selected during the installation process. After installation is complete, an item for **Learn On-Demand** appears automatically in the **Programs** submenu. The **Learn On-Demand** shortcut appears in this item's submenu.

Uninstalling Learn On-Demand Titles and Software

Learn On-Demand includes an uninstall program. The uninstall program is included in the **Learn On-Demand** program folder. You can access this folder from the **Start** menu. You can use this program to remove titles from **Learn On-Demand**. The same program can be used to uninstall the **Learn On-Demand** software. **Learn On-Demand** automatically uninstalls when you use **uninst.exe** to remove the final title.

Use the following procedure to uninstall a title from **Learn On-Demand**:

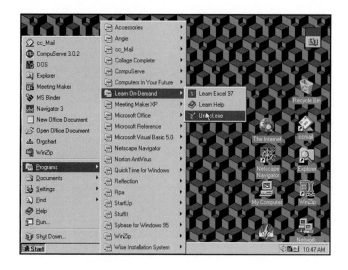

1 Select **Start**.

2 Select **Programs**.

3 Select **Learn On-Demand**.

4 Select **Uninst.exe**.

Starting Learn On-Demand

To start Learn On-Demand:

1 From the taskbar, select the **Start** menu. The **Start** menu appears.

2 Select **Programs**.

The **Programs** menu appears.

3 Select the **Learn On-Demand** program group. The Learn On-Demand submenu appears.

4 Select **Learn Access 97**.

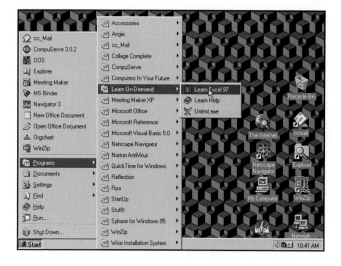

5 The **Learn On-Demand** toolbar floats on the Windows desktop. **Learn On-Demand** is now ready for use. At this point, you need to start **Access.**

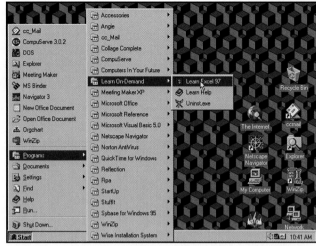

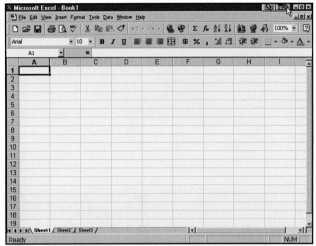

6 The **Learn On-Demand** toolbar appears on the application title bar.

Using Learn On-Demand

Specific tasks in Learn On-Demand are covered in topics. You can learn about a topic by using any of the four **Learn On-Demand** playback modes: **Concept, Concurrent, Teacher,** or **Demo.** These modes are individually covered later in this tutorial.

The **Interactive Training—Lesson Selection** dialog box is the central location from which you can find and view available training modules, lessons, and topics. From this location, you can launch a desired topic in any of **Learn On-Demand**'s training modes. The dialog box contains three tabbed pages: **Contents, Search,** and **Topics for.** The purpose of each page is to help you view and locate training relevant to your specific needs, which are reviewed later in this tutorial.

 Click the Teacher button on the application title bar to open **The Interactive Training—Lesson Selection** dialog box. You are now ready to select the desired topic and training mode.

❶ Displays all the modules, lessons, and/or topics available. Click the plus box to expand the listings and click the minus box to contract the listings. A description of each selected topic appears below the list box.

❷ Enables you to quickly locate topics of interest. You can enter a keyword to find all related topics.

❸ Displays only those topics that relate to your working application. A description of each selected topic appears below the list box.

❹ When selected, displays the lessons within the modules.

❺ When selected, groups the topics by lesson. Expanding lessons displays the topics within them.

❻ When selected, displays all available topics.

❼ Provides a description of the key concept of the current topic.

❽ Enables you to learn while you work.

❾ Prompts you to enter mouse clicks or keystrokes as you complete tasks in a simulated environment.

❿ Displays an animated demonstration of the task being completed in a simulated environment.

⓫ Closes the **Interactive Training—Lesson Selection** dialog box and returns you to your application. This button does not close Learn On-Demand. The Learn On-Demand icon still appears on your application title bar.

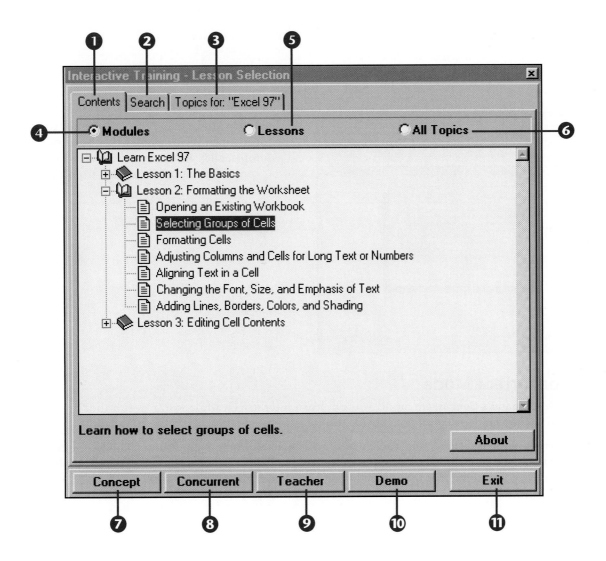

Using Concept Mode

While it is important to learn how to perform a task, it is also important to learn when and why a task is performed. **Learn On-Demand**'s **Concept** mode displays the key concept of a topic to help you gain a better understanding of how the topic relates to everyday uses of the application.

Use the following procedure to learn how to use **Learn On-Demand's Concept** mode:

1 Select a topic describing the task you want to learn how to complete. Click the **Concept button**.

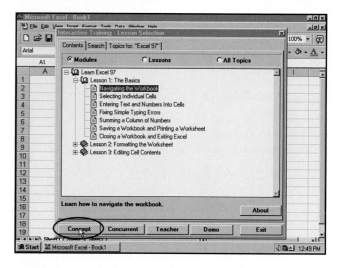

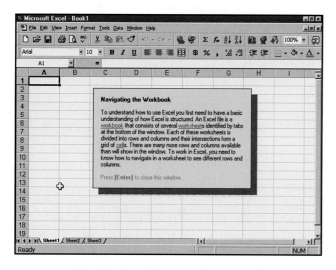

2 **Learn On-Demand** displays the key concept for the topic. When you have finished viewing the topic, click anywhere or press any key. The concept information disappears from your screen.

Using Concurrent Mode

With **Learn On-Demand's Concurrent** mode, you can learn interactively while working with the "live" application and data. This unique mode makes it possible for you to accomplish real tasks with actual data.

When **Concurrent mode** is selected, the **Topic** dialog box opens within the application. This dialog box includes a series of steps that need to be followed in sequence to complete the selected task. As steps are completed, a red check mark appears, indicating that the step has been completed. **IMPORTANT NOTE:** You must follow these steps exactly as directed.

1 Concurrent mode prompts the student with a hotspot around the area of the screen needing action.

2 The hotspot is outlined with a red marquee.

3 The red line drawn from the hotspot to the current step provides easy and clear onscreen directions.

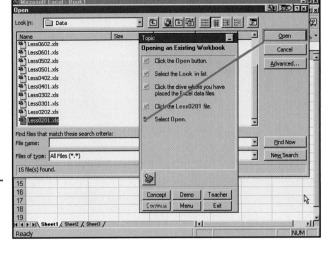

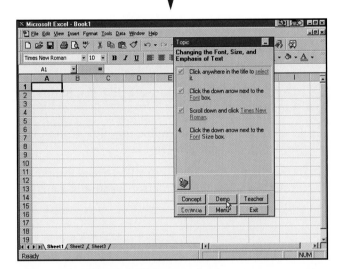

If you need further assistance during your **concurrent** training session, you can switch to another training mode by clicking the **Concept**, **Demo**, or **Teacher** mode button.

Using Teacher Mode

Teacher mode prompts you to enter the necessary mouse clicks or keystrokes to complete tasks in a simulated environment. When you are working in **Teacher** mode, **Learn On-Demand** places a **hotspot** over the location where you need to complete an action. The **hotspot** is outlined with a red marquee. If you make a mistake, **Learn On-Demand** prompts you to try again. Notice that **Teacher** mode provides a simulated environment, so active data and system settings in your application are protected. You can control **Teacher** mode by using the following buttons, which appear at the bottom of the **Teacher** mode screen. Use the following procedure to learn how to complete a task in **Learn On-Demand's Teacher** mode:

 Click the **Teacher** button to open the **Interactive Training—Lesson Selection** dialog box, if necessary.

1 Select a topic describing the task you want to learn how to complete. With the topic selected, click the Teacher button.

2 **Learn On-Demand** displays an opening screen with the objective of the topic in Teacher mode.

3 ▶ Click the forward button to begin training. The training for the selected topic appears in **Teacher** mode.

Buttons appear at the bottom of the Topic dialog box.

You can use the buttons, which are described in the following figure, to perform additional Learn On-Demand functions.

❶ Enables you to move to the beginning screen within a topic. (Applicable for multiple-step topics only.)

❷ Enables you to move backward one step at a time.

❸ Pauses **Teacher** mode.

❹ Enables you to move forward one step at a time.

❺ Enables you to move to the last screen within a topic.

❻ Returns you to the **Interactive Training—Lesson Selection** dialog box. From this dialog box, you can select another topic.

❼ Exits **Teacher** mode.

❽ **In Depth:** Detailed look at a topic or procedure or another way of completing a task.

❾ **Quick Tip:** Faster or more efficient way of doing something.

❿ **Pothole:** Area where trouble may be encountered and ways of recovering from mistakes.

⓫ Displays the key concept for the selected topic. Tells you when you would use a software function and why.

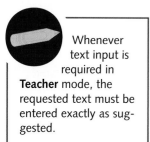

Whenever text input is required in **Teacher** mode, the requested text must be entered exactly as suggested.

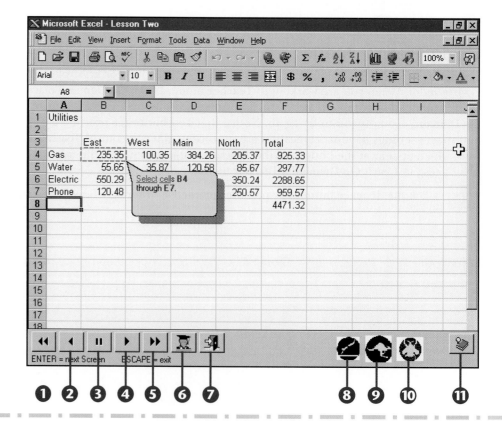

In addition to the buttons, pressing the ⏎Enter key advances Teacher mode one frame at a time. Pressing the Esc key exits Teacher mode.

Using Demo Mode

Demo mode enables you to learn by watching an animated demonstration of operations being performed. All required activities, such as moving the mouse and selecting menu items, are completed automatically.

When you are working in **Demo** mode, you can stop the demonstration at any time by pressing the Esc key. You can also pause the animation by holding the ⇧Shift key. Releasing the ⇧Shift key resumes the demonstration.

Use the following procedure to learn how to complete a task in **Learn On-Demand's Demo** mode:

1 🎓 Click the **Teacher** button to open the **Interactive Training—Lesson.**

The **Interactive Training—Lesson Selection** dialog box opens.

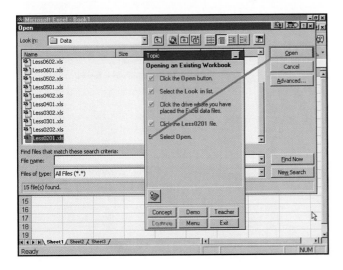

2 Select the topic describing the task you want to learn how to complete. Click the **Demo** button. **Learn On-Demand** displays an animation that demonstrates how to complete the task.

3 You can obtain more information about a topic at any time while using **Demo** mode by pressing the F1 key to display the **Concept** button. Clicking this button once displays conceptual information about the task, and clicking it again removes the information from your screen. Pressing the Esc key removes the button. Depending on the topic being viewed, other buttons may also appear, including the **In Depth**, **Speed**, and/or **Pothole** buttons.

Searching by Topic

After you have started **Learn On-Demand** and are in the application (with your file open) for which you want training, you can select a topic. Simply choose a selection from the list of available modules, lessons, and/or topics from the **Search Tab** in the **Interactive Training—Lesson Selection dialog box**.

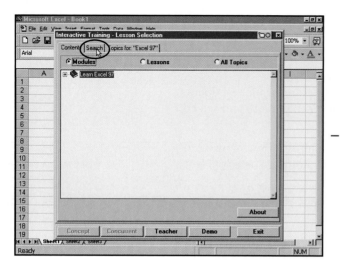

1 Click the **Search** tab. The **Search** page appears.

2 Type the keyword **format**.

3 Related keywords of **format** appear in the **Select a keyword from the list box**. Select format from the list.

4 Related topics appear in the **Pick the topic** list box.

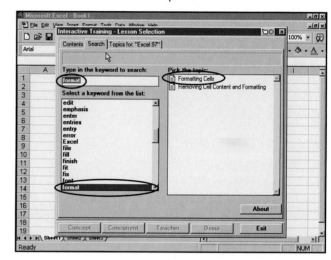

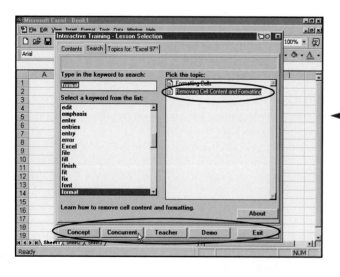

5 Select a topic from the **Pick the topic** frame.

6 Select your desired mode: **Concept**, **Concurrent**, **Teacher**, or **Demo**. Follow the steps as outlined on your screen.

Exiting Learn On-Demand

Use the following procedure to exit **Learn On-Demand:**

 1 Click the **Learn On-Demand** button on the application title bar. The **Learn On-Demand** menu appears.

2 Select the **Exit** command. The Learn On-Demand—Exit dialog box opens.

3 Select **Yes**.

Learn On-Demand closes.

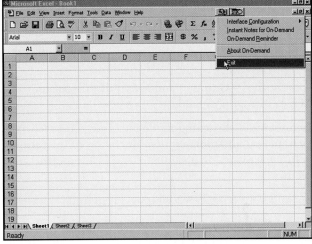

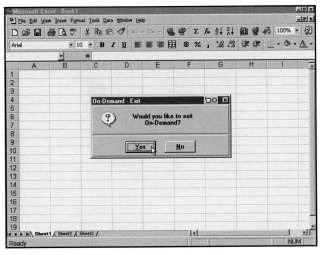

Technical Support

Should you need assistance installing and/or operating **Learn On-Demand**, call Macmillan Technical Support at (317) 581-3833 or send an email to support@mcp.com.

Glossary of Terms

checklist—Steps listed in the Topics dialog box in **Concurrent** mode. To perform the topic, these steps must be followed exactly as they appear.

Concept mode—Learning mode displaying the key concept of a topic. Explains when, where, and why you would use a program's features, as well as any other important conceptual information about a topic.

Concurrent mode—Learning mode enabling you to learn interactively while you work without leaving your "live" application.

content files—Graphics and lesson files associated with Learn On-Demand.

Demo mode—Learning mode enabling you to learn by watching an animated demonstration of operations being performed in a simulated application environment.

hotspot—Area where user input is required.

keyword—A word or phrase used to find a specific training topic. Users enter keywords on the **Search** page in the **Interactive Training—Lesson Selection** dialog box.

reminder—After a period of inactivity, **Learn On-Demand** Reminder displays a message reminding you that **Learn On-Demand** is active.

Teacher mode—Learning mode enabling you to learn interactively by prompting you to enter mouse clicks or keystrokes as you complete tasks in a simulated application environment.

topic—The most specific level of organization within PTS courseware titles. Each topic provides all the information required to complete a specific task within an application.

Table of Contents at a Glance

Table of Contents

Lesson 4: Extract Useful Information from Large Databases 94

Lesson 5: Using Two or More Tables In Combination 128

Lesson 1
Create a Database Using the Database Wizard

Task 1 Creating an Address Database Using the Database Wizard

Task 2 Using the Main Switchboard to View a Database Form and Add Text to a New Record

Task 3 Entering Data in Fields that Use Input Masks and Special Data Types

Task 4 Using the Reports Switchboard to Preview Database Reports

Task 5 Examining the Database Table Using the Database Window

Task 6 Using the "What's This?" Help Tool to Learn About the Design of a Form and a Report

Task 7 Closing the Database and Exiting Access

Introduction

Access is a computerized *database* management system that allows you to store, retrieve, analyze, and print information. It is a system for managing large amounts of data. Companies use databases for many purposes: to manage customer files, to track orders and inventories, and for marketing purposes. An individual might set up a database to track household expenses or manage a list of family, friends, and business addresses. Teachers often set up a database to track students' grades and other class information. A database allows the user to access and manage thousands of pieces of data in an organized, efficient, and accurate manner.

To begin to use Access there are a number of terms that you need to understand. An Access database consists of *tables, queries, forms, reports, macros* and *modules* known generally as *objects*. These objects work together to store, search, input, report, and automate the data. The purpose of these objects is explained in the preface to this book. Please refer to this material for a more detailed overview. The objects of the database are viewed from the *Database window*, which is the window that opens when you open a database.

The approach used in this book emphasizes the coordination of the six objects so that you understand their interaction. The first lesson uses the Database Wizard to give you an overview of a database and each of the objects in the database. In later lessons each object in the database will be examined in more detail.

Visual Summary

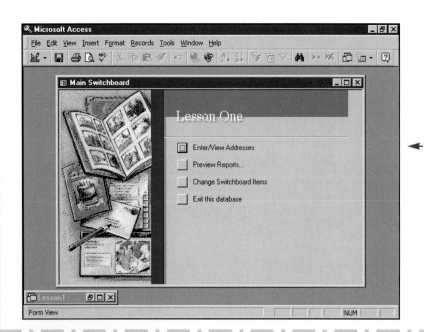

When you are done with this entire lesson, you will have created a database that looks like this:

Task 1

Creating an Address Database Using the Database Wizard

Why would I do this?

The Access *Database Wizard* is a program that helps you create a database, step by step, by presenting you with a series of options. In each of the steps you make selections that will be used to create your database. The advantage of using the Wizard is that it creates all of the necessary objects for you to be able to operate the database. For someone new to databases, this is a quick way to see how the different objects work together. Later in this book you will learn how to create each of the objects separately.

As you will see, Access contains 22 design templates of the most commonly used databases, including templates for addresses, inventory control, household inventory, a music collection, and students and classes. A design *template* is a pre-designed form or format that can be used instead of creating one of your own.

In this task, you learn how to use the <u>D</u>atabase Wizard to guide you through the process of creating an address database, using a design template.

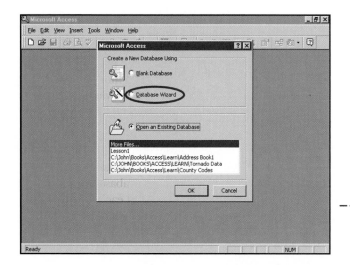

1 Launch Microsoft Access. The Microsoft Access dialog box opens and provides three choices.

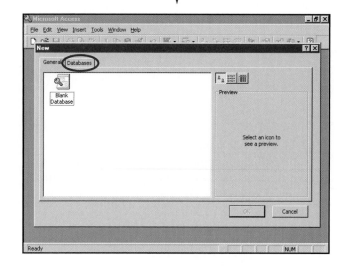

2 Click the **Database Wizard** option and click **OK**. The **New** dialog box opens.

3 Click the **Databases** tab, if necessary. The selection of existing database design templates is displayed. Click the **Address Book** icon.

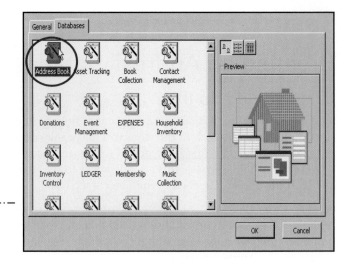

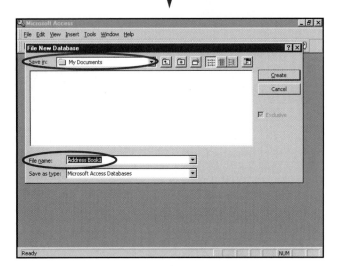

4 Click **OK**. The **File New Database** dialog box opens.

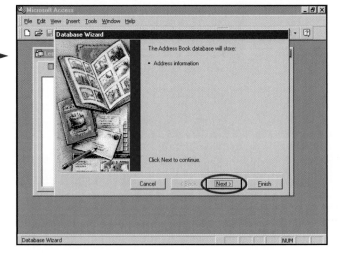

5 Click the **File name** box and type **Lesson1**. Use the **Save in** box to locate the folder where your instructor has suggested that you save your files. Click **Create**. The **Database Wizard** dialog box opens.

6 Click <u>N</u>ext. Another **Database Wizard** dialog box opens. Scroll down the list of fields in the **Fields in the table** box. These are the fields that will be included in your address database. The fields shown in italics are optional. Click the **Yes, include sample data** option at the bottom of the dialog box.

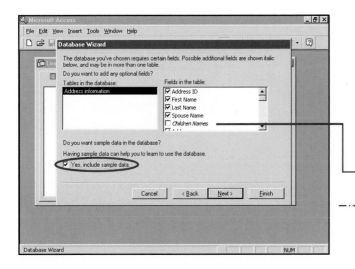

———— Optional field

Pothole: If you did not click the "Yes, include sample data" box, your database will not include any data. Choose the Back button to return to the previous screen and click this option. This will ensure that data is included in your database.

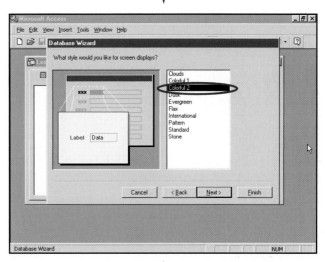

7 Click <u>N</u>ext. A **Database Wizard** dialog box opens that allows you to pick from several backgrounds. **Click Colorful 2.**

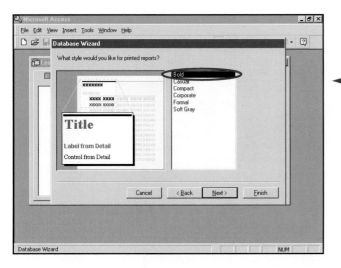

8 Click <u>N</u>ext. A **Database Wizard** dialog box opens that allows you to pick a font style. Click **Bold**.

9 Click <u>N</u>ext. The next **Database Wizard** dialog box allows you to enter a title for your database. This title will display at the top of forms and reports. Replace the default title with **<u>Lesson One</u>**.

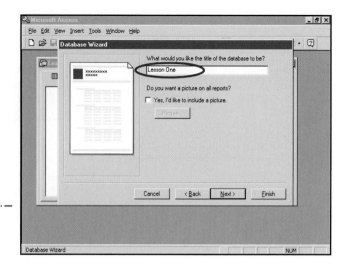

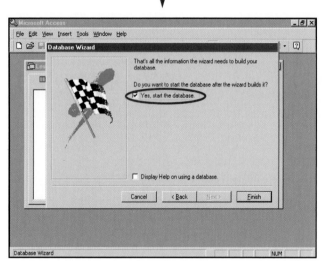

10 Click <u>N</u>ext. A **Database Wizard** dialog box opens that allows you to choose whether you want to start using the database. Make sure that the option **Yes, start the database** is checked to begin using the database.

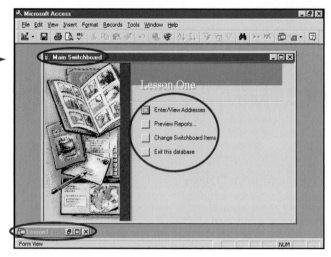

11 Click <u>F</u>inish. The wizard created the database objects and displays a Database window icon in the lower left corner of the screen. The **Main Switchboard** menu opens, which allows you to use the database objects by clicking action buttons.

Task 2

Using the Main Switchboard to View a Database Form and Add Text to a New Record

Why would I do this?

The advantage of using the Wizard program to create a database is that you can enter data, look at records and print reports with very little knowledge of the inner workings of the database. As you saw in the first task, the Wizard program creates a Main Switchboard that serves as a menu from which different tasks can be accomplished. By selecting different menu options, someone with little knowledge of Access can keep records up-to-date and print reports. This is a good way to gain a basic understanding of how to use the different objects in a database to manage information.

In this task, you learn how to use the Main Switchboard to look at records and add text to a new record in your database.

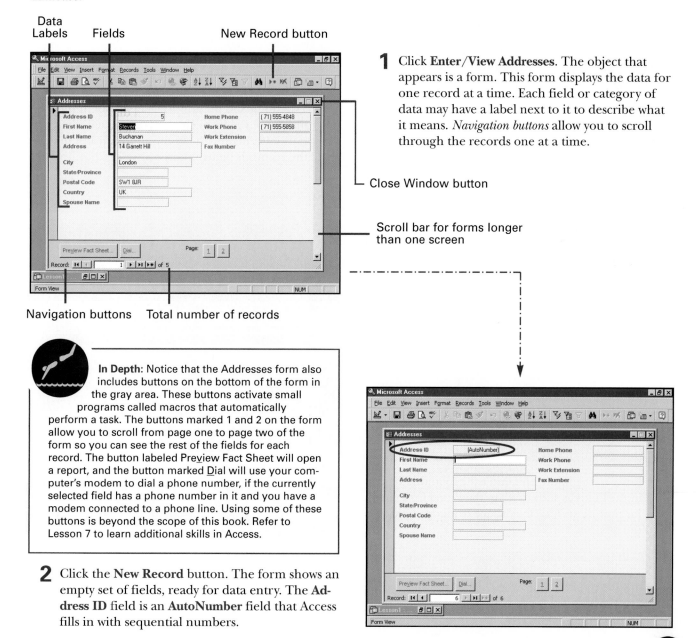

Data Labels   Fields   New Record button

Close Window button

Scroll bar for forms longer than one screen

Navigation buttons   Total number of records

1 Click **Enter/View Addresses**. The object that appears is a form. This form displays the data for one record at a time. Each field or category of data may have a label next to it to describe what it means. *Navigation buttons* allow you to scroll through the records one at a time.

In Depth: Notice that the Addresses form also includes buttons on the bottom of the form in the gray area. These buttons activate small programs called macros that automatically perform a task. The buttons marked 1 and 2 on the form allow you to scroll from page one to page two of the form so you can see the rest of the fields for each record. The button labeled Preview Fact Sheet will open a report, and the button marked Dial will use your computer's modem to dial a phone number, if the currently selected field has a phone number in it and you have a modem connected to a phone line. Using some of these buttons is beyond the scope of this book. Refer to Lesson 7 to learn additional skills in Access.

2 Click the **New Record** button. The form shows an empty set of fields, ready for data entry. The **Address ID** field is an **AutoNumber** field that Access fills in with sequential numbers.

3 Click the **First Name** field to place the cursor in it, if necessary. It is now ready to receive new data.

Cursor ——————

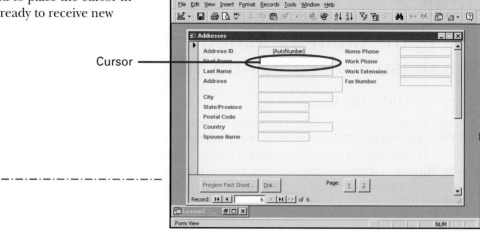

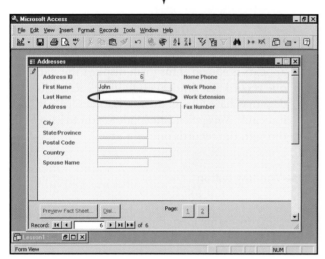

4 Type **John** and press Tab⇄. The symbol in the left margin of the form changes to a pencil when you start entering information. This indicates that the record is being entered.

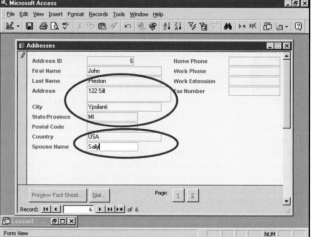

5 Refer to the figure and enter the following data in the fields as shown. (Skip the Postal Code field for now.) Use Tab⇄ to advance from one field to the next.

Task 3
Entering Data in Fields that Use Input Masks and Special Data Types
Why would I do this?
When you create a database, one of the goals is to be able to retrieve the data. To help ensure that data will be retrieved, it is useful to design your database so the information is entered in a consistent manner. There are a number of tools in Access that you can use to help ensure consistency of data entry. Some data, such as phone numbers and social security numbers, are usually entered with extra characters such as parentheses or dashes. An *input mask* is a field property designed to guide the user when entering data so that data containing dashes or parentheses is entered in a consistent way.

When you create a table the type of data that will be entered in each field is determined. The *data type* tells the computer how to interpret the data. Most data that is entered is *text*, a data type that consists of short phrases, words, or numbers that will not be used in calculations, such as phone numbers or social security numbers. Text is the default data type. Some types of data, however, are used for special purposes. Examples are dates, numbers, currency, logical Yes/No, and memos.

In the previous task, all of the information you entered used text as the data type. In this task, you learn how to enter data into fields that use input masks or use some of the other data types. This will help you understand how a database can be designed so people entering data are guided in entering the correct type of data in the correct format.

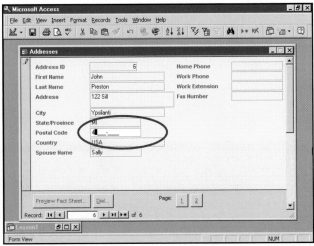

1 Click the **Postal Code** field to select it. Use the arrow keys on the keyboard to position the cursor at the far left, and type the first number of the code, **4**. The field displays space for five numbers, a dash, and space for four more numbers. This is called an input mask.

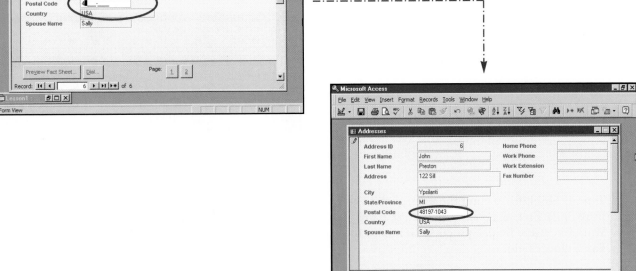

2 Type the rest of the Postal Code, <u>81971043.</u> Notice that you did not have to type the dash.

3 Press (Tab⁺) three times to advance to the **Home Phone** field. Notice that the selection jumped from the bottom of the first column of fields to the top of the second column. The sequence of fields on each page of the form the (Tab⁺) key advances to is called the *tab order*.

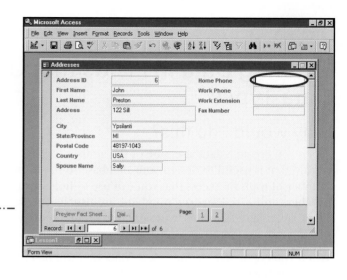

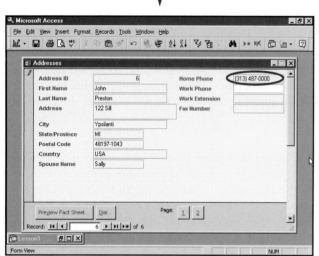

4 Type **3134870000** and press (Tab⁺). Notice how the input mask automatically adds the parentheses and dashes.

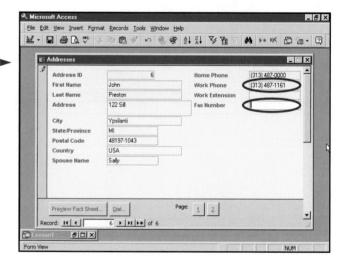

5 Type **3134871161** to enter the work phone and press (Tab⁺). Press (Tab⁺) once more to skip the Work Extension field. Your cursor is now in the **Fax Number** field.

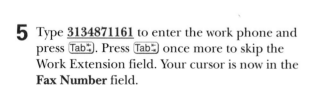

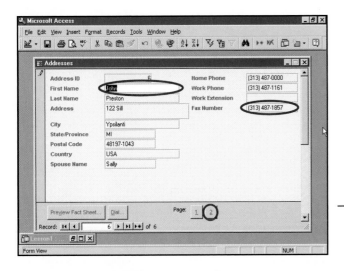

6 Type <u>3134871857</u> to enter the Fax number and press `Tab⇆`. The cursor will return to the **First Name** field on the form.

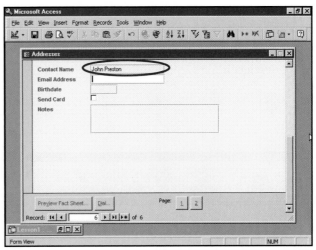

7 Click the **2** button to go to the second page of the form. Notice that the **First Name** and **Last Name** fields have been combined to create **Contact Name**. This is an example of a *concatenated field*.

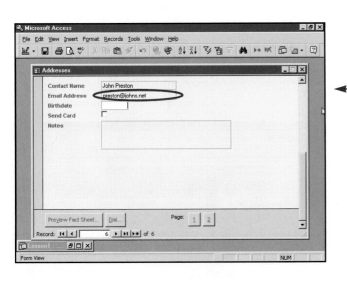

8 Type <u>preston@johns.net</u> in the **Email Address** box and press `Tab⇆` to advance to the **Birthdate** box.

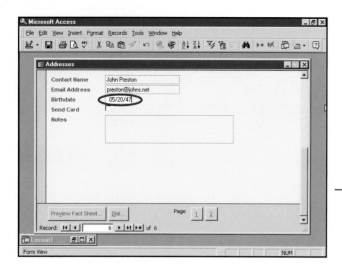

9 Type <u>052047</u>. Notice that the input mask adds slashes and that the date requires a leading zero. This is an example of a field that uses *date* as the data type.

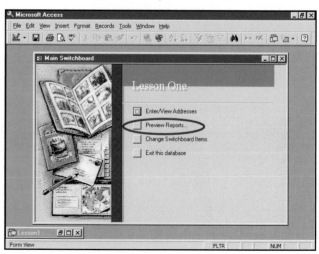

10 Click the check box next to the **Send Card** label. This is an example of a field that uses the *Yes/No* data type. If you were to click it again, it would deselect it.

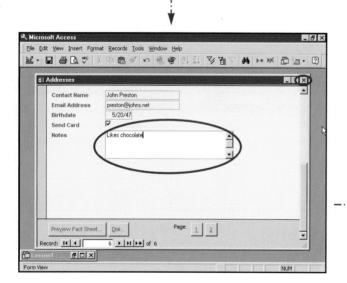

11 Click in the **Notes** box and type **Likes chocolate**. This is an example of a field that uses the *memo* data type where unstructured and unlimited comments can be added.

12 Click the **Close Window** button to return to the **Main Switchboard**.

Task 4

Using the Reports Switchboard to Preview Database Reports

Why would I do this?

The form you used in the previous task displayed records one at a time. In managing a database, you will also need to print several records at a time. When you need to print records you will want to use a report. Reports can be based on tables or queries and can consist of a simple listing of all the records, or they can consist of groups of selected or filtered records. A *filter* is used to limit records to those that meet certain requirements.

In this task, you learn how to use the Reports Switchboard to look at the different reports that were created as part of this database. Reports are viewed in a print preview mode so you can examine how the report will look before it is printed.

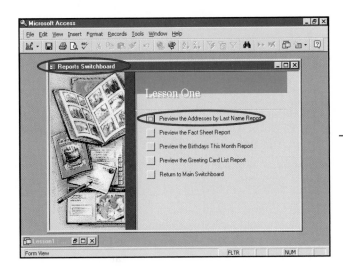

1 Click the **Preview Reports** button. The **Main Switchboard** opens the **Reports Switchboard**, which displays several choices.

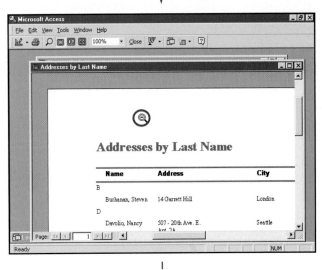

2 Click the **Preview the Addresses by Last Name Report** button. A preview of the report opens and the pointer turns into a magnifying glass.

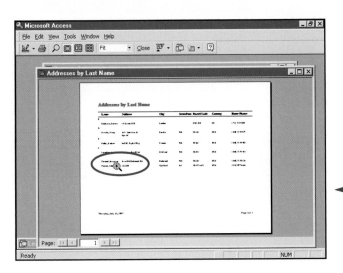

3 Move the pointer onto the report and click. The view zooms out to show the whole page. Move the pointer onto the last record in the report.

4 Click the mouse. The view zooms in on the last record. Notice that the record that you entered is now part of this report. This is an example of a report that groups records. In this case the groups are based on the first letter of the last name.

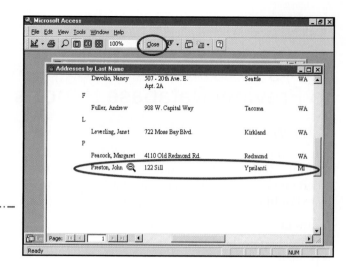

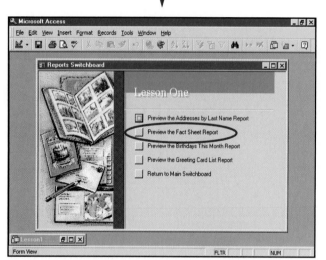

5 Click the **Close** button on the toolbar to return to the **Reports Switchboard**.

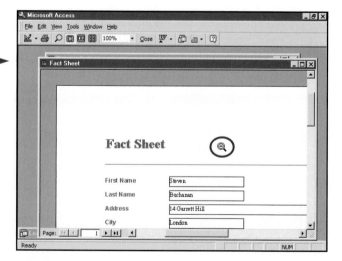

6 Click the **Preview the Fact Sheet Report** button. The report is displayed and the cursor turns into a magnifying glass.

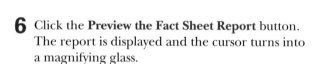

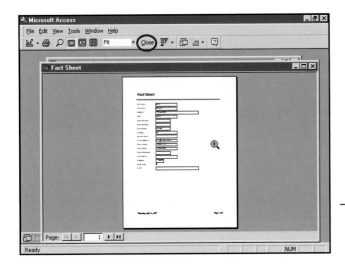

7 Click anywhere in the report to switch the zoom to a full page view. This is an example of a *columnar report* which is designed to print one record per page in a single-column format.

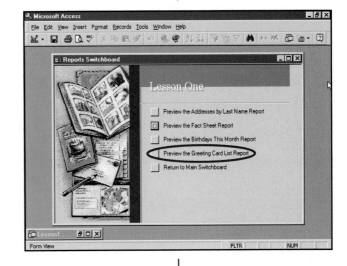

8 Click the **Close** button on the toolbar to return to the **Reports Switchboard**.

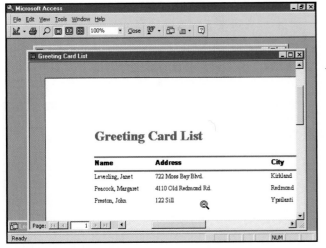

9 Click the **Preview the Greeting Card List Report** button. This is an example of a report that uses a filter to restrict the records displayed to those that meet a certain criteria. In this case, the records shown are those that were checked for a greeting card.

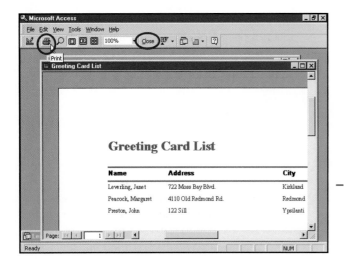

10 Click the **Print** button on the toolbar to send this report to the printer.

11 Click the **Close** button on the toolbar to return to the **Reports Switchboard**.

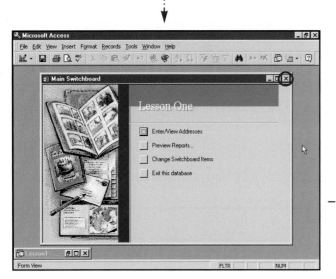

12 Click **Return to Main Switchboard**. Do not exit the database at this time.

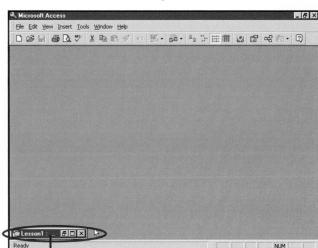

13 Click the **Close Window** button at the corner of the **Main Switchboard** to close the switchboard but leave the database open.

Reduced Database window

Task 5

Examining the Database Table Using the Database Window

Why would I do this?

In this lesson, a Wizard was used to create a sample database. If you use Wizards to create databases, you may find that not all of the objects are exactly what you want or need. If you want to customize the database objects to fit your specific needs, you will need to use the Database window to modify the design of the objects. Likewise, when you create a database without using a Wizard you will use the Database window to create new objects, to open objects, or to change the design of objects. The Database window is similar to a switchboard in that it opens forms and reports you use to enter or print data. But the Database window also allows you to create or modify objects in your database. It is a central control window that gives you access to all areas of your database.

In this task, you will examine the table that was created for this database. You will learn how to add and then delete a record. You will look at the design of the table to see how an input mask property looks. In future lessons, you will use the table design window to create tables. This exercise gives you an introduction to the design and use of a table.

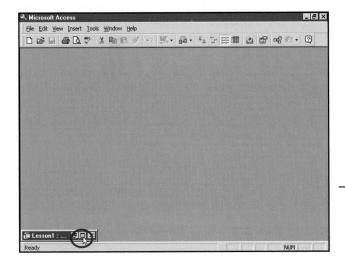

1 Move the pointer to the **Maximize** button in the title bar of the Database window.

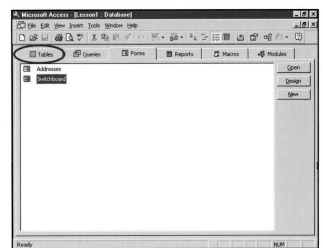

2 Click the **Maximize** button. The Database window displays six tabs showing the database objects: Tables, Queries, Forms, Reports, Macros, and Modules.

3 Click the **Tables** tab. You see a list of the tables that were created for this database.

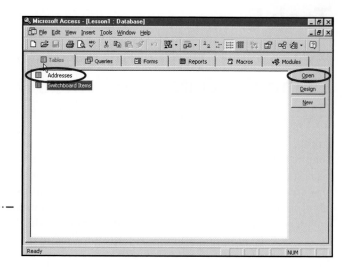

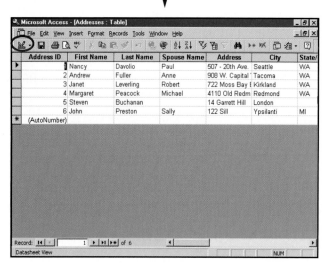

4 Click **Addresses** and then click the **Open** button. The Addresses table opens in *Datasheet View*. This view shows the field names at the top of each column and the records in rows. Tables may be viewed in either of two ways: the Datasheet View you see, or the *Design View*, which is used to design or modify the table. The View button is used to switch between views.

Key field ⟶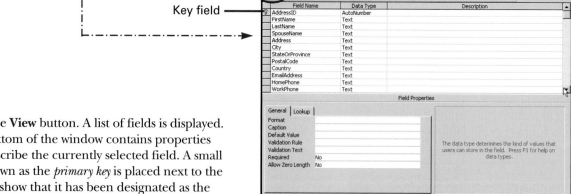

5 Click the **View** button. A list of fields is displayed. The bottom of the window contains properties that describe the currently selected field. A small key known as the *primary key* is placed next to the field to show that it has been designated as the field that contains a unique value for every record.

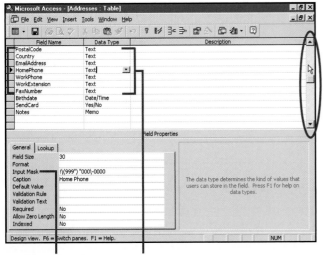

Input mask   Text fields

6 Scroll down to see the last ten field names and click the **HomePhone** data type column. Notice that the **Field Properties** window displays the input mask that is used to insert the parentheses and dashes. Notice, too, that even though you entered numbers in the PostalCode and Home-Phone fields, their data type is text. Number data types are generally used only for fields that have an intrinsic numeric value that may be used in a mathematical calculation.

7 Click the data type for the **Birthdate** field. Notice the input mask used for dates.

In Depth: Input masks look difficult, but you will learn how to use a wizard that will create them for you.

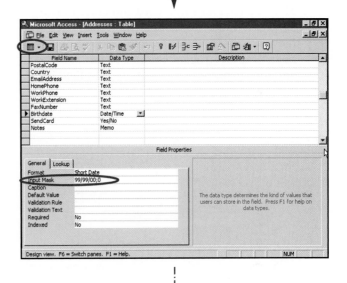

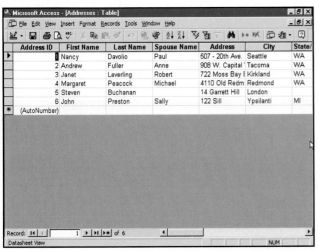

8 Click the **View** button to switch back to Datasheet View.

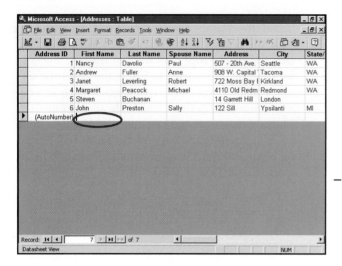

9 Click the **First Name** field in the empty record at the bottom of the list of records.

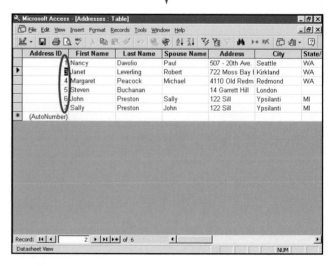

10 Make up data for this record and enter it. Use Tab⇄ to advance from one field to the next as you move across the screen. After you enter the last field, press Tab⇄ again; the new record is saved and the cursor jumps back to the first field in the next record.

Record selector

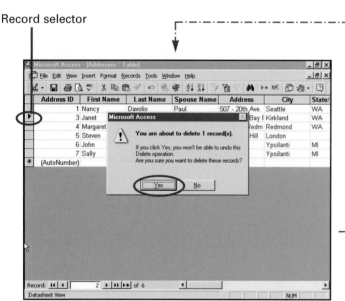

11 Click the small box at the far left side of the second record. This box is called the *record selector*. Press Del to delete the record. A dialog box opens with a message warning you that the data will be deleted and there is no way to bring it back.

12 Click **Yes**. The record is deleted but the Address ID numbers in the other records do not change.

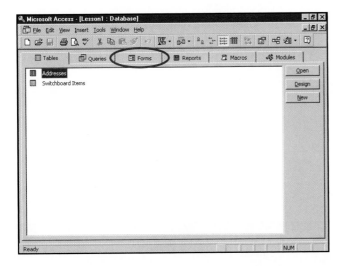

13 Click the **Close Window** button to close the Datasheet View of the table to return to the Database window.

Task 6

Using the "What's This?" Help Tool to Learn About the Design of a Form and a Report

Why would I do this?

You have seen how a table is displayed in rows and columns of data in Datasheet View. You have also seen the window that is used to design a table. Likewise, you can view data in your forms and reports, or you can look at the design of these objects to create or modify them.

In most cases, you will use a Wizard to create your forms or reports, but you may need to make some modifications after the object is created. This is done in Design View of the particular object you are changing. For example, if you are copying data from paper forms, you will find it easier to do if the fields on the screen are arranged in the same order as those on the paper forms. Similarly, you may wish to reorganize the fields in a report to create a different type of report. In order to customize reports or forms, you need to be familiar with how they are designed.

In Tasks 2, 3, and 4 you worked with the Form View of a form and the Preview View of reports. These views are used to display the data. In this task, you will examine the Design View of the forms and reports created for this database. To help you understand the different parts of these objects and how they are designed you learn how to use the "What's This?" help tool. This is a part of the Help options that will be examined in more detail in Lesson 7. In this task, the Help option is used to provide you with information about forms and reports.

1 Click the **Forms** tab, click **Addresses**, and click the **Design** button. The **Addresses** form is displayed in Design View.

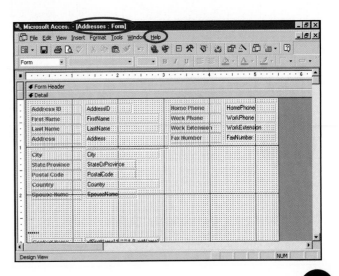

> **Pothole:** When the Design View of a form or report opens, the Toolbox may also appear on the screen. To give you a better view of the design, simply close the Toolbox by clicking the Close button (**X**) in the upper right-hand corner of the Toolbox.

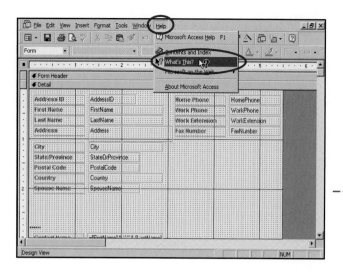

2 Choose **Help** and **What's This?** from the menu. The pointer will turn into an arrow with a question mark attached.

3 Click the label for the **First Name** field. Read the message box that describes the *label box*. This is a control on a form or report that contains descriptive text such as a title or caption.

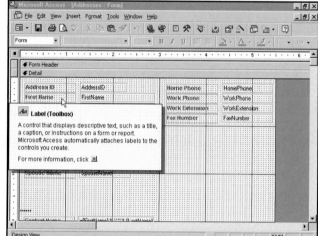

4 Click an empty space in the form to close the message box.

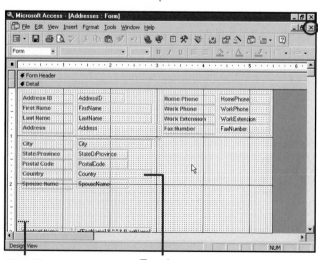

Page Break   Text box

5 Repeat steps 2 through 4 for a **text box** and the **page break**.

In Depth: The design of a form or report contains many kinds of controls. A *control* is a graphical object on a form or report that is used to display data, perform an action, or make a form or report easier to read. You have just looked at a *text box*, which is a type of control that is bound to the database and is used to display the data. Another type of control is the page break. Controls like these help to make a form or report function the way you want.

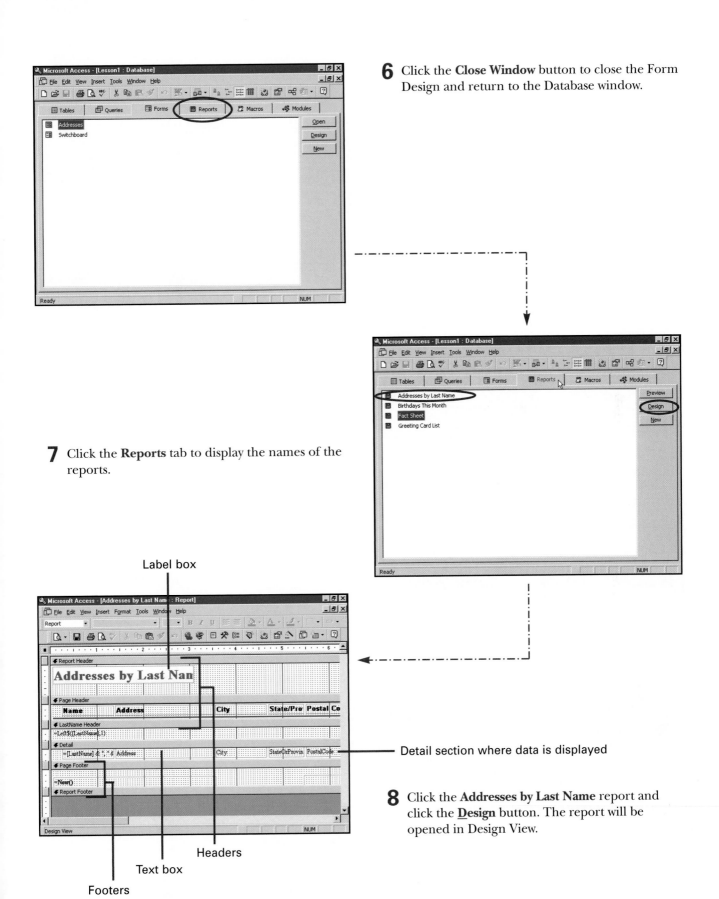

6 Click the **Close Window** button to close the Form Design and return to the Database window.

7 Click the **Reports** tab to display the names of the reports.

Label box

Detail section where data is displayed

8 Click the **Addresses by Last Name** report and click the **Design** button. The report will be opened in Design View.

Headers

Text box

Footers

9 Choose **Help, What's This?** Click an empty space in the Report Header and read the description.

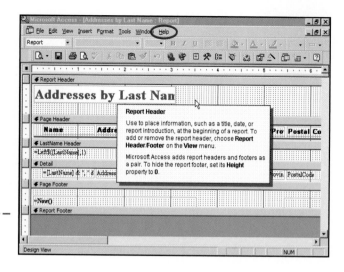

10 Click an empty space on the screen to close the message box.

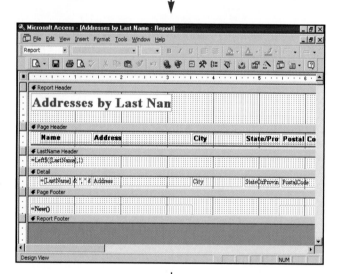

Pothole: When clicking in each area of the report design, it is important that you click in an open area and do not click on top of a text or label box. In the Page Header and Detail sections click to the left of the boxes. This open area will result in a description of the Page Header and the Detail sections of the report. When you click in the LastName Header you will see a description for Group Header. In this report, the Last Name field was used to group the data by the first letter of the last name, which resulted in this group header in the report design. In a report, you will see a group header for each field that you have grouped the data on.

11 Repeat this process for the **Page Header**, **LastName Header**, **Detail**, and **Page Footer** sections.

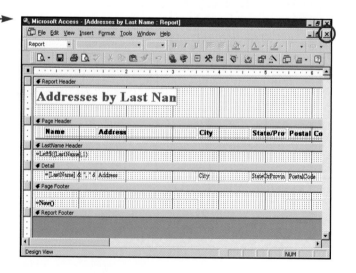

12 Close the **Addresses by Last Name** report.

Task 7

Closing the Database and Exiting Access

Why would I do this?

Access is designed to work with files that may be too large to fit in the computer's *RAM* memory, so most of the file remains on the disk while the program loads part of it into RAM memory. The program also assumes that the file is on your computer's hard disk. If you are storing a database on a floppy disk, it becomes very important that you are careful about closing a database properly and that you *never* swap floppy disks while a database is open. In this task, you learn how to close the database and then exit the Access program. If you simply turn off the computer while a database is open, you may corrupt the database beyond repair.

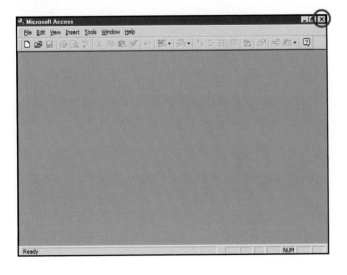

1 Click the **Close Window** button on the Database window. Notice that it does not ask you if you want to save changes. Changes are made continuously to the database on the disk—they do not need to be saved.

2 Click the **Close Window** button on the **Microsoft Access** title bar. The program closes.

Student Exercises

True-False

Circle either T or F.

T   F   **1.** Access contains over 30 templates.

T   F   **2.** Input masks are designed to prevent the user from accidentally adding data to protected fields.

T   F   **3.** Dates, numbers, currency, and memos are examples of non-text data types.

T   F   **4.** The Main Switchboard can be used to view database forms and reports.

T   F   **5.** Two views of a table are Datasheet View and Edit View.

T   F   **6.** When viewing records in Datasheet View, the record selector is used to select all the fields of a record.

T   F   **7.** If a table includes an AutoNumber field and you delete a record, AutoNumber automatically renumbers all of the following records.

T   F   **8.** It is OK to turn off the computer if a database is open. It will recover automatically when you launch Access again.

T   F   **9.** If you add or delete records while a database is open, Access will ask if you want to save the changes when you close the database.

T   F   **10.** The part of a report that will print at the top of each page of a multi-page report is called the Report Header.

Identifying Parts of the Access Screen

1. Refer to the figure and identify the numbered parts of the screen. Write the letter of the correct label in the space next to the number.

1. _____
2. _____
3. _____
4. _____
5. _____

A. Navigation buttons
B. Labels
C. Fields
D. View button
E. Close Window button

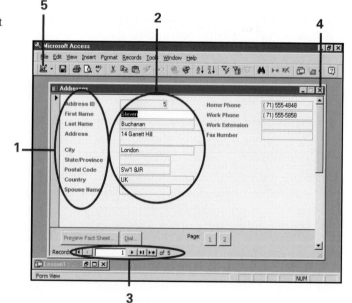

2. Refer to the figure and identify the numbered parts of the screen. Write the letter of the correct label in the space next to the number.

1. _____
2. _____
3. _____
4. _____
5. _____

A. Input mask
B. Non-text data types
C. Scroll bar
D. Field properties
E. View button

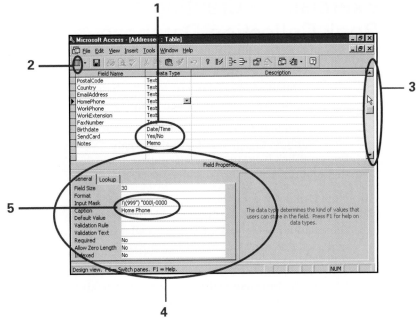

Matching

Match the statements below to the word or phrase that is the best match from the list. Write the letter of the matching word or phrase in the space provided next to the number.

1. ___ Automatically adds parentheses and dashes when you enter data

2. ___ Guides you through the process of creating a database through a series of dialog boxes

3. ___ A button on a table in Datasheet View that allows you to select all of the fields in a record

4. ___ A type of field used to store data that can have only two logical states

5. ___ Buttons that scroll from one record to another in a form

6. ___ Indicates a field that contains a unique value for each record

7. ___ A category of information

8. ___ Collection of data about one individual, event, or object

9. ___ Used in a table to specify the kind of information that will be entered in a field

10. ___ Works like a menu to open forms and reports

A. Primary key

B. Navigation

C. Main Switchboard

D. Input mask

E. Yes/No

F. Data type

G. Record

H. Page Header

I. Database Wizard

J. Field

K. Record selector

Application Exercises

Exercise 1 – Creating a Book Collection Database

1. Launch Access.

2. Use the Database Wizard to create a database using the **Book Collection** design template.

3. Save your database as **Book Collection** in the File New Database dialog box. Click the **Create** button. Click **Next** in the first Database Wizard dialog box.

4. Notice that the database contains five tables. Select the **Author Information** table and select the optional field, **Nationality**. Keep all of the default fields already checked. Click the option box **Yes, include sample data.**

5. Choose the **International** screen display style and the **Soft Gray** printed report style.

6. Call the database **Book Collection** and start the database when given the option.

7. Select **Preview Reports** and **Preview the Titles by Author** from the Switchboard.

8. Print the report and then close it to return to the switchboard.

Exercise 2 – Adding Information Using the Form View

1. Select **Enter/View Books** from the Switchboard.

2. Click the **New Record** button to move to a blank record.

3. In the Title field type **Access for Fun and Profit**.

4. Use the drop-down menu in the Topic field and select **Business**. Type **Macmillan** as the publisher and the cover type as **Soft**.

5. In the Notes field type **A useful guide to setting up a business using Access**.

6. Enter **19.95** as the price. Notice that when you move to the next field a dollar sign is added. This is because the Price field uses a currency data type.

7. Type **1997** as the Copyright Year, **12/24/97** as the Date Purchased, and **365** as the number of Pages.

8. The Author area in the lower-left corner of the Form window is actually information taken from a different table. To add a new author to this table, double-click in the Author field. Type your first name and your last name in the appropriate fields and close the Author window.

9. In the Author area click the drop-down menu arrow and select your name from the list.

10. Choose **File**, **Print** from the menu. Click the **Selected Record(s)** action button and then **OK** to print just the current record. Close the form and return to the main switchboard.

Exercise 3 – Adding and Deleting Information Using the Table View

1. Close the **Main Switchboard**, but not the database.

2. Maximize the **Database Window** in the lower-left corner of the screen.

3. Select the **Tables** tab and open the **Topics** table.

4. Add two new topics, **History** and **Philosophy**.

5. Delete the **Psychology** topic.

6. Print a copy of the datasheet. Write your name on the datasheet to hand in.

7. Close the **Topics** table. Leave the workbook open for use in the next exercise.

Exercise 4 – Printing a Report

1. Click the **Forms** tab, select **Switchboard**, and click **Open**.

2. Choose **Preview Reports**.

3. Choose the **Preview the Titles by Author Report**.

4. Scroll down to make sure your name and the book you wrote is listed on this report.

5. Click the report to preview the whole page, then click it again to magnify the page.

6. Choose **File**, **Print**.

7. Click the **Setup** button. Change the top margin to **2"** and the left and right margins to **.5"**.

8. Print the report, then close the report and exit Access.

Lesson 2
Create a Customized Database

Task 1 Creating a New Database Using the Blank Database Option

Task 2 Creating a Table and Defining its Fields

Task 3 Entering Records into a Table

Task 4 Adding and Deleting Fields

Task 5 Creating a Form Using the Form Wizard

Task 6 Arranging Text and Label Fields in a Form and Adding a Label

Task 7 Setting the Tab Order in a Form

Task 8 Creating a Report Using the Report Wizard

Task 9 Modifying and Printing a Report

Introduction

There are three ways to use Access once it is launched. You can use the Database Wizard, open an existing database file, or create a new database. In this lesson, you create a new database by creating and defining a set of fields for a personnel file for a fictional company called Armstrong Pool, Spa, and Sauna Co. Normally you would spend time thinking about how the database would be used, what information was needed, and what kinds of reports you would need to produce. Like any other computer application, a database is only as useful as the information that it contains. Once you decide on the information you need in your database, you create it by designing tables and adding records.

In this lesson, the content of the database will contain basic employee information. You will create the database and a personnel table. You will enter records, create and modify a form, and print a report.

Visual Summary

When you are done with this entire lesson, you will have created a database report that looks like this:

Personnel File by Department

Department	Last Name	First Name	Social Security Number	Telephone	Hourly Pay	Employed
Sales						
	Dent	Arthur	323232322	(313)941-0000	$9.00	10/1/90
	Johnson	Deborah D.	111223333	(313)555-1234	$9.50	5/25/95
	Johnson	John J.	123456789	(313)555-1234	$9.50	5/25/95
	Prefect	Ford	232323233	(313)461-0000	$9.00	10/1/90
Service						
	Robinson	Robert R.	987654321	(313)487-0000	$12.80	1/2/89
Stock						
	Abercrombie	Aaron A.	222334444	(810)437-0000	$5.00	6/12/97
	Wilson	Wendy W.	221212211	(313)769-0000	$5.00	7/17/97

Task 1

Creating a New Database Using the Blank Database Option

Why would I do this

Using the Database Wizard to create a database with pre-defined fields can be very helpful, if your database requirements match one of the 22 Access templates. There will be many occasions, however, when none of the templates are appropriate. For example, most businesses have needs for maintaining records that are unique to their type of business. When this happens, you will want to create your own customized database that is designed to meet your particular needs.

In this task, you will create a database that you design. You will launch Access, choose Blank Database, give the database a name, and choose where to store the file. Unlike other applications, when you create a database, the first action you will take is to name the database and designate where you will be saving the file. Only after the file has been created and saved can you actually begin to add data to the database.

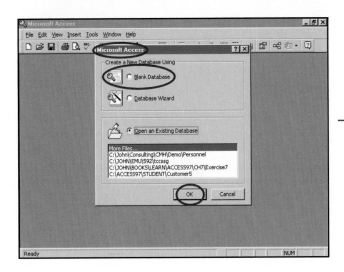

1 Launch Microsoft Access. The Microsoft Access window opens and allows you to **Open an Existing Database**, or to create a new database using the **Database Wizard** or **Blank Database** options.

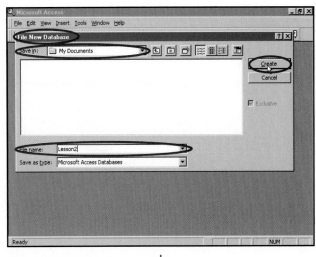

2 Click the **Blank Database** option and click **OK**. The **File New Database** dialog box opens. In the **Save in** box choose where you want to save your file. Type **Lesson2** in the **File name** box.

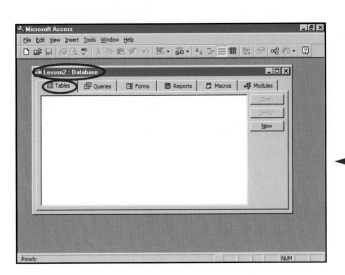

3 Click **Create**. The Database window opens with the **Tables** tab selected. The name of the database is shown in the database title bar.

Task 2

Creating a Table and Defining Its Fields

Why would I do this?

Once you have opened a new blank database, the next thing you must do is create a table. A table defines the content of your data by establishing the fields that will be included in each table.

In this task, you will create a table in Design View, assigning each field a name, data type, and description. Your field names will show as column headings in the table, the data type tells the computer what type of data will be entered, and the description appears on the status line of the table to aid in entering data.

1 With the **Tables** tab selected, click the **New** button. The **New Table** dialog box is displayed. Select the **Design View** option.

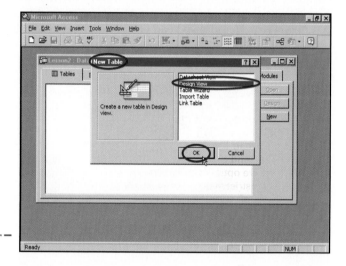

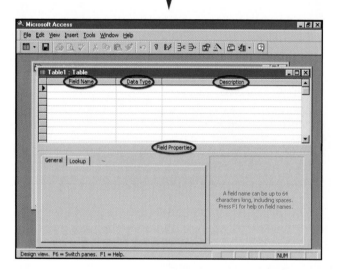

2 Click **OK**. The table **Design View** window opens. It contains three columns: **Field Name**, **Data Type**, and **Description**. There is also a section to modify the **Field Properties**.

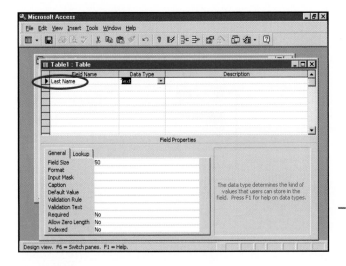

3 With the cursor in the first Field Name box, type **Last Name** and press ⏎Enter. The first Field Name is entered and the cursor jumps to the Data Type column.

In Depth: Once you have entered a field name and moved to the Data Type column, the Field Properties section becomes available. Each field has associated properties, such as field size and format. The types of properties that are available will depend on the data type that is selected. Field properties are optional tools that can be used to help control or restrict a field, or to improve its function in a table. Some of the available field properties are discussed in Lesson 3.

4 Since the first field will be text, press ⏎Enter to accept the **Text** data type. Type **Employee's last name** in the **Description** box and press ⏎Enter. The cursor jumps to the next Field Name box and the row selector moves to the second field.

Row Selector

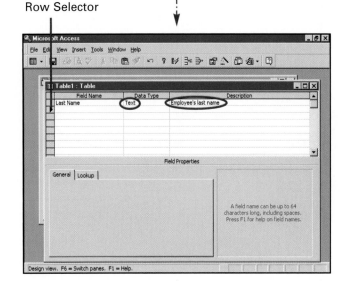

In Depth: Whatever you type in the Description box will appear in the Status bar at the bottom of the screen when the table is shown in **Datasheet View**. This allows you to place instructions for anyone entering data in case there is any question about the information that is to be entered in a field.

5 In the second field, type **First Name**, accept the **Text** data type, and enter **Employee's first name and middle initial**. Press ⏎Enter to move to the third field.

6 Type **Age** for the third field, then press (←Enter). Click the arrow on the **Data Type** drop-down box to reveal all of the data types.

Data Type drop-down box ⎯⎯⎯⎯⎯⎯⎯⎯⎯

View button

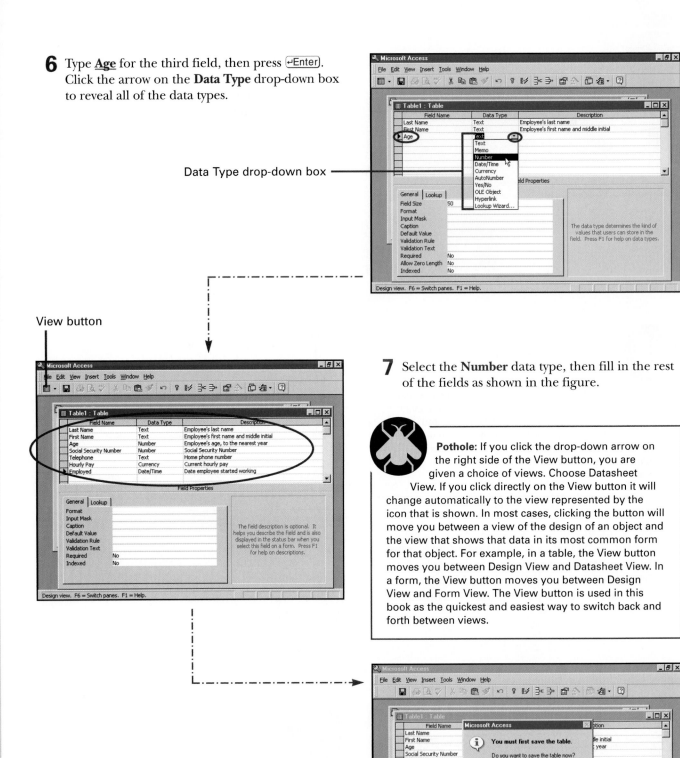

7 Select the **Number** data type, then fill in the rest of the fields as shown in the figure.

Pothole: If you click the drop-down arrow on the right side of the View button, you are given a choice of views. Choose Datasheet View. If you click directly on the View button it will change automatically to the view represented by the icon that is shown. In most cases, clicking the button will move you between a view of the design of an object and the view that shows that data in its most common form for that object. For example, in a table, the View button moves you between Design View and Datasheet View. In a form, the View button moves you between Design View and Form View. The View button is used in this book as the quickest and easiest way to switch back and forth between views.

8 Click the **View** button on the Standard toolbar to go to **Datasheet View**. A dialog box prompts you to save the table.

9 Click <u>Yes</u>. The **Save As** dialog box opens. Type **Personnel File** in the Table <u>N</u>ame box.

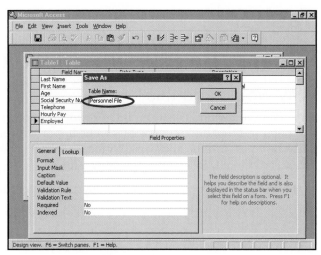

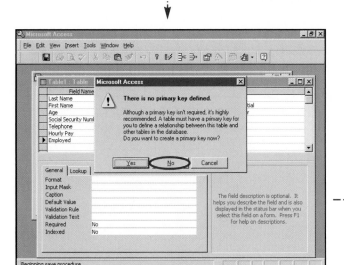

10 Click **OK**. A dialog box warns you that you haven't selected a primary key and asks if you want to create one.

Maximize button

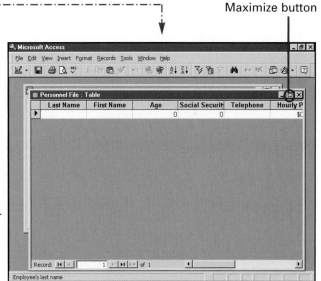

11 Click <u>N</u>o. You will deal with the primary key later. The table is now displayed in **Datasheet View** and is ready to accept data.

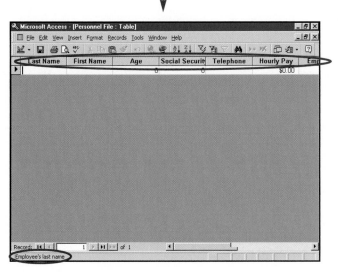

12 Click the **Maximize** button to give you the full screen to work in. Notice the field names are shown as column headings, and the description of the field shows in the status bar.

Task 3

Entering Records into a Table

Why would I do this?

The main function of a database is to provide a source of information about a topic. Data can be entered into the computer in three different ways: it can be imported from another source, it can be captured from a Web site, and it can be entered at the keyboard. With customized databases, this last method is the most common. Records can be entered directly in a table or by using a form.

In this task, you will enter records directly into a table and by using a form

1 With the cursor in the Last Name field, type **Johnson** and press ↵Enter). Notice that the description you entered when you created the field appears in the status bar. Also note that the record selector looks like a pencil, meaning that the record is being edited but has not yet been saved. Lastly, note that when you enter the first piece of data, a new empty record is displayed with an asterisk for the record selector.

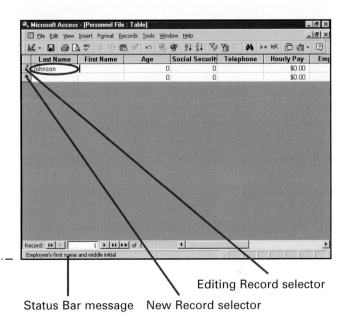

Editing Record selector

Status Bar message   New Record selector

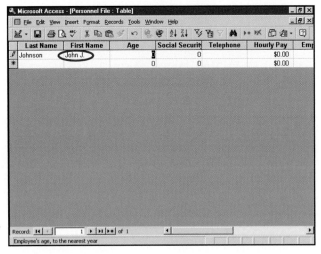

2 Type **John J.** in the First **Name field** and press ↵Enter).

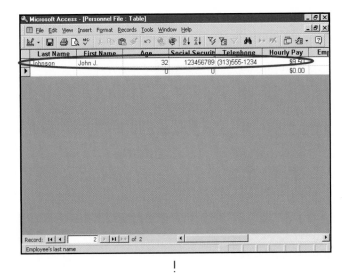

3 Enter <u>32</u> for the Age, <u>123456789</u> (no dashes) for the Social Security Number, <u>(313)555-1234</u> for the telephone number, <u>9.50</u> for the Hourly Pay, and <u>5/25/95</u> for the date Employed. Press ↵Enter after each entry. After you enter the last field, the cursor moves to the first field of the new record.

In Depth: You will notice that you are entering social security numbers without dashes and are typing parentheses and dashes in the phone numbers. In the previous lesson, an input mask was used to format these fields. We will add an input mask for the fields in this task in Lesson 3. By entering data without the Input Mask tool, you can compare the difference, and learn by experience, how different properties aid in data entry.

New Object: Auto Form button

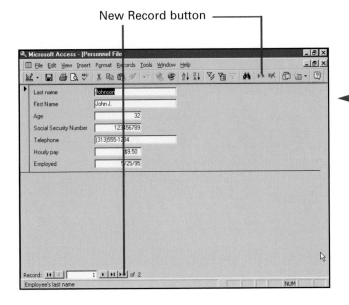

4 Fill in the next record as follows:

Last Name	**Robinson**
First Name	**Robert R.**
Age	**47**
Social Security Number	**987654321**
Telephone	**(313)487-0000**
Hourly Pay	**12.80**
Employed	**1/2/89**

A form can be created automatically that will list all of the fields in a table. This *AutoForm* can be used to enter data.

New Record button

5 Click the **New Object: AutoForm button**. An Auto-Form is created. Notice that the form places all of the fields in one vertical column. Using a form to enter records can be easier because all of the fields are visible on the screen and you see only one record at a time.

6 Click the **New Record** button on either the
Standard toolbar or at the right end of the navigation buttons to move to an empty record. Use
the AutoForm to enter the next four records listed
below. Press Tab⇄ or ←Enter to move from field to
field. After the last record is entered, the status bar
will show that six records have been entered.

Last Name	**Johnson**
First Name	**Deborah D.**
Age	**30**
SSN	**111223333**
Telephone	**(313)555-1234**
Hourly Pay	**9.50**
Employed	**5/25/95**
Last Name	**Abercrombie**
First Name	**Aaron A.**
Age	**16**
SSN	**222334444323232322**
Telephone	**(810)437-0000**
Hourly Pay	**5.00**
Employed	**6/12/97**
Last Name	**Prefect**
First Name	**Ford**
Age	**34**

SSN	**232323233**
Telephone	**(313)461-0000**
Hourly Pay	**9.00**
Employed	**10/1/90**
Last Name	**Dent**
First Name	**Arthur**
Age	**28**
SSN	**323232322**
Telephone	**(313)941-0000**
Hourly Pay	**9.00**
Employed	**10/1/90**

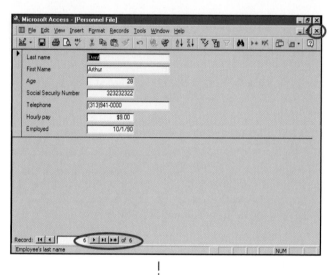

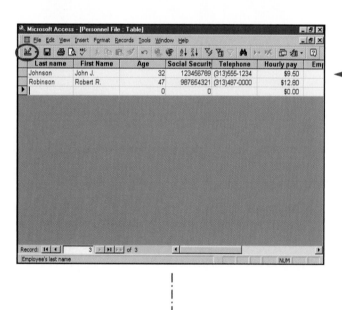

7 Click the **Close Window** button to close the AutoForm. When it asks if you want to save the form,
choose **No**.

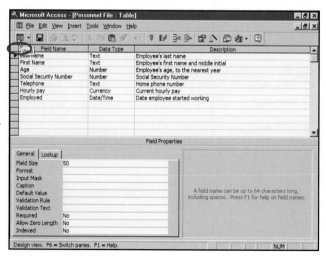

8 The table datasheet that was opened when you
created the AutoForm is now visible; however,
only the first two records show. To see the rest of
the records, you need to refresh the window.
Click the **View** button to change to Design View.

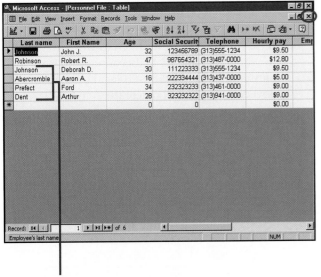

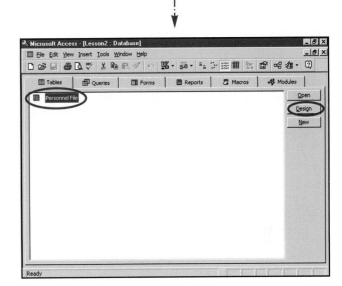

9 Click the **View** button again to return to Datasheet View. Now you can see all of the records you have entered.

Records added by using Autoform

10 Click the **Close Window** button. The **Tables** tab now shows the **Personnel File** table.

Task 4

Adding and Deleting Fields

Why would I do this?

Prior planning is critical when designing a customized database. This helps to avoid problems at a later date. No matter how well you plan, however, there will be times when you need to add new fields to your database. You will also discover that some fields are extraneous and need to be removed.

In this task, you learn how to modify a table by adding new fields and deleting others. When you make changes to the design of a table after records have been entered, Access gives you warning messages that the changes may affect your data. For this reason, it is recommended that you back-up your file before you begin. If you know the content of your data you will be able to judge the impact of the warnings. Be aware of the following:

✳ If you delete a field, all of the data in that field will be deleted as well.

✳ If you delete a field from a table, it must also be removed from other objects. If you forget and do not remove the deleted field, any query that uses the field will not work and forms or reports will display an error message.

✳ If you rename a field in a table you must also rename it in any object that uses that field.

✳ If you resize a field to a smaller size, Access will warn you that data may be lost because it may not fit in the new smaller field.

✳ If you change a field's data type, Access will try to convert the data in that field.

In this task, you learn how to add and delete fields and have the opportunity to see some of these warnings.

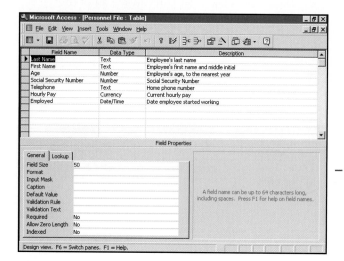

1 Click the **Design** button to go to **Design View** of the Personnel File table. Because there is some question about whether it is legal to keep an employee's age, you will delete the **Age** field.

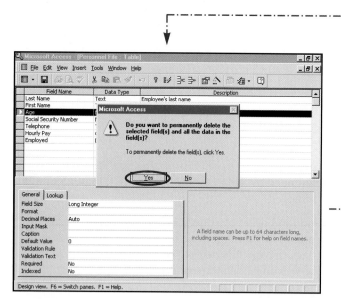

2 Click in the **Row Selector** column to the left of the **Age** field. The entire row is now selected.

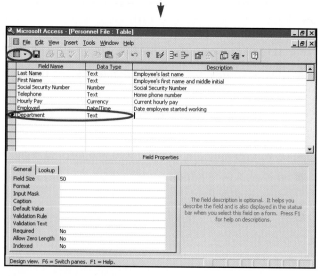

3 Press Del. A dialog box warns you that the deletion will be permanent, and asks if you want to delete the field(s). Click **Yes**.

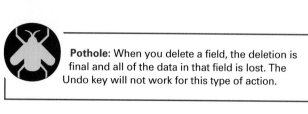

Pothole: When you delete a field, the deletion is final and all of the data in that field is lost. The Undo key will not work for this type of action.

4 To add another field, place the cursor in the Field Name box of the first blank row. Type **Department** as the new field name, accept the **Text** data type, and leave the Description area blank.

5 Click the **View** button to change to **Datasheet View**. A dialog box opens and prompts you to save the table.

In Depth: Anytime you change the structure of a database object, such as the change you made to the Personnel File table in step 4, you must save the change when it is made. You must save your changes before you go to Datasheet View, or they will be lost.

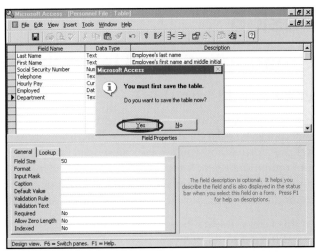

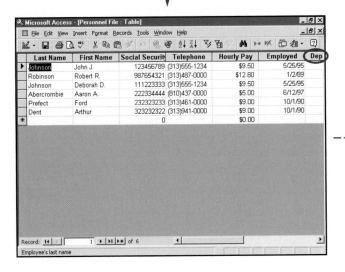

6 Click **Yes** to save your changes. The datasheet no longer contains an Age field, but does show the **Department** field on the right.

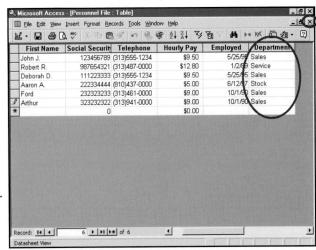

7 Fill in the **Department** field as shown.

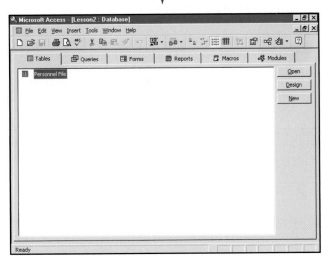

8 Click the **Close Window** button to close the table.

Task 5

Creating a Form Using the Form Wizard

Why would I do this?

In small databases, where all of the fields can be seen on the screen, you can easily enter records in the table Datasheet View. With larger databases, scrolling back and forth to view a field becomes tedious; in that case, a form is helpful. Forms allow you to place more fields on the screen at a time. You can see more information about a record, and unlike Datasheet View, you can view one record at a time. In Task 3 you created a form using the AutoForm option. This form is created based on the open or selected table. With an Autoform you do not have the opportunity to modify the order in which the fields appear, choose the fields that appear, or select a style or background.

In this task, you learn how to use the Form Wizard to create a form. Using the Wizard allows you to arrange fields in a different order, select only those fields that you want to use, and select a background and style for the form. This task is designed to introduce you to the Form Wizard so you can see the different options that are available. While the form you will create is similar to the Autoform, the process used is different. This form will be used in the next task to show you how to modify a form design.

1 Click the **Forms** tab. The Forms tab shows that no forms exist in the Lesson2 database.

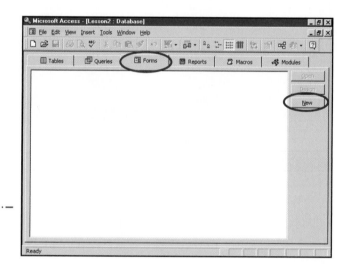

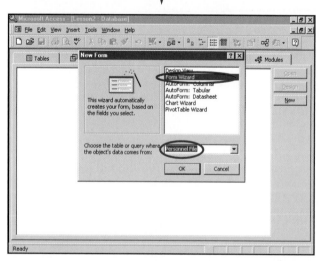

In Depth: You could use the **AutoForm: Columnar** option to create the same form you will create here with the Form Wizard. The Form Wizard, however, gives you much more control over the choice of fields and the color and design of the form background.

2 Click **New**. The **New Form** dialog box opens. Select **Form Wizard** and then select **Personnel File** from the table or query drop-down box.

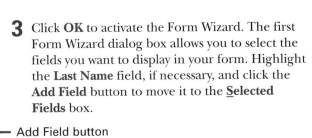

3 Click **OK** to activate the Form Wizard. The first Form Wizard dialog box allows you to select the fields you want to display in your form. Highlight the **Last Name** field, if necessary, and click the **Add Field** button to move it to the **Selected Fields** box.

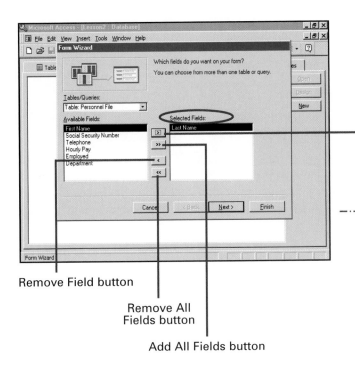

— Add Field button

Remove Field button

Remove All
Fields button

Add All Fields button

4 Click the **Add All Fields** button to place the rest of the fields in the **Selected Fields** box.

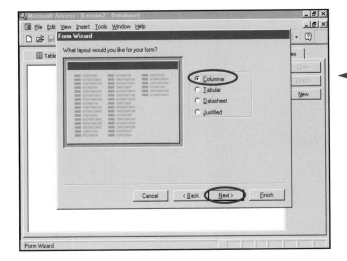

5 Click **Next**. The second **Form Wizard** dialog box prompts you to structure the form. Choose **Columnar**, if necessary.

6 Click **Next**. The third **Form Wizard** dialog box
prompts you to select a background style. Choose
Standard, if necessary. A preview is shown on the
left side of the dialog box.

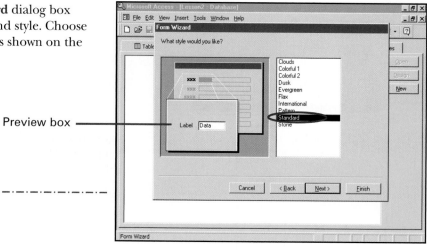

Preview box ————

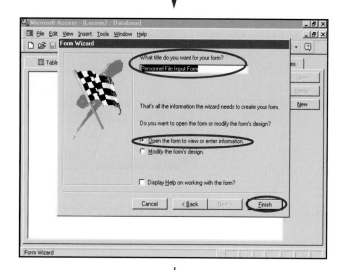

7 Click **Next**. The fourth (and final) **Form Wizard**
dialog box prompts you to name the form. Type
Personnel File Input Form. Make sure that the
Open the form to view or enter information
option is selected.

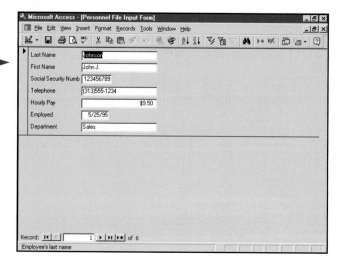

8 Click **Finish**. Access generates the columnar form
with the fields and background you selected. If
your form is not maximized, click the **Maximize**
button.

Task 6

Arranging Text and Label Fields in a Form and Adding a Label

Why would I do this?

When you use Form Wizard or AutoForm, Access arranges the data labels and the data boxes in a preset order. There will be many times when you would like to rearrange the fields to match the layout of a paper form. With practice you can design an Access form to look exactly like a printed form.

In this task, you learn how to move around in a form and change the layout of the text and label boxes.

Toolbox   Toolbox button

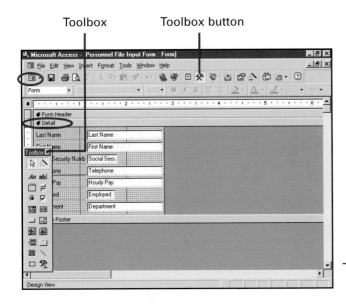

1 Click the **View** button to move to **Design View**. The form design window is displayed, along with the Toolbox. (Note: If the Toolbox is not displayed on your screen, click the **Toolbox** button on the Standard toolbar.) All of the fields are shown in the *Detail section* of the form.

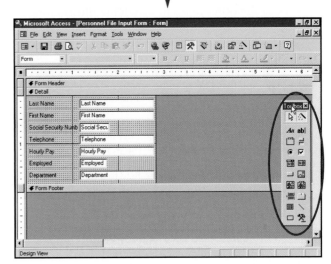

2 Click the Toolbox title bar and drag the Toolbox to the right side of the screen.

3 Click and drag the **First Name** field to the right of its current location, as shown in the figure.

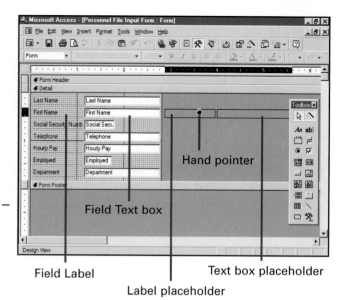

Field Label

Label placeholder

Field Text box

Hand pointer

Text box placeholder

In Depth: While you are dragging the field, a hand replaces the arrow pointer. Field *place-holders* show where the field will be located when you release the mouse button. It doesn't matter whether you drag the field *label* (in this case, the field name) or the field *text box* (which contains the data).

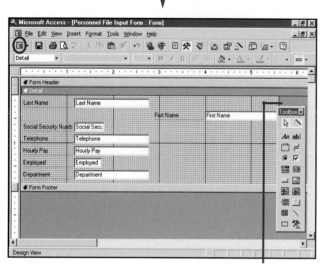

Detail work area border

5 Drag the other fields to match the illustration.

Pothole: Be patient with yourself. Repositioning fields takes some practice. If you follow the steps below, you will find it easier to master the technique.

To move a field with one motion, position the mouse pointer on top of the field you want to move. Click and hold down the left mouse button. The mouse pointer will turn into an open-hand symbol. When the mouse pointer is in the shape of a hand, drag the field to a new position.

To move a field using two motions, position the mouse pointer on top of the field you want to move. Click and release the mouse to select the field. You can tell when a field is selected by the handles that surround the outer edges. Now, move the mouse around the edge of the field until the cursor turns into a hand. When you see the hand, click and drag the field to its new location. Do not release the mouse until the field is positioned where you want it.

Whichever method you choose, the key is that the mouse pointer must be in the shape of a hand to move the field label and text box together.

4 Release the mouse button. The **First Name** field is now on the right half of the screen. The Detail work area automatically increased to accept the new field location.

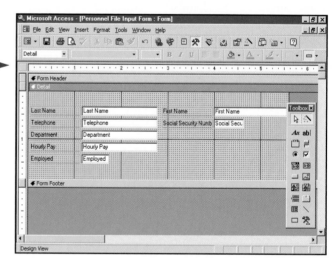

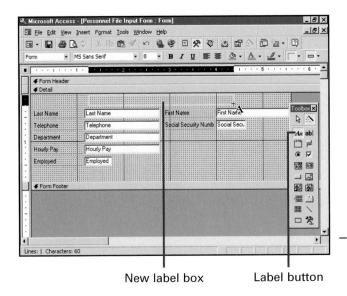

New label box   Label button

6 Click the **Label** button on the Toolbox toolbar. When you move the pointer to the **Detail** area, it changes to a crosshair with the letter **A** attached. Draw a new label box as shown in the figure.

Pothole: To begin drawing, click the mouse above the Last Name field and drag down and to the right above the First Name field. Do not release the mouse until you have finished drawing the new label box. If you release the mouse too soon, repeat the process and try again.

7 Type **Armstrong Pool, Spa, and Sauna Co.** in the label box. Click outside the new label, then click it again. Black handles surround the outer edge, showing that the box is selected.

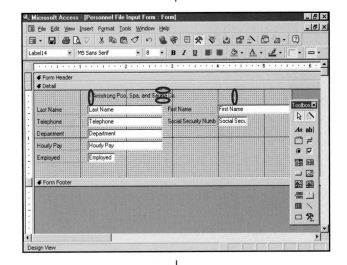

Font Size button ─┐   ┌─ Bold button

Font button   Center button

8 Click the **Bold** button and then the **Center** button on the Formatting toolbar. In the Font box, change the font to **Arial**, if necessary. Use the Font Size box to increase the font size to **12** point.

In Depth: If the formatted label no longer fits in the box, adjust the size of the box by clicking a black handle and then stretching the box to enlarge it. You may need to increase both the length and the height of the box.

9 Click the **View** button to return to **Form View**. Notice the effect of your changes.

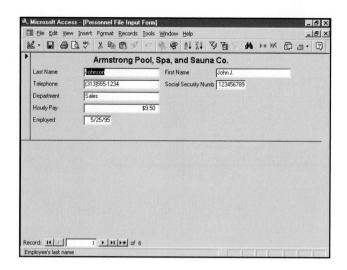

Task 7

Setting the Tab Order in a Form

Why would I do this?

The layout of your newly modified form may now make great sense, but when you start entering data, you will find that the cursor moves from field to field in the same order that the fields were entered in the table. The order the cursor follows in moving from field to field is called the *tab order*. By changing the tab order to match the new layout of the form, it will be easier to enter data.

In this task, you learn how to change the tab order to match the design of your form.

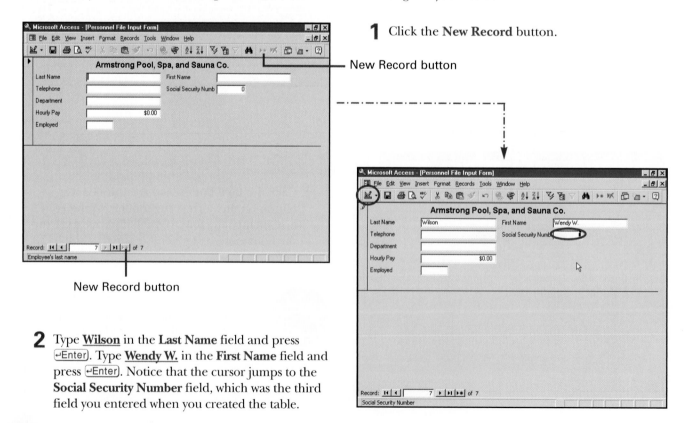

New Record button

1 Click the **New Record** button.

New Record button

2 Type **Wilson** in the **Last Name** field and press (←Enter). Type **Wendy W.** in the **First Name** field and press (←Enter). Notice that the cursor jumps to the **Social Security Number** field, which was the third field you entered when you created the table.

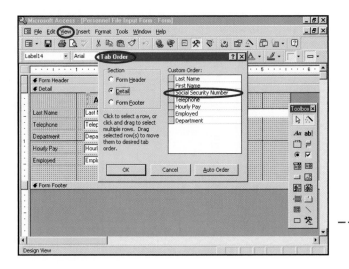

3 Click the **View** button to move to **Design View**. Choose **V**iew, **Tab** Order. The **Tab Order** dialog box opens with the Social Security Number shown as the third field.

4 Click the **Auto Order** button. The order of data entry automatically changes to match the fields so it will go from left to right and top to bottom.

In Depth: To change the tab order manually, click the selector box to the left of the field name. Release the mouse button, then click the selector box for that field again and drag the field up or down.

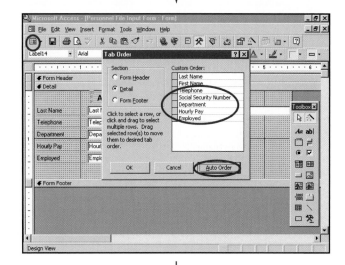

Print Preview button

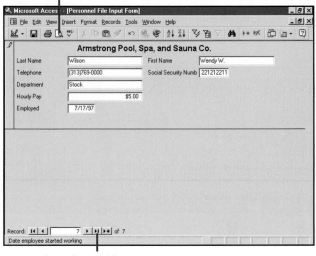

Last Record button

5 Click **OK**. Then click **View** to change to **Form View**. Click the **Last Record** button to return to the record you were adding. Finish filling in the information as shown.

6 Click the **Print Preview** button. The forms created show in a print preview window. Click the **Print** button to print the forms.

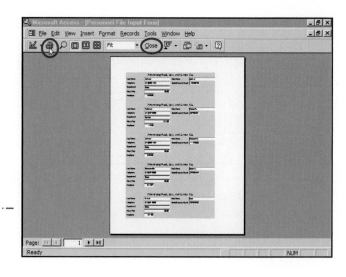

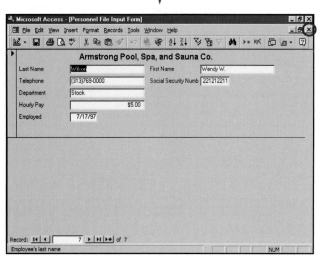

7 Click the **Close** button to return to Form View.

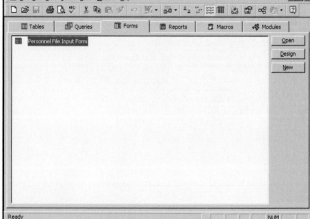

8 Click the **Close Window** button to close the form and move to the database window. Save your changes when prompted.

Task 8

Creating a Report Using the Report Wizard

Why would I do this?

When you have spent a great deal of time creating a database structure and entering data, you will want to print the information. A report gives you the flexibility to print the records and fields you select. You can also sort and group the records in a number of ways.

In this task, you use the Report Wizard. The Wizard helps you create a customized report that includes the fields you want, grouped and sorted in the manner you select. Reports, like forms, can be modified once they have been created. In this task, you will also create a report based on the Personnel File table that is grouped by department and sorted on last and then first name.

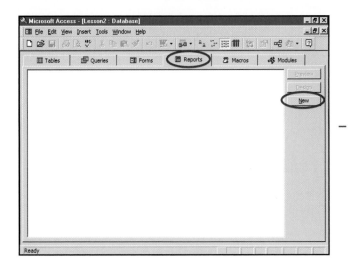

1 Select the **Reports** tab. No reports are shown since none have been created in this database.

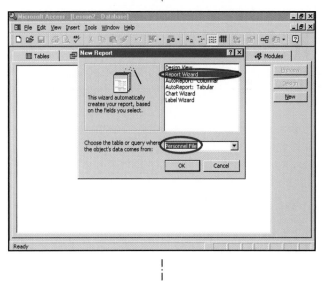

2 Click the **New** button. The **New Report** dialog box opens. Select **Report Wizard** and select the **Personnel File** table from the drop-down box.

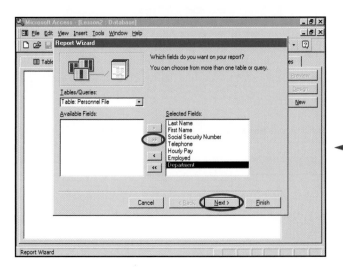

3 Click **OK**. The first Report Wizard dialog box opens. Click the **Select All** button to move all of the fields from the **Available Fields** box to the **Selected Fields** box.

4 Click **Next**. The second Report Wizard dialog box allows you to group data. Select the **De-partment** field and click the **Select Field** button.

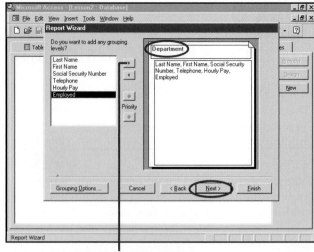

Select Field button

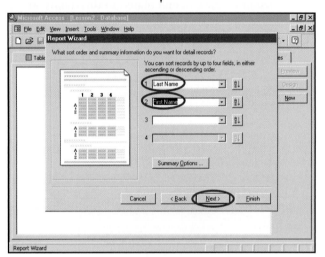

5 Click **Next**. The third Report Wizard dialog box allows you to sort data. You can sort on up to four fields. Select the **Last Name** field in the first sort drop-down box. Select the **First Name** field in the second drop-down box.

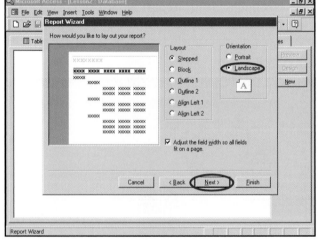

6 Click **Next**. The fourth Report Wizard dialog box allows you to choose the report layout. Select the **Landscape** button to print the report horizontally.

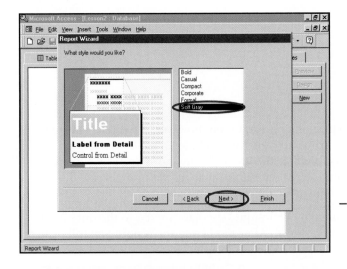

7 Click **Next**. The fifth Report Wizard dialog box allows you to choose the report design. Select **Soft Gray**, if it is not already selected.

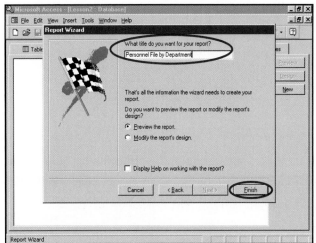

8 Click **Next**. The sixth Report Wizard dialog box asks for a report name. Call the report **Personnel File by Department**.

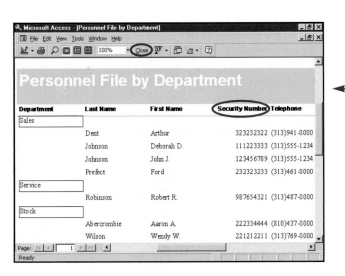

9 Click **Finish**. A Report Preview is displayed. Notice that the form looks quite good, but still needs a little editing, because some of the field names are cut off and the spacing of the columns needs improvement.

Task 9

Modifying and Printing a Report

Why would I do this?

The Report Wizard is a great tool to create the overall structure of a report. Often, however, the report may need some modifications to align fields under headings properly, or to show the full field name. In the report that was just created, the Social Security Number column heading is cut off on the left and only shows Security Number. Spacing between the columns is uneven, and the report would look better if the spacing was more evenly distributed. Once the report looks the way you want, it is easy to print a copy.

In this task, you learn a few techniques for modifying a report. The techniques used are similar to the ones used in Task 6 when you changed the design of the Personnel File Input Form. After modifying the report, you will print it.

1 Click the **View** button to return to the Report Design window.

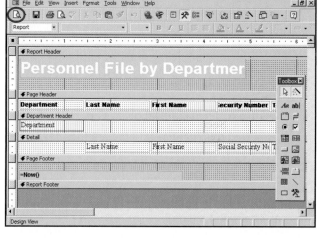

Handles

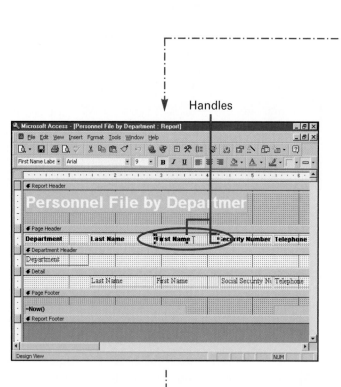

2 Click the **First Name** label in the Page Header to select it. The small squares around the edge of the box are called handles. These are used to modify the size and shape of a label or text box.

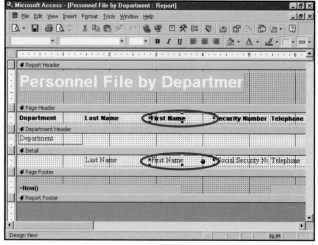

3 Hold down the (•Shift) key and click the **First Name** text box in the Detail section to select it. Both the label and the text boxes are now selected and can be modified together.

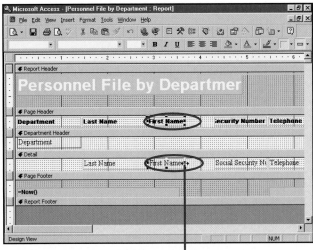

Double-headed arrow

4 Point to the handle in the middle of the right end of the **First Name** text box. When the pointer turns into a double-headed arrow, click and drag the end of the box to the left to shorten the length of the box as shown in the figure. Now there is room to lengthen the size of the Social Security Number label.

5 Click the **Security Number** label to select it. Hold down the ⬆Shift key and click the **Social Security Number** text box to select it.

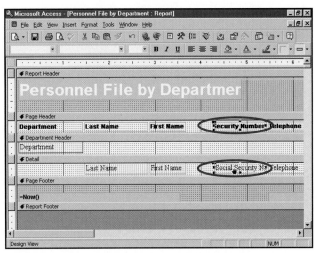

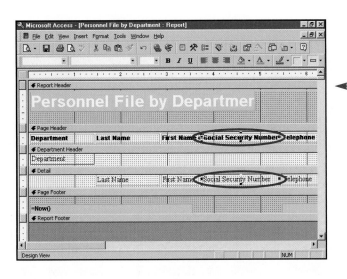

6 Point to the handle in the middle of the left end of the Security Number label box. Click and drag the end of the box to the left to lengthen it as shown in the figure.

7 With both the label and text box still selected, click the **Center** alignment button on the Formatting toolbar. This centers the numbers under the label in the report.

Center button

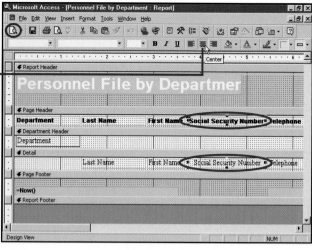

8 Click the **View** button to see the effect of your changes. Scroll to the right and notice that the Hourly Pay and Employed fields are too close together.

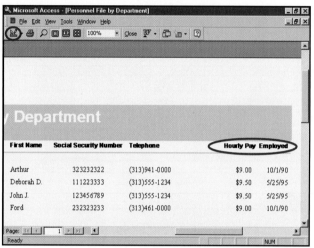

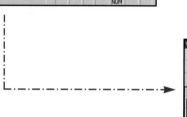

9 Click the **View** button to return to **Design View**. Click the **Hourly Pay** label, hold down the ⇧Shift key, and click the **Hourly Pay** text box.

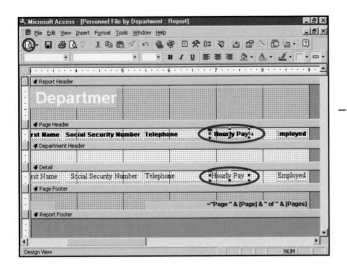

10 Point to the handle on the right end of the **Hourly Pay** label box. Click and drag the end of the box to the left to shorten both the label and text box as shown in the figure.

Print button

Mouse pointer shaped as magnifying glass

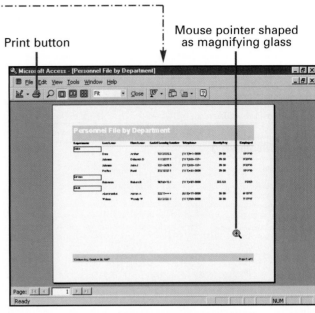

11 Click the **View** button to see the effect of your changes. The mouse pointer is in the shape of a magnifying glass. Click the report to see a full-page view of the report. The columns are more evenly spaced now, and the column headings are fully displayed. If necessary, adjust the width of the Employed field so the title is fully displayed.

Personnel File by Department

Department	Last Name	First Name	Social Security Number	Telephone	Hourly Pay	Employed
Sales						
	Dent	Arthur	323232322	(313)941-0000	$9.00	10/1/90
	Johnson	Deborah D.	111223333	(313)555-1234	$9.50	5/25/95
	Johnson	John J.	123456789	(313)555-1234	$9.50	5/25/95
	Prefect	Ford	232323233	(313)461-0000	$9.00	10/1/90
Service						
	Robinson	Robert R.	987654321	(313)487-0000	$12.80	1/2/89
Stock						
	Abercrombie	Aaron A.	222334444	(810)437-0000	$5.00	6/12/97
	Wilson	Wendy W.	221212211	(313)769-0000	$5.00	7/17/97

Friday, November 07, 1997

Page 1 of 1

12 Click the **Print** button to print a copy of the report.

13 Click the **Close** button to return to **Design View**.

Close button —

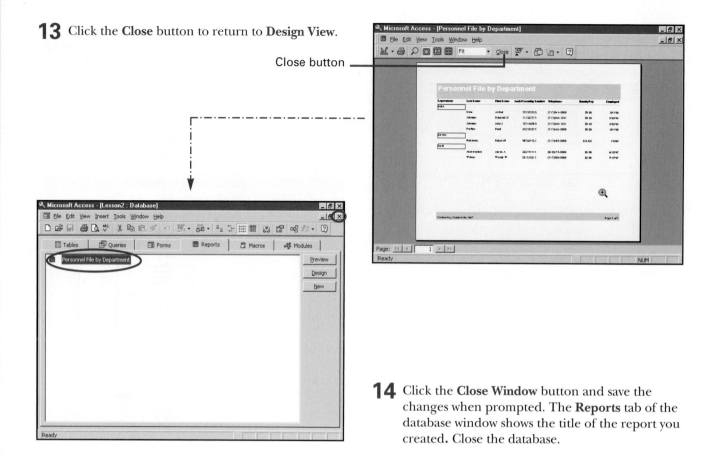

14 Click the **Close Window** button and save the changes when prompted. The **Reports** tab of the database window shows the title of the report you created. Close the database.

Student Exercises

True-False

Circle either T or F.

T F **1.** To create a customized Access database you need to launch Access, choose <u>B</u>lank Database, name the file, and select a file location.

T F **2.** Once you have created a new database, the first thing you have to do is to create a form for data entry.

T F **3.** When creating a table in <u>D</u>esign View, whatever you type in the Description column will appear in the Datasheet title bar.

T F **4.** When you make changes in the structure of a table, you need to save the table in order for your changes to take effect.

T F **5.** The first step in deleting a field is to click on the field's row selector.

T F **6.** If you delete a field, you can recover the data using the Undo button.

T F **7.** Data that you enter into a form or table is saved automatically.

T F **8.** You can see only one record at a time in a Columnar form.

T F **9.** The AutoForm: Columnar option gives you more control than the Form Wizard when creating a new form.

T F **10.** In a report, you can sort records up to four fields.

Identifying Parts of the Access Screens

Refer to the figures and identify the numbered parts of the screen. Write the letter of the correct label in the space next to the number.

1. _____
2. _____
3. _____
4. _____
5. _____
6. _____
7. _____
8. _____
9. _____
10. _____

A. Label button
B. Toolbox button
C. View button
D. Undo button
E. Maximize button
F. Close Window button
G. Detail area
H. Text box
I. Label
J. Row selector

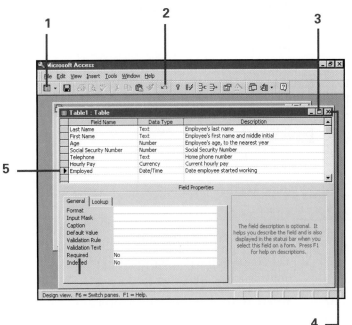

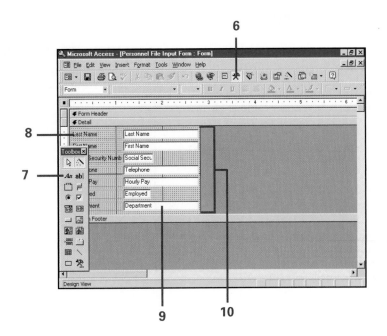

Matching

Match the statements below to the word or phrase that is the best match from the list. Write the letter of the matching word or phrase in the space provided next to the number.

1. ___ A toolbar of Access design tools

2. ___ Option which allows you to create a customized database

3. ___ Sets the tab order from left to right and top to bottom

4. ___ Indicates you are editing a record that isn't saved yet

5. ___ The shape of the pointer when you are moving a text box on a form

6. ___ Indicates that a text box or label is selected

7. ___ Indicates an empty record

8. ___ Horizontal report orientation

9. ___ The shape of the pointer when you are drawing a label box

10. ___ Where the data is shown on a form

A. Hand pointer

B. Asterisk record selector

C. Text box

D. Toolbox

E. Crosshair pointer with an attached A

F. **B**lank Database

G. Handles

H. **A**uto Order

I. Pencil record selector

J. **P**ortrait

K. **L**andscape

Application Exercises

Exercise 1 – Creating a Database and a Table

1. Launch Access. Choose the **Blank Database** option. Name the new database **EX0201**.

2. Use the skills that you have learned in this lesson to create the **Pool Parts Inventory** table as shown in the figure. See the steps below for more detail.

3. Make sure the **Table** tab is selected. Choose **New**.

4. Select the **Design View** option from the **New Table** dialog box.

5. Enter the fields as shown.

6. Click the **View** button to move to **Datasheet View**. Name the table **Pool Parts Inventory**.

7. Let Access create a **primary key** for you.

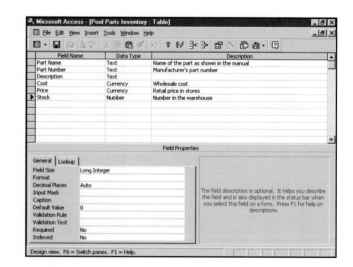

Exercise 2 – Entering Records into the Inventory Table

1. Make sure you are in **Datasheet View** of the **Pool Parts Inventory** table.

2. Use the skills that you have learned in this lesson to enter the data into the table as shown in the figure. See the steps below for more detail. You can create an AutoForm to enter the data if you prefer. (Note: The widths of the columns in this table have been resized to show all of the fields.)

3. Enter the data for each field as shown. Press (Tab↹) or (↵Enter) after each entry and at the end of each record.

4. Choose **File**, **Page Setup**, and **Landscape** orientation.

5. Choose **File**, **Print** to print a copy of the table.

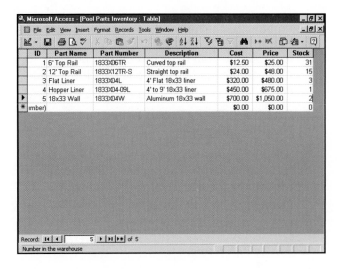

Exercise 3 – Adding and Deleting Fields

1. Click the **View** button to return to **Design view**. Because this information is to be printed for a customer price list, you will remove the **Cost** field. You will also add a **Sale Price** field.

2. Use the skills that you have learned in this lesson to create the **Pool Parts Inventory** table as shown in the figure. See the steps below for more detail.

3. Click the **row selector** for the **Cost** field and press (Del). Agree to permanently delete the data.

4. Move the cursor to the first blank row and type **Sale Price**. Choose the **Currency** data type. Type **10% off** in the Description area.

5. Click the **View** button to move back to **Datasheet view**. Save the changes to the table.

6. Fill in the **Sale Price** field as shown.

7. Choose **File**, **Print** and print a copy of the table in **Landscape** orientation. Close the table.

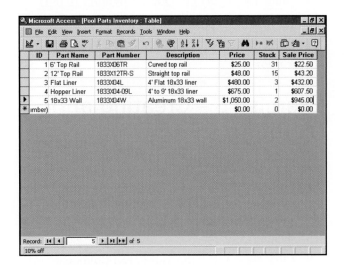

Exercise 4 – Creating a Report Using the Report Wizard

1. Click the **Reports** tab.

2. Use the skills that you have learned in this lesson to create the **Pool Parts Inventory** report as shown in the figure. See the steps below for more detail.

3. Click **New**. Choose **Report Wizard** and the **Pool Parts Inventory** table.

4. Select all of the fields, then highlight the **ID** field and remove it from the selected fields. (Note: To remove the ID field, click the ◁ button. The ID field moves back to the <u>A</u>vailable Fields box.)

5. Do not group on any of the fields.

6. Sort by **Part Name**.

7. Select a **Tabular** report printed in the <u>L</u>andscape orientation.

8. Select the **Corporate** style.

9. Name the report **Pool Parts Inventory Report**.

10. Preview the report, then print it.

11. Close the report and return to the database window.

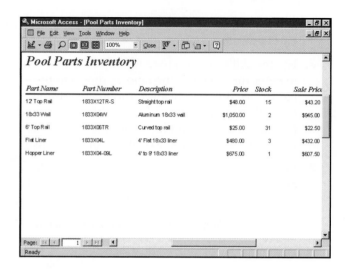

Exercise 5 – Creating and Modifing a Form

1. Click the **Forms** tab.

2. Use the skills that you have learned in this lesson to create the **Pool Parts Inventory Input Form** as shown in the figure. See the steps below for more detail.

3. Click **New**. Select the **AutoForm: Columnar** and the **Pool Parts Inventory** table. (Note: You may have a different background to your form.)

4. Click the **View** button to change to **Design View**. (Note: If necessary, click the Maximize button to enlarge the view.)

5. Rearrange the fields as shown. Choose **View**, **Tab Order**, **Auto Order** to reset the order of entry.

6. Return to **Form View**. Print a copy of the current record, Record 1, only.

7. Close the database and exit Access.

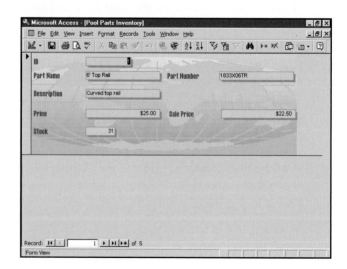

Lesson 3
Modify the Structure of an Existing Database

Task 1 Changing the Data Type of a Field

Task 2 Adding Input Masks to Aid Data Entry

Task 3 Setting Default Values

Task 4 Assigning a Primary Key Field

Task 5 Adjusting Table Column Widths

Task 6 Adding a List Box to a Form

Task 7 Adding a Combo Box to a Form

Task 8 Adding Headers, Footers, and Page Breaks to a Form

Introduction

When you create a custom database, there are many modifications you can make so that the database is easier to read and more useful for the end-user. There are a number of field property changes you can make to improve the data-entry process. You can apply an input mask to format a field so it looks like the information you are entering, such as you saw with telephone numbers or Social Security numbers in Lesson 1. You can make common values appear in a field automatically, and you can create lists of common field entries so the user does not have to type the same information over and over. You can also add explanatory information to forms and reports to make them more useful.

In this lesson, you change some of the properties in a table and add a combo box, list box, header, footer, and a page break to a form.

Visual Summary

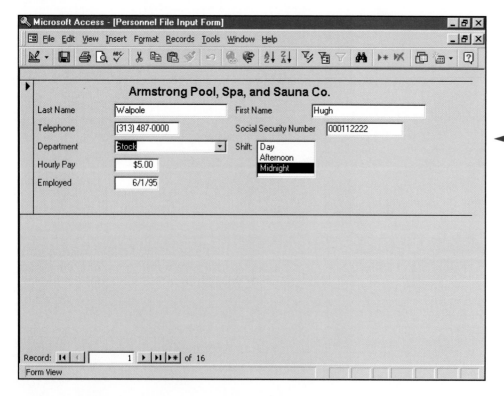

When you have completed this entire lesson, you will have created a form in a database that looks like this:

Task 1

Changing the Data Type of a Field

Why would I do this?

If you plan your database carefully, you should not have to change a field data type very often. If you create enough databases, however, you will eventually need to modify the data type.

In this task, you learn how to change a number field to a text field so you can add an input mask later. In Lesson 1, the database created by the Database Wizard used input masks to help format phone numbers and zip codes. As you will recall, an input mask applies special field structures to help the user enter data. Input masks are primarily used in Text and Date/Time fields but can be manually applied to number or currency fields. To make it easier, you will change the data type to text so the Input Mask Wizard can be used to apply an input mask in Task 2.

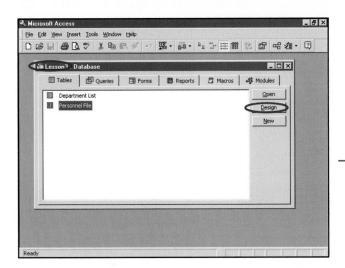

1 Using Windows Explorer, copy **Less0301** and rename the file **Lesson3**. (Follow your instructor's directions for the location to copy and rename the file.) Launch Microsoft **Access**. Choose **Open an Existing Database**, find the file **Lesson3**, and open the file. This is a slightly expanded version of the file you worked on in Lesson 2.

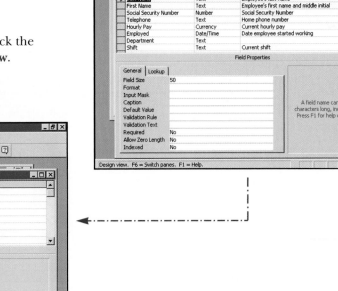

2 Select the **Personnel File** table and click the **Design** button to switch to **Design View**.

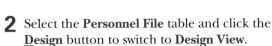

Data Type drop-down menu

3 Place the cursor in the **Data Type** column of the **Social Security Number** row. Click the arrow to activate the drop-down menu.

4 Choose the **Text** option from the **Data Type** drop-down menu.

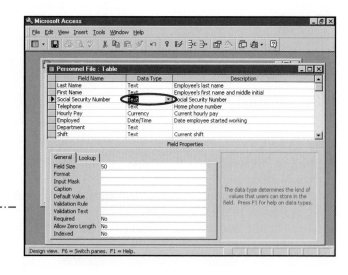

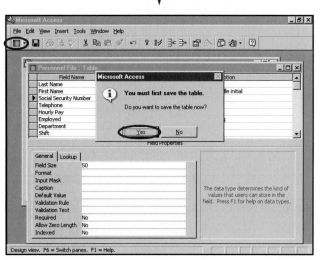

5 Click the **View** button to switch to **Datasheet View**. Click **Yes** when prompted to save your table.

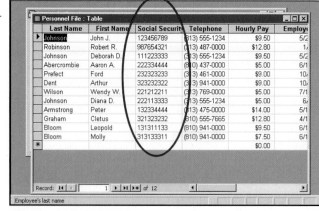

6 Notice that the numbers in the **Social Security Number** field are left-aligned, now that you have designated them as a text data type.

Task 2

Adding Input Masks to Aid Data Entry

Why would I do this?

Many types of information, such as telephone numbers, Social Security numbers, and dates include dashes and parentheses as part of their structure. In Lesson 1, you entered data in some fields that used a pre-formatted structure, while in Lesson 2, the table you designed did not contain that same formatting. Entering data is much easier when the format needed has already been applied to the field structure in the table.

In this task, you learn how to use the Input Mask Wizard to create a formatting structure for the Social Security Number field.

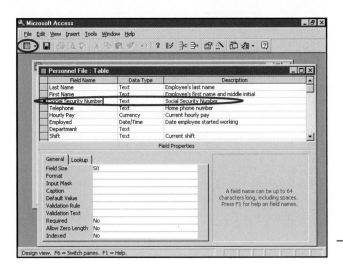

1 Click the **View** button to change to **Design View**. Click anywhere in the **Social Security Number** field.

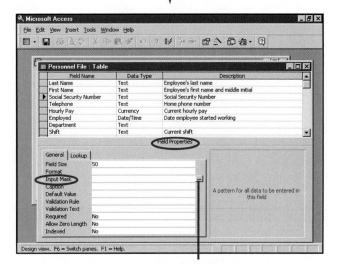

Build button

2 In the **Field Properties** section click in the **Input Mask** box. A **Build** button is displayed on the right edge of the box.

3 Click the **Build** button. The first **Input Mask Wizard** dialog box opens. Select the **Social Security Number** option.

> **Pothole:** If your system was set up with a standard installation, you will get a warning that this feature is not installed. This feature is part of the Advanced Wizard package that can be installed as part of a custom installation. Consult with your instructor for further direction. If you are unable to install the Wizard, continue reading this task and you can manually enter the necessary coding. See the In Depth note following Step 6 for assistance.

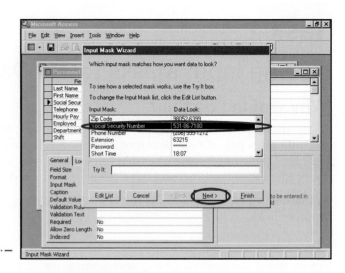

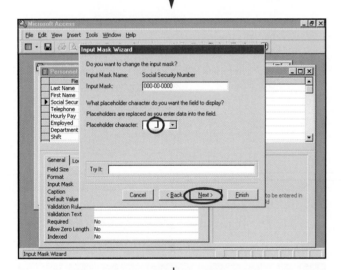

4 Click **Next**. The second **Input Mask Wizard** dialog box opens. Accept the underscore as the placeholder.

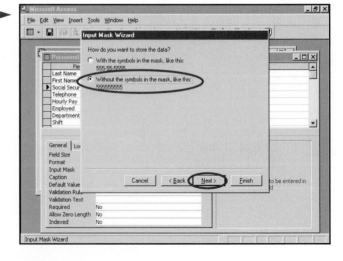

5 Click **Next**. The third **Input Mask Wizard** dialog box opens. Choose to store the data without the dashes. This will take less storage space, but the dashes will still be displayed.

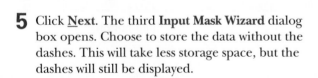

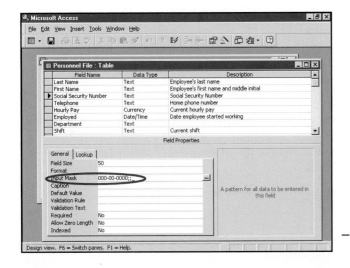

6 Click **Next**. The last **Input Mask Wizard** dialog box opens. It requires no input. Click **Finish** to close the **Input Mask Wizard**. The input mask is shown in the **Input Mask** box.

In Depth: You can manually enter an input mask if you know the proper coding. If you were unable to use the Input Mask Wizard, enter the coding you see in the figure on the Input Mask line for the Social Security Number field.

7 Click the **View** button to move to **Datasheet View**. Save changes when prompted. Notice that all of the Social Security numbers have dashes in the proper locations.

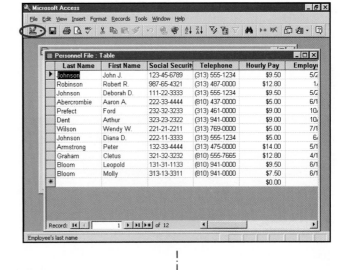

Pothole: When you add an input mask to a field in a table that is already used as the basis for a form or record, the input mask will not affect the appearance of the field in either the form or report. You will need to add an input mask to each object.

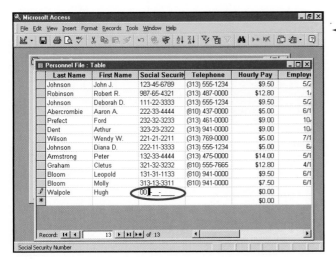

8 Add another record with the following data: **Walpole**; **Hugh**; **000112222**; **(313) 487-0000**; **5**; **6/1/95**; **Stock**; **Midnight**. Watch how the structure of the Social Security number is displayed as you enter the number.

Task 3

Setting Default Values

Why would I do this?

Default values are values that are entered into a field as soon as you start editing a record. For example, if most of your employees hire in at $5.00 an hour, you can have the program automatically put that number in the Hourly Pay field every time a new employee record is created. This can save time in entering data if it is used when there will be few exceptions. It also ensures that a field is not left blank.

In this task, you learn how to add the current date to the Employed field, since the only new records you will be adding will be for new employees.

1 Click the **View** button to move to **Design View**. Click anywhere in the **Employed** field.

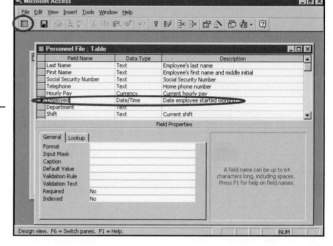

2 In the **Field Properties** section click in the **Default Value** box. A **Build** button is displayed on the right edge of the box.

3 Click the **Build** button. The **Expression Builder** dialog box opens.

4 Double-click the **Functions** option. A subdirectory called **Built-In Functions** is displayed.

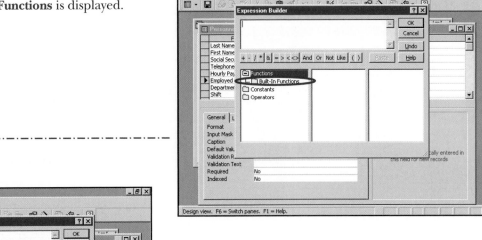

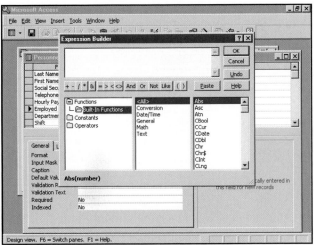

5 Click the **Built-In Functions** subdirectory. Two new options columns are displayed.

6 Select **Date/Time** from the middle column. A group of date and time options are displayed in the third column.

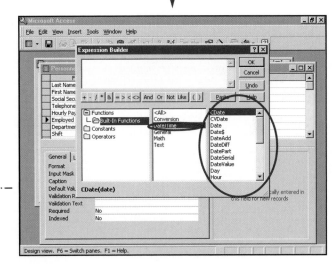

7 Select **Date** from the third column and click the **Paste** button. The **Date()** option is pasted into the **Expression Builder** work area. This function automatically enters the current date into the Employed field.

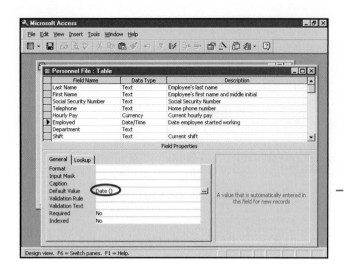

8 Click **OK**. The **Date()** function is now displayed in the **Default Value** box for the **Employed field**.

9 Click the **View** button to move to **Datasheet View**. Save changes when prompted. Notice that the default date already appears in the **Employed** field of the empty record at the bottom of the table.

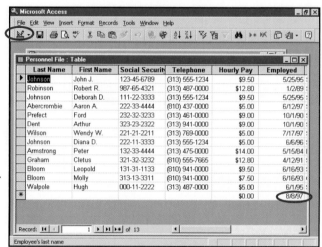

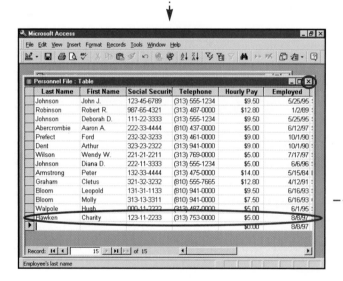

10 Add another record with the following data as shown: **Hawken**; **Charity**; **123112233**; **(313) 753-0000**; **5**; (accept the current date); **Stock**; **Day**.

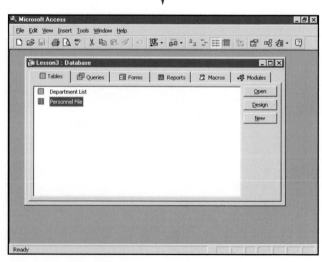

11 Click the **Close** button to return to the Database window.

Task 4

Assigning a Primary Key Field

Why would I do this?

Primary key fields are fields that are used to speed up sorting and finding data in a large table and to link tables together. A primary key field must contain unique data for each record; that is, there can be no duplication in that field from one record to the next. Some tables use sequential numbers, known as counters, as primary keys. Others use fields that are naturally unique, such as Social Security numbers or employee identification numbers.

In this task, you learn how to designate the Social Security Number field as your primary key field.

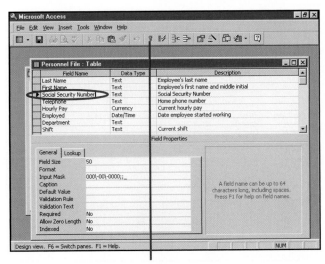

Primary Key button

1 With the **Personnel File** table still selected, click the **Design** button to move to **Design View**. Click anywhere in the **Social Security Number** field.

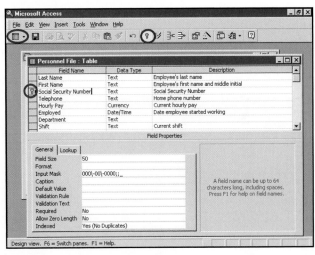

2 Click the **Primary Key** button in the Table Design toolbar. A key symbol is placed in the row selector column to the left of the field name.

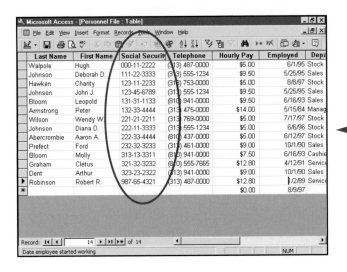

3 Click the **View** button to move to **Datasheet View**. Save changes when prompted. Notice that the table is now sorted in order of Social Security number.

Task 5

Adjusting Table Column Widths

Why would I do this?

In some small tables you will be using the Datasheet View of the table to enter information. Even with bigger tables, you will still often use Datasheet View to browse through your data. The default column widths in a table are seldom the right width, allowing far too much room for some fields, and cutting off the view of longer fields. There is an easy way to adjust the column widths. In this task, you learn how to adjust the column widths and save the changes to your layout.

1 Click the **Maximize** button to maximize the size of the Datasheet window. Notice that several of the columns are too wide, and not all of the columns are shown on the screen.

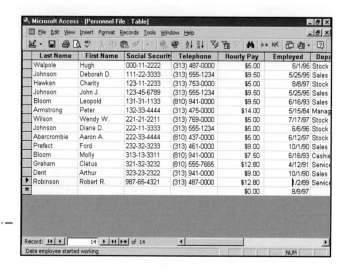

Field selector

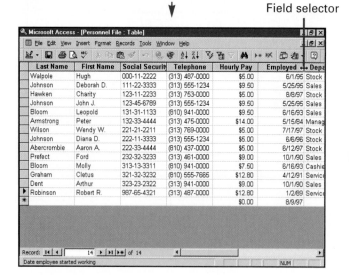

2 Move the pointer to the right edge of the *field selector* for the **Employed** field. The pointer changes to a two-sided arrow.

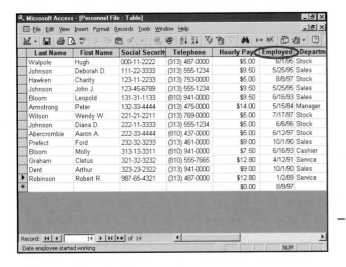

3 Click and drag the right edge of the **field selector** until the column width is just large enough to show the **Employed** label. It may take more than one try.

4 Change the column widths of the other columns as shown in the figure. In some cases, part of the field name in the **field selector** will be hidden. That's ok. The objective is to view all of the record data, without scrolling.

> **Quick Tip:** You can automatically adjust a column width by double-clicking on the right edge of the field selector. You can also adjust more than one field at a time by clicking in the middle of a field selector and dragging to the right or left to select multiple columns. You can double-click on the right edge of any one of the selected columns to automatically adjust all of them at once.

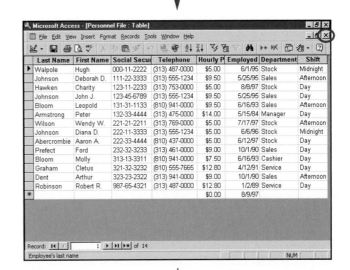

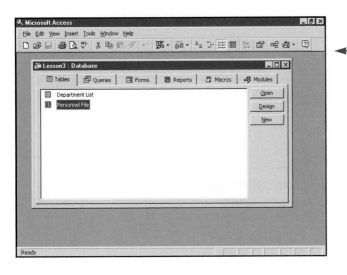

5 Click the **Close Window** button. Save changes when prompted.

Task 6

Adding a List Box to a Form

Why would I do this?

When there are only a few possible values for a field, a *list box* makes it easy to select the correct entry. By clicking on one of the items in a list box, you also assure that the entry will be spelled correctly. List boxes have certain restrictions. The entries shown in the box are the only possible entries; nothing else can be entered in that field. Also, the list box remains on the screen at all times.

In this task, you learn how to add a list box to the Shift field, which has only three possible values.

1 Click the **Forms** tab and select the **Personnel File Input Form**.

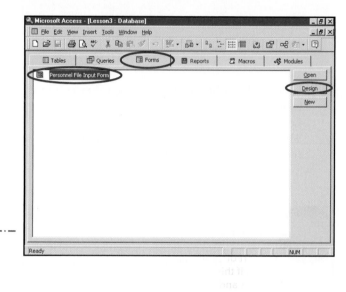

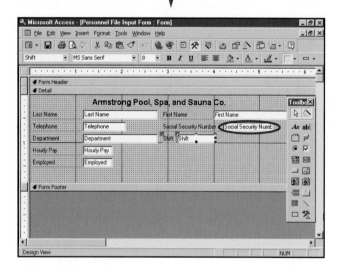

2 Click the **Design** button to switch to **Design View**. If necessary, move the **Toolbox** so it doesn't interfere with any of the fields. Click the **text box** in the **Shift** field to select it.

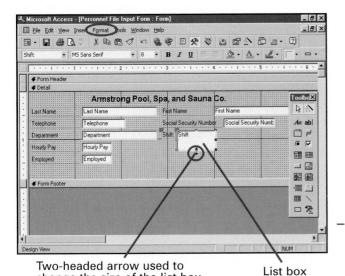

Two-headed arrow used to
change the size of the list box

List box

3 Choose **Format, Change To, List Box**. A box opens to the right of the **Shift** label. Grab the bottom handle on the box and resize it as shown in the figure so three lines of text will fit.

Pothole: If the **List Box** option is not available from the menu, it means you selected the **label** instead of the **text box** for the **Shift** field. Click the Shift field text box and try again.

4 Click the **Properties** button on the Form Design toolbar. The **List Box: Shift** properties dialog box is displayed.

Pothole: It is important that the properties dialog box is titled **List Box: Shift**. This indicates that the property box opened is for the list box you just created for the Shift field. If the box has any other title, it means that you clicked the mouse in another part of your screen before clicking the **Properties** button. If this happens, click the title bar of the properties box and drag the box to another part of the screen until you can see the list box. Then click the Shift list box and the properties box will change to the properties box for the selected field.

Properties button

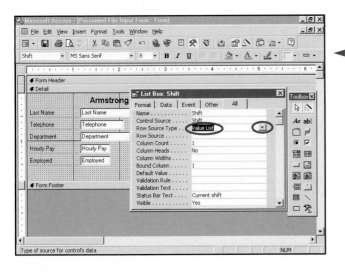

5 Click in the **Row Source Type** box. Click the drop-down arrow at the right of the box, and choose **Value List**.

6 Click in the **Row Source** box. Type the three possible entries exactly as shown: **Day; Afternoon; Midnight**. Make sure you include the semicolons between each item. These three items will appear in the **list box**.

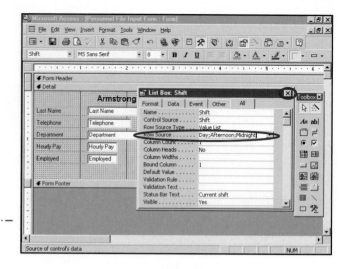

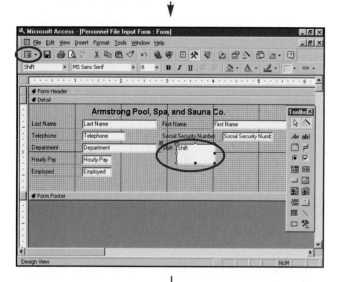

7 Click the **Close** button to close the **List Box: Shift** properties dialog box. The list box does not show the individual items in Design View.

8 Click the **View** button to switch to **Form View**. You should be able to see all three items in the **list box**.

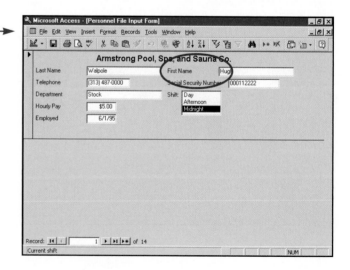

Pothole: If the list box has a scroll bar on the right and does not show all of the items, it means that you made the box too small. Return to **Design View**, select the **list box**, and resize it using the middle handle on the bottom edge of the box.

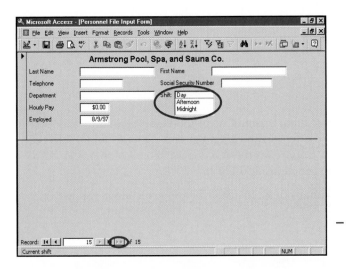

9 Click the **New Record** button to add a new record. Notice that none of the items in the **list box** are selected.

10 Enter the information for the new record as shown. When you reach the **Shift** field, click **Day** to select the Day shift.

In Depth: Notice that today's date shows automatically in the employed date field because of the default property that was set for this field.
The Social Security number is not formatted in the form, however, because the input mask was added to the table after the form had been created, and you have not added the input mask formatting to the form.

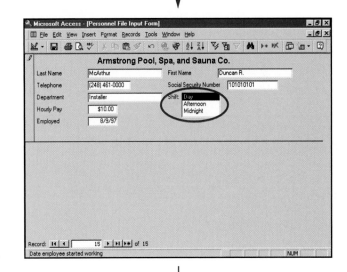

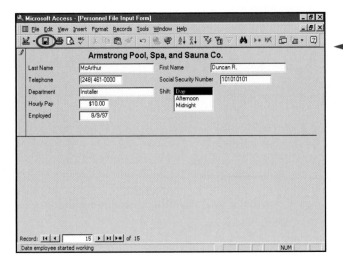

11 Click the **Save** button to save the changes made to the form.

Task 7

Adding a Combo Box to a Form

Why would I do this?

A list box is handy in some cases, but in others, a *combo box* is far more useful. A combo box is similar to a list box because it helps in the data-entry process. A list of items is presented from which the correct data can be selected. A combo box, however, uses a drop-down list, so it takes up less space on the screen. You can also enter items not found in the data source, whereas the list box restricts you to the items in the list.

In this task, you learn how to add a combo box to the Department field. Instead of typing the items, you will use another table as the data source.

1 Click the **View** button to switch to **Design View** of the **Personnel File Input Form**.

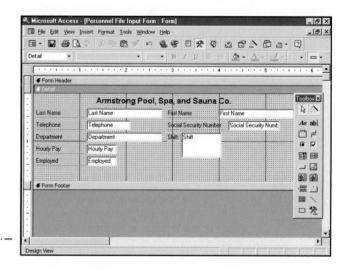

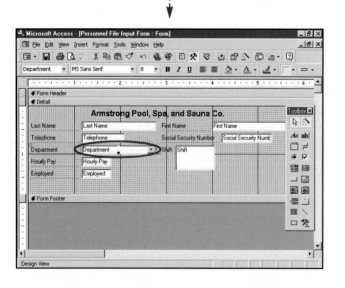

2 Click the **Text Box** of the **Department** field to select it.

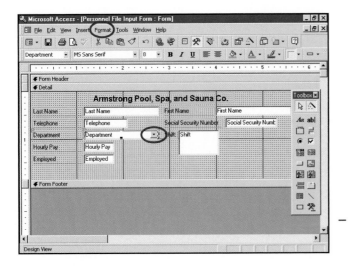

3 Choose **Format**, **Change To**, **Combo Box**. A drop-down arrow is displayed on the right side of the **text box**.

Pothole: If the **Combo Box** option is not available from the menu, it means you selected the **label** instead of the **text box** for the **Department** field. Click the Department field text box and try again.

4 Click the **Properties** button. The **Combo Box: Department** properties dialog box is displayed. **Table/Query** is the default choice for the **Row Source Type**.

In Depth: When you created the list box in the previous task, you selected the option **Value List** in the **Row Source Type** box. This allowed you to type a list of values. In this case, you will accept the default choice to use the **Table/Query** option in the **Row Source Type** box, because you are using a table as the source of the list for the combo box. You could, however, use one of the other options for the Row Source Type with a combo box.

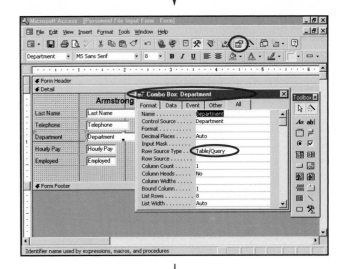

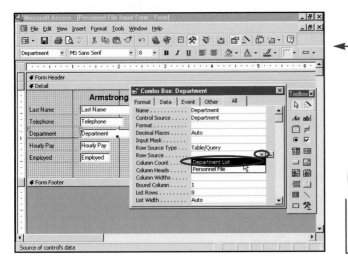

5 Click in the **Row Source** box. Click the drop-down arrow to display the tables and queries available as data sources. Select **Department List**.

In Depth: The Department List is a table that has just one field. This field lists all five of the current departments in the company. You will see the departments listed when you move to Form View to test the combo box.

6 Click the **Close** button to close the **Combo Box: Department** properties dialog box. The combo box does not show the department list in Design View.

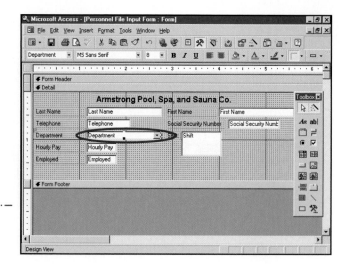

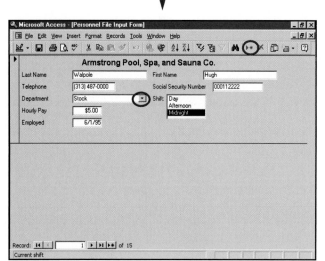

7 Click the **View** button to move to **Form View**. Notice that the **Department** field has a drop-down arrow on the right side of the **text box**.

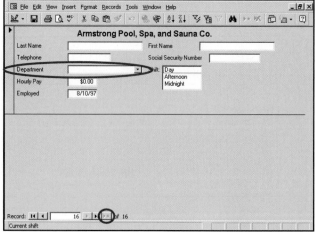

8 Click the **New Record** button to add a new record. Notice that none of the items in the **combo box** are selected.

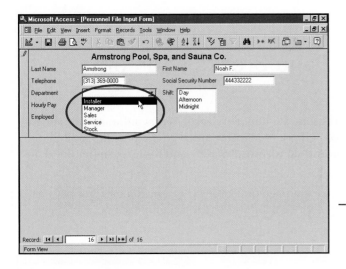

9 Enter the information for the new record as shown. When you get to the **Department** field, click the drop-down arrow to view the available items.

10 Select <u>Installer</u> from the **combo box**, then finish filling in the record as shown.

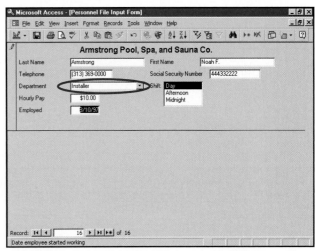

Quick Tip: A quick way to select items from a combo box or a list box is to type the first letter of the option you want. The program will choose the option based on the first letters that are typed. When you see your choice in the field text box you can press Enter to select it and move to the next field.

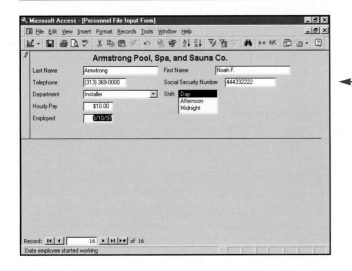

11 Click the **Save** button to save the changes made to the form.

Task 8

Adding Headers, Footers, and Page Breaks to a Form

Why would I do this?

When you created the Personnel File by Department report using the Report Wizard, Access automatically added headers and footers to the report. A *Page Header* or *Page Footer* gives added information to the person reading the report. Since it is often useful to print out a form to view individual records, headers and footers can be useful on forms, too.

In this task, you learn how to add a header and footer and insert a page break so you can print one form per page. This would be useful if you wanted to print individual records for distribution or for filing in each person's personnel file.

1 Click the **View** button to switch to **Design View**. Notice that there are **Form Header** and **Form Footer** sections available.

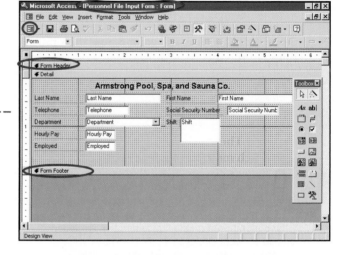

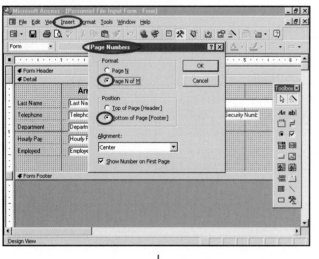

2 Choose **Insert**, **Page Numbers**. The **Page Numbers** dialog box opens. Click the **Page N of M** option button and the **Bottom of the Page [Footer]** option button. Leave the other options as shown.

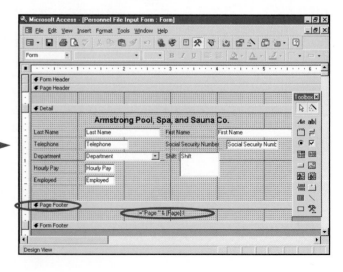

3 Click **OK**. The page number is placed in the **Page Footer**. This means that the page number will appear at the bottom of each page.

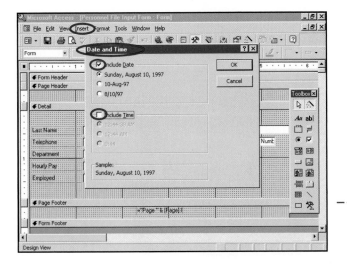

4 Choose **Insert, Date and Time**. The **Date and Time** dialog box opens. Accept the long date option from the **Include Date** area as shown, but turn off the **Include Time** option by clicking the check box.

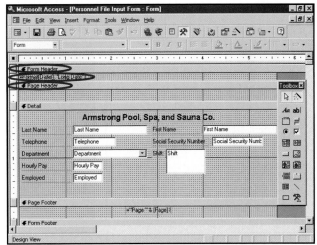

5 Click **OK**. The date is placed in the **Form Header** area, which means it will appear only on the first page. A **Page Header** is also displayed.

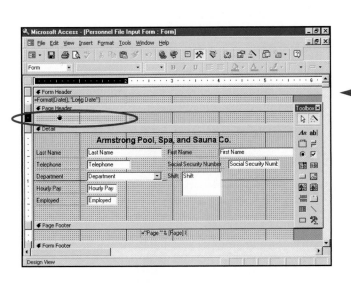

6 Click the date and hold down the mouse button. The pointer changes to a hand. Move the date down to the **Page Header** area as shown.

7 Release the mouse button to place the date in the **Page Header** area.

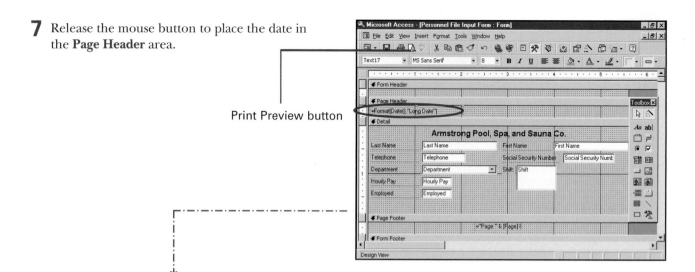

Print Preview button

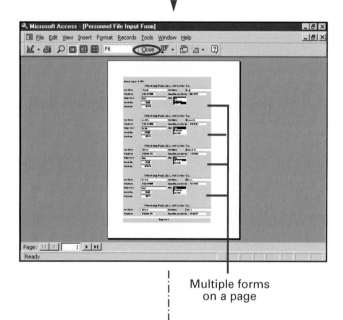

Multiple forms on a page

8 Click the **Print Preview** button to see what the printed form will look like. Notice that there are four forms printed on a page.

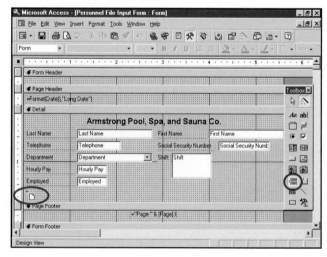

9 Click **Close** to close the **Print Preview** window. Click the **Page Break** button on the **Toolbox** (do not hold down the mouse button), then move the pointer to the left side of the screen as shown in the figure. The pointer turns into a crosshair with a page attached.

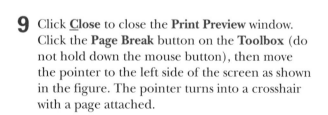

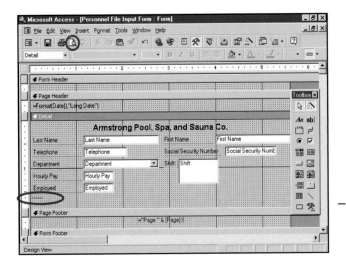

10 Click the pointer just below the **Employed** label to insert a page break. Three dots are inserted to designate a page break after the employed field.

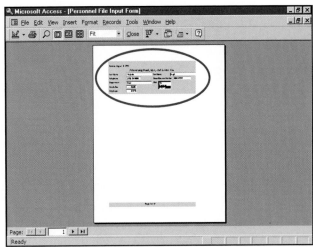

11 Click the **Print Preview** button. Notice that there is only one form per page.

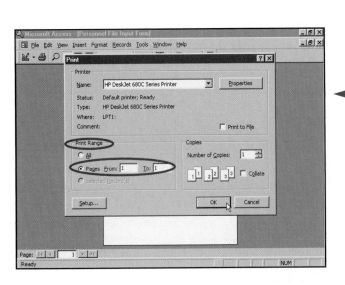

12 Choose **File**, **Print**. In the **Print Range** area, select the **Pages From** option and type **1** in the **From** and **To** boxes.

13 Click the **OK** button to print the first page of the forms. Click the **Close** button to close the **Print Preview** window, then click the **Close Window** button to close the **Form Design** window. Save changes when prompted. Close the database.

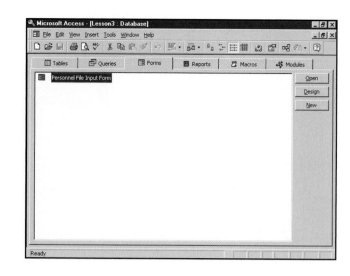

Student Exercises

True-False

Circle either T or F.

T   F   **1.** Input masks are used to apply specific formats to text fields.

T   F   **2.** Default values work only with fields that have a Number data type.

T   F   **3.** An input mask added to a field in a table will also appear in previously created forms or reports that include that field.

T   F   **4.** Assigning a primary key can help speed up searching or sorting.

T   F   **5.** You can automatically adjust a column width in Datasheet View by double-clicking the right edge of the field selector.

T   F   **6.** If the entry you are looking for is not in the List Box you can always type in a new item.

T   F   **7.** A Combo Box gives you a list to choose from and also allows you to type a new entry.

T   F   **8.** You can insert page numbers in either the Page Header or the Page Footer.

T   F   **9.** The Page Break button is found on the Toolbox toolbar.

T   F   **10.** There can be no duplicate entries in a Primary Key field.

Identifying Parts of the Access Screens

Refer to the figures and identify the numbered parts of the screen. Write the letter of the correct label in the space next to the number.

1. _____
2. _____
3. _____
4. _____
5. _____
6. _____
7. _____
8. _____
9. _____
10. _____

A. Primary Key button
B. Build button
C. Properties button
D. Page Break button
E. Primary Key indicator
F. Input Mask field property
G. Default Value field property
H. Page number
I. Date
J. List box

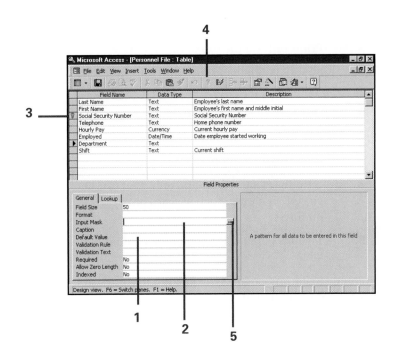

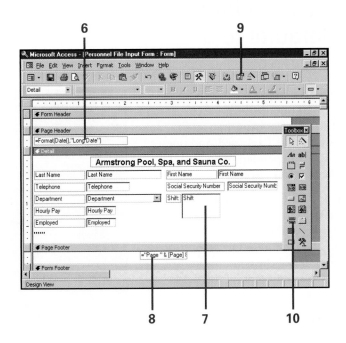

Matching

Match the statements below to the word or phrase that is the best match from the list. Write the letter of the matching word or phrase in the space provided next to the number.

1. ___ Where the items for a list box or combo box come from

2. ___ Button on the Toolbox toolbar which allows printing of one form per page

3. ___ Prints only on the top of the first page

4. ___ Applies special field structure for phone numbers, zip codes, etc.

5. ___ Displays the current date

6. ___ A field containing unique values

7. ___ Prints on the bottom of every page

8. ___ Used to select built-in functions that can be placed on a form, such as dates or page numbers

9. ___ The label area at the top of the column in a table

10. ___ In a form, creates a drop-down list of possible data for a field

A. Primary key

B. Expression Builder

C. Field selector

D. Page Footer

E. Row Source

F. Input mask

G. Page break

H. Date()

I. Combo box

J. Form Footer

K. Form Header

Application Exercises

Exercise 1 – Adding Input Masks and Defaults to a Table

1. Using Windows Explorer, make a copy of **Ex0301** and rename the copy of the file **Exercise3**. Launch Microsoft Access. Choose **Open an Existing Database**, find the file **Exercise3**, and open the file. This is a slightly expanded version of the exercises you worked on in Lesson 2.

2. Use the skills that you have learned in this lesson to create **input masks** for the Phone and Zip fields and a **Default Value** for the State field as shown in the figure. See the steps below for more detail. (Note: The widths of the columns in this table have been resized to show all of the fields you will be working on.)

3. Make sure the **Table** tab is selected.

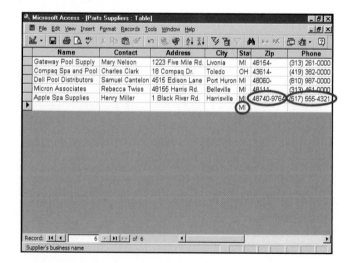

4. Select the **Design View** option for the **Parts Suppliers** table.

5. Select the **Zip** field. Click in the **Input Mask** box in the **Field Properties** area.

6. Click the **Build** button and choose the pre-set **Zip Code** option. Store the **Zip** field information without the dash.

7. Select the **Phone** field (save the table when prompted). Click in the **Input Mask** box in the **Field Properties** area.

8. Click the **Build** button and choose the pre-set **Phone Number** option. Store the **Phone** field information without the symbols.

9. Select the **State** field. Click in the **Default Value** box and type **MI**, since most of the suppliers will be from Michigan.

10. Switch to **Datasheet View** and save your changes when prompted. Enter the following new record, using the input masks and default value you just created: **Apple Spa Supplies**; **Henry Miller**; **1 Black River Rd.**; **Harrisville**; **MI**; **487409764**; **5175554321**; **60 Day**.

11. Adjust the column widths to show all of the data. Choose **File**, **Print** and print a copy of the table in **Landscape** orientation. (In the print dialog box, click the Properties button, click the Paper tab and select Landscape orientation.) Close the table.

Exercise 2 – Assigning a Primary Key and Adjusting Column Widths

1. Switch to **Design View** of the **Pool Parts Inventory** table.

2. Use the skills that you have learned in this lesson to enter the data into the table as shown. See the steps below for more detail.

3. Click anywhere in the **Part Number** field. (Note: This field will be used as a primary key because each part number is unique.)

4. Click the **Primary Key** button.

5. Move to **Datasheet View**. Save your changes when prompted.

6. Resize the columns as shown.

7. Print a copy of the table in Landscape orientation, then close it. Save your changes when prompted.

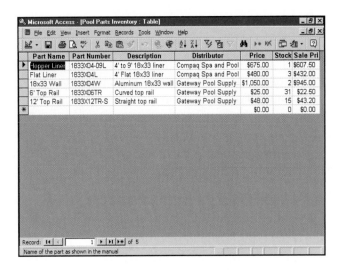

Exercise 3 – Adding a List Box to a Form

1. Click the **Forms** tab. Open the **Parts Suppliers Input Form** in **Design View**.

2. Use the skills that you have learned in this lesson to add a **list box** to the **Billing** field.

3. Click the **text box** of the **Billing** field.

4. Choose **F**ormat, **C**hange To, **L**ist Box.

5. Click the **Properties** button on the Form Design toolbar. Choose **Value List** from the **Row Source Type** drop-down menu.

6. In the **Row Source** box type the following entries exactly as shown: **10 Day**; **30 Day**; **45 Day**; **60 Day**.

7. Close the **List Box: Billing** properties dialog box and move to **Form View**.

8. Switch back to **Form View** and resize the **list box** as necessary.

9. Move to record 5 if necessary. Choose **F**ile, **P**rint, and click the **Selected R**ecord(s) option button to print only the current record. Close the form and save your changes when prompted.

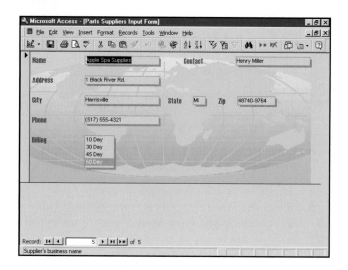

Exercise 4 – Adding a Combo Box to a Form

1. Open the **Pool Parts Inventory Input Form** in **Design View**.

2. Use the skills that you have learned in this lesson to add a **combo box** to the **Distributor** field.

3. Click the **text box** of the **Distributor** field.

4. Choose **F**ormat, **C**hange To, **C**ombo Box.

5. Click the **Properties** button on the Form Design toolbar. Choose **Table/Query** from the **Row Source Type** drop-down menu.

6. In the **Row Source** box select the **Parts Suppliers** table. The **combo box** will read the information in the first field in that table.

7. Close the **Combo Box: Distributor** properties dialog box and switch to **Form View**.

8. Switch back to **Design View** and resize the **combo box**, if necessary.

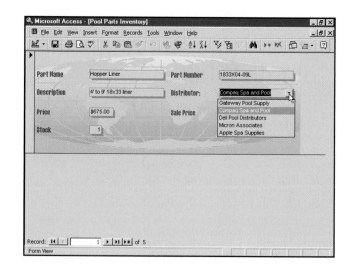

9. Choose **File**, **Print** and click the **Selected Record(s)** option button to print only the current record. Close the form and save your changes when prompted.

Exercise 5 – Adding a Header and Footer to a Form

1. Open the **Parts Suppliers Input Form** in **Design View**.

2. Use the skills that you have learned in this lesson to add information to the header and footer areas of the form.

3. Choose **Insert**, **Page Numbers**. Place a simple page number on the right-hand side of the **Page Footer**.

4. Choose **Insert**, **Date and Time**. Insert the full date and time as shown on the figure.

5. Move the date and time box from the **Form Header** to the right side of the **Page Header**.

6. Click the **Label** button in the Toolbox. Draw a label box in the left side of the Page Header area. Type the company name: **Armstrong Pool, Spa, and Sauna Co.**

7. Change the font size of the company name to 14 point. (See Task 6 of Lesson 2 to review how to do this, if needed.)

8. Adjust the size of the label box as necessary.

9. Use the **Page Break** button to place a page break just under the **Billing** list box.

10. Switch to **FormView**. Choose **File**, **Print** and click the **Selected Record(s)** option button to print only the current record. Close the form and save your changes when prompted.

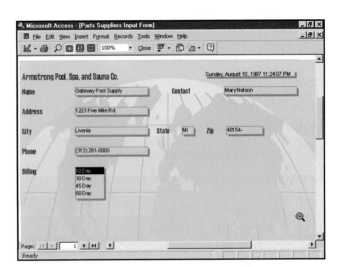

Lesson 4
Extracting Useful Information from Large Databases

Introduction

Extracting information from databases is crucial in running many businesses, and is the basis for many types of research. In this lesson, you learn how to work with a database that contains data of all tornadoes occurring in the United States from 1950 through 1995. This database has over 38,000 records, but with the skills you learn in this lesson, you will be able to find the answers to questions such as "How many people have been killed or injured in my county?" "Which states have the most tornadoes?" "Where have the biggest tornadoes occurred?" This is an example of how scientists conduct such research. Because you are dealing with real data, you have the opportunity to ask new questions, discover new relationships, and experience the excitement of doing real research!

In this lesson, you learn how to use form filters and how to create queries.

Visual Summary

Path Width

Year	Killed	Injured	Path Width (ft)
95	5	60	2110
95	3	32	3000
95	3	24	900
95	3	6	2100
95	3	5	750
95	2	11	2640
95	2	1	300
95	1	70	2110
95	1	55	3900
95	1	20	1320
95	1	12	600
95	1	3	450
95	1	3	510
95	1	1	150
95	1	0	60
95	1	0	90
95	0	122	120
95	0	45	2640
95	0	36	450
95	0	28	220
95	0	23	2640
95	0	22	150
95	0	22	600
95	0	20	300

Year	Killed	Injured	Path Width (ft)
95	0	17	360
95	0	13	220
95	0	12	1500
95	0	12	1500
95	0	11	60
95	0	10	60
95	0	9	1200
95	0	8	210
95	0	8	300
95	0	8	300
95	0	8	600
95	0	8	90
95	0	7	600
95	0	6	980
95	0	6	2640
95	0	6	240
90	0	5	90
95	0	5	1050
95	0	5	30
95	0	5	900
95	0	5	750
95	0	5	220
95	0	4	900

When you have completed Task 8, you will have created several filters and saved a query that looks like this:

Task 1

Opening a Database

Why would I do this?

In the first three lessons you learned how to create and modify a database. Once a database has been created, you need to find and open it in order to use it again. The value of a database is derived from using it to find answers to questions and to extract data that meets certain conditions.

In this task, you learn how to open an existing database.

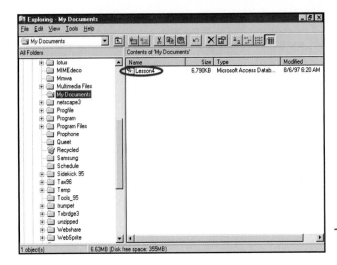

1 Find the **Less0401** file that was supplied with your book. Use **Windows Explorer** to make a copy of the file and rename the copy **Lesson4**. (Follow your instructor's directions for the location to use when copying and renaming the file.)

2 Launch **Microsoft Access 97**. A dialog box opens that provides two choices for creating a new database and an option for opening an existing database.

Pothole: If you are using a computer in a laboratory, you might not have enough room for the 6 megabyte Less0401 file, which covers 45 years. If this is the case, use the 1.4 megabyte **Less0402**, which has ten years' data (1986-1995). Follow all of the other directions in step 1.

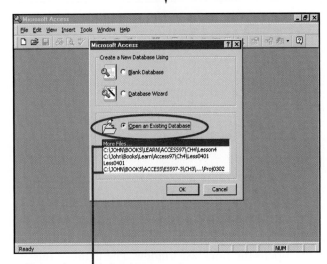

Recently used databases

3 Make sure that the **Open an Existing Database** option is selected and click **OK**. The **Open** dialog box is displayed.

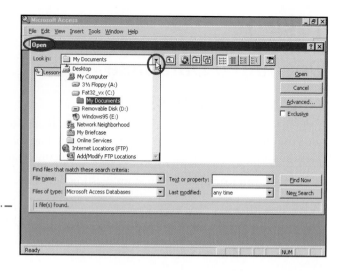

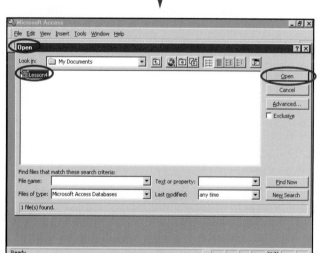

4 Click the arrow at the right of the **Look in** list and locate the **Lesson4** file that you copied and renamed.

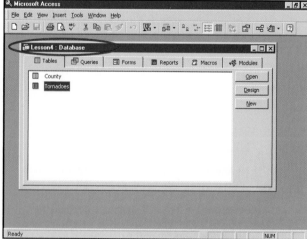

5 Click the **Lesson4** file and then **Open**. Access opens the **Database window**. The name of the database is shown in the title bar.

Task 2

Moving between Records and Columns of a Table

Why would I do this?

When you are dealing with a large database, it is important to know how to navigate the records. Simply scrolling through 38,000 records looking for what you want will not work well. It is also important to examine the data to understand the kind of information contained in each field. There are some techniques that can be used to move quickly from the beginning to the end of data, and to have columns shift to appear next to each other for easy comparison.

In this task, you learn how to freeze selected columns and how to move to the last record and then the first record in the table.

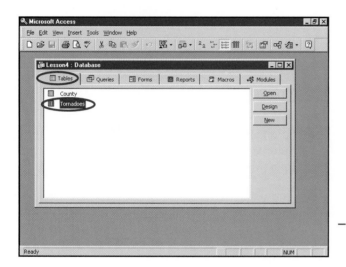

1 Click the **Tables** tab, if necessary, and select **Tornadoes**.

2 Click the **Open** button. The **Tornadoes** file opens and displays the records. The first column is a sequential number that is used as the key field and the second column indicates the year of the tornado.

Pothole: The records you see on the screen will not match the ones shown if you are using the smaller version of the database (Less0402). This will occur several times in lessons 4 and 5, but will not affect the outcomes of the tasks.

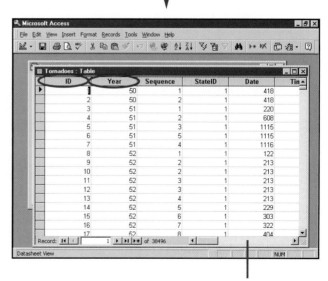

horizontal scroll bar

3 Use the horizontal scroll bar to scroll the view all the way to the right. The last column contains a code that identifies the county. The first two digits in the code are the state code and the last three digits are the county code.

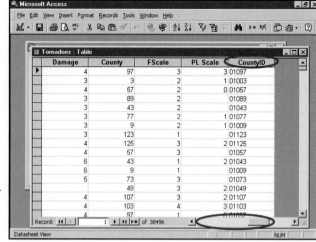

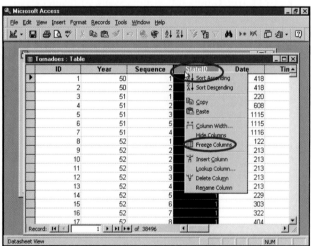

4 Scroll all the way back to the left. Right-click the **StateID** header to select this column and bring up a shortcut menu.

5 Click **Freeze Columns**. Notice that the column is automatically moved to the far left.

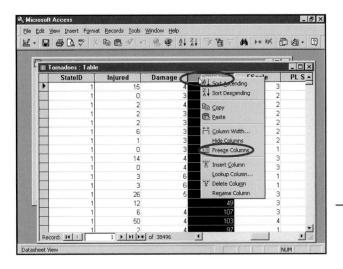

6 Scroll to the right. Right-click the **County** header to select this column and to bring up the shortcut menu.

7 Click **Freeze Columns**. The **County** column moves and is now the second column next to the **StateID** column.

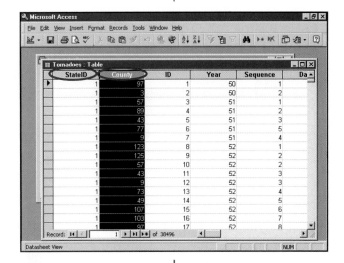

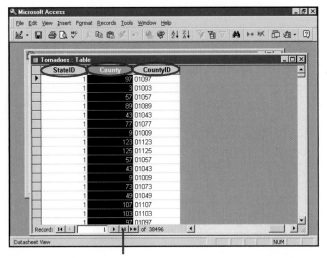

Last Record button

8 Scroll to the right until there are only three columns displayed: **StateID**, **County**, and **CountyID**. Notice how much easier it is to compare the three columns using the Freeze Columns feature. You can now verify that the **CountyID** field is a combination of the **StateId** and **County** numbers.

9 Click the **Last Record** button. Notice that the **StateID** code is 56. The codes used in this database skip some numbers and include some U.S. territories.

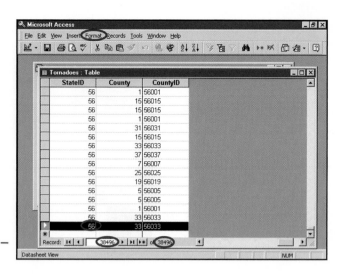

10 Choose **Format** and **Unfreeze All Columns** to remove the freeze. Notice that the StateID and County columns are still located at the left.

In Depth: The effect of freezing the StateID and County fields is that the columns have been temporarily moved to the left. The **Unfreeze All Columns** action removes the freeze but does not immediately move the columns back to their original position. If you close the table without saving these changes to the layout, the columns will appear in their original location the next time you open the table. However, you can save these changes to the layout for the next time the table is opened. Saving the changes to the layout does not affect the original organization of the fields in the table design.

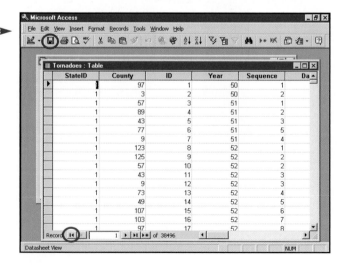

11 Click the **First Record** button to move to the beginning of the table. Click the **Save** button to save the changes in layout.

Task 3

Finding Records

Why would I do this?

Sometimes it is not necessary to use a filter or write a query to find the information you need. You may need to locate a particular record to change some information. For instance, in a personnel database you may need to change an employee's address, marital status, or pay rate. In this case, you want to find one record and make the necessary changes. Other times you may want to find a particular record or do a quick search to see if the database contains a record. When you are looking for one particular record, often the quickest way to find it is to use the Find feature.

In this task, you learn how to use the Find feature to determine how many tornadoes have occurred on New Year's Day.

Find button

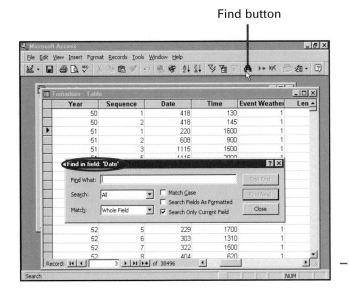

1 Click anywhere in the **Date** column and then click the **Find** button on the **Table Datasheet** toolbar. The **Find in field:'Date'** dialog box opens.

2 Make sure that the **Search Only Current Field** box is checked and the **Match** box displays **Whole Field**.

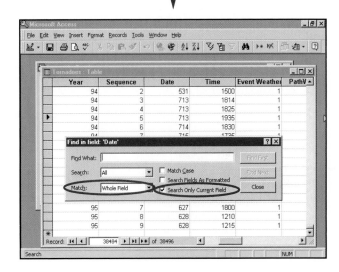

3 Click the **Find What** box and type <u>101</u>.

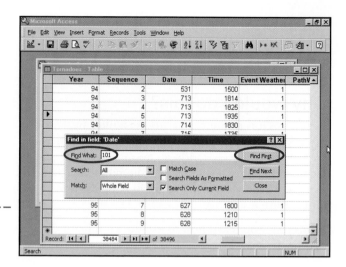

4 Click **Find First**. The first record in the table that has a date of 101 is number 969.

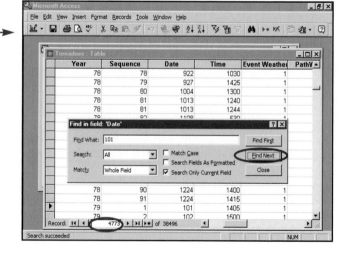

5 Click **Find Next**. Notice how quickly the program scans the records to find the next occurrence in record number 4773.

Pothole If you are using the smaller version of the database (Less0402) there will be only one tornado that occurred on New Year's Day.

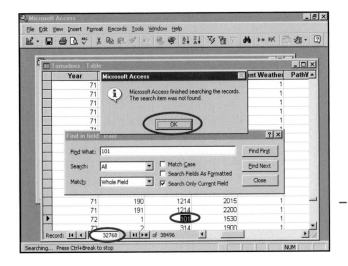

6 Click **Find Next** twice. Access will find one more occurrence (record 32768). Then, you will see a message stating that Access is finished searching. There are no more records to find. You have determined that there have been only three tornadoes on New Year's Day in the United States from 1950 to 1995.

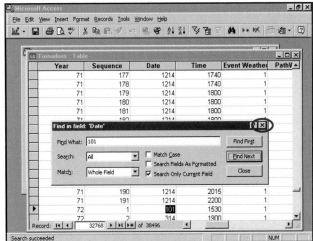

7 Click **OK** to close the message box.

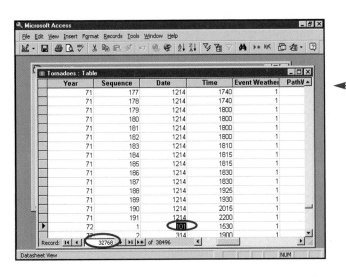

8 Click the **Close** button on the **Find** dialog box. The table remains open at the last record that was found.

Task 4

Sorting and Indexing Records

Why would I do this?

In this table, the records are arranged by date of occurrence, but you have the option of sorting the records by any of the other fields as well. Sorting tools are available that can be used to sort a database on one particular field. Sometimes, however, it is helpful to first index a database before it is sorted. An index can speed up the sorting process on very large databases.

In this task, you learn how to sort the records by the FScale field in descending order. The numbers in this field indicate the intensity of the tornado, where higher numbers indicate stronger tornadoes. You also learn how to index a field to increase sorting speed.

1 Scroll to the right and click anywhere in the **FScale** column.

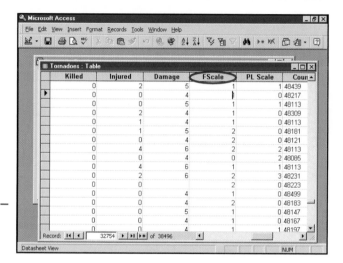

Sort Descending
button

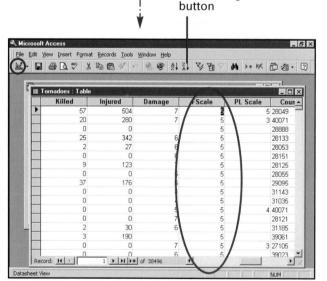

2 Click the **Sort Descending** button. After a few seconds, the records are reorganized and displayed in descending order according to the contents of the **FScale** field.

In Depth: The time it takes to sort depends on your computer's processor speed. A Pentium processor operating at 133 megahertz takes three or four seconds to sort this table of 38,000 records.

3 A delay of a few seconds is usually not a problem, but if you have a table with ten or one hundred times as many records, the delay can affect your productivity. Click the **View** button to switch to **Design View**.

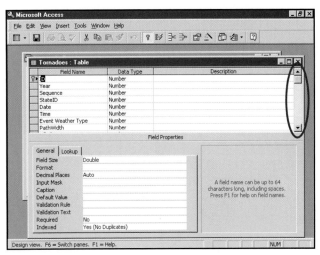

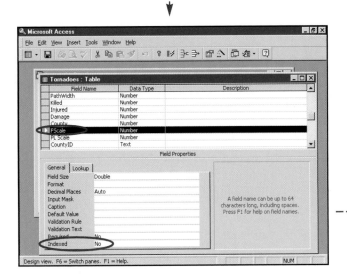

4 Scroll down the list of fields and click the **Fscale row selector**. The field properties for the **FScale** field are displayed.

5 Click the **Indexed** box. A list arrow appears at the right end of the box.

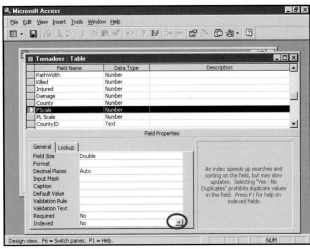

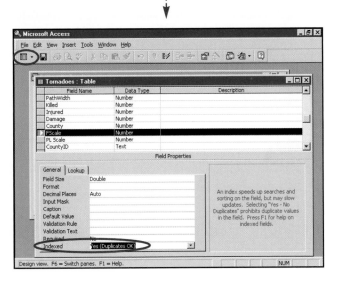

6 Click the list arrow and click **Yes (Duplicates OK)**.

In Depth: The program calculates the order of the records if they are sorted by this field and stores this calculation for later use. If you decide to sort on this field again it will not have to calculate the proper order, so the display will be updated more quickly. The order will have to be recalculated whenever a record is added or deleted, however, so it is better to wait until most of the records have been created before you index the fields.

7 Click the **View** button and click **Yes** to save the change. The table is displayed in **Datasheet View**.

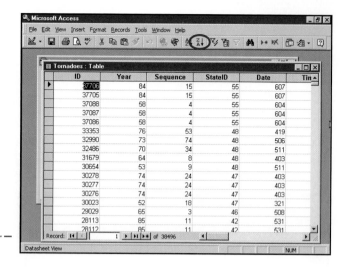

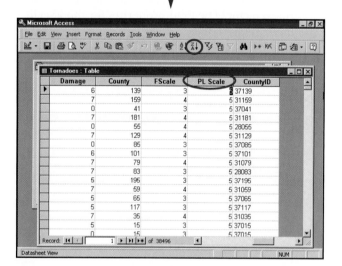

8 Click anywhere in the **PL Scale** column and click the **Sort Descending** button. Observe how long it takes to sort the table.

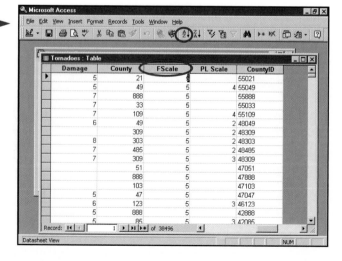

9 Click anywhere in the **FScale** column and click the **Sort Descending** button. Notice how much faster the sort takes place now that the table is indexed by that field.

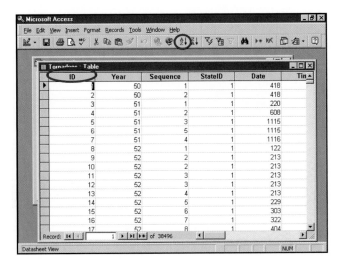

10 Scroll to the left and click anywhere in the **ID** column. Click the **Sort Ascending** button. This returns the table to its original organization.

Task 5

Using a Form to Define a Filter

Why would I do this?

There will be times when you want to view only a few of the many records in a database. To show only the records you are interested in viewing, you can create a *filter* that will specify *criteria* which will allow only certain records to be displayed. Using a form filter is a simple way to limit records based on criteria. Generally, if you will want to be able to look at your data with the same filter over and over, you will create a query that can be saved. Form filters are not usually saved, but can provide a quick method for searching your data. Filters also provide a good introduction to some of the concepts you will learn in Task 6 when you create a query. Form filters use the same logical and/or operators, but may seem more intuitive in this format.

In this task, you learn how to use a form to create a filter. You will use it first to restrict the records to those from a particular year. Then you learn how to create more complex filters.

New Object button

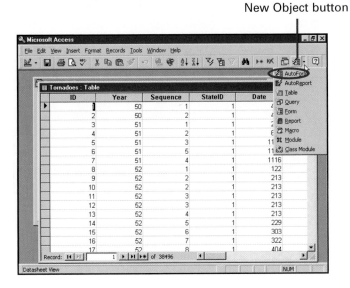

1 Click the list arrow next to the **New Object** button.

2 Click **AutoForm** and click <u>Y</u>es to save the previous changes. The program creates a simple form that displays the fields in the **Tornadoes** table.

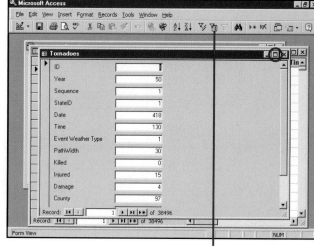

Filter By Form button

3 Click the **Maximize** button and then click the **Filter by Form** button. The form is cleared of entries and the ID field is selected.

In Depth: Each field box in the form displays a list arrow when the box is selected. This list allows you to select either all the records which have no entry (is null) for the field or all the records that do have an entry (is not null) for the field.

Apply Filter button

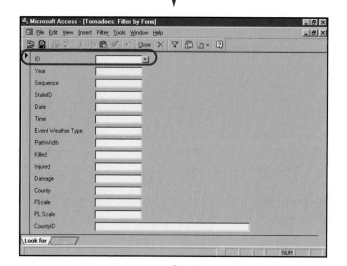

4 Click in the **Year** field box and type **92**.

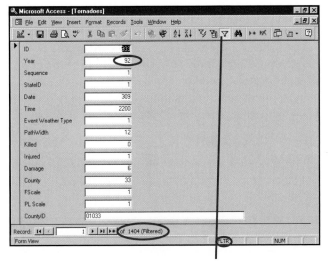

Remove filter button

5 Click the **Apply Filter** button. Notice that there were 1404 tornadoes in 1992.

> **In Depth:** Notice that the screen tip for the **Apply Filter** button now says **Remove Filter**. This is a toggle button that will apply and remove the filter that has been created. Also notice that **FLTR** is highlighted on the status bar which indicates that a filter is currently applied to the data.

6 Click the **Filter by Form** button again. Click in the **FScale** field box and type **5**.

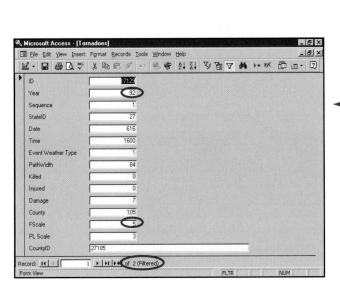

7 Click the **Apply Filter** button. Notice that only 2 of the 1404 tornadoes in 1992 were rated a 5.

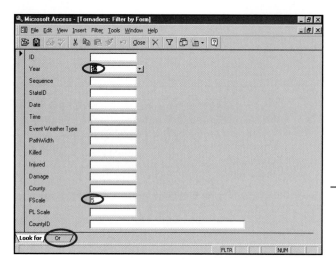

8 It is also possible to use more than one filter at a time. Click the **Filter by Form** button. Notice that the Year and FScale boxes still contain the previous filter conditions. Also notice the tab at the bottom labeled **Or**.

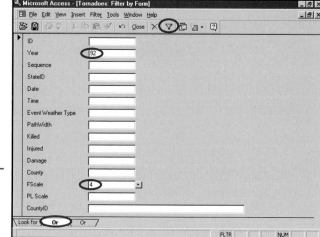

9 To also look for tornadoes rated 4 in 1992, click the **Or** tab. Type **92** in the Year field box and **4** in the **FScale** field box.

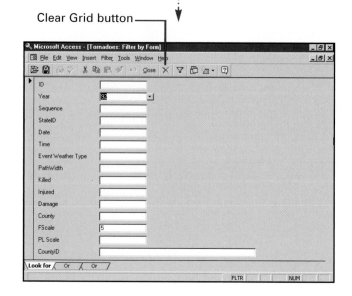

10 Click the **Apply Filter** button. Notice that there were 30 tornadoes in 1992 rated 4 or 5.

Clear Grid button

11 Click the **Filter by Form** button.

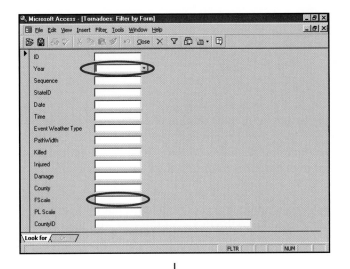

12 Click the **Clear Grid** button. This removes the values entered for both filters.

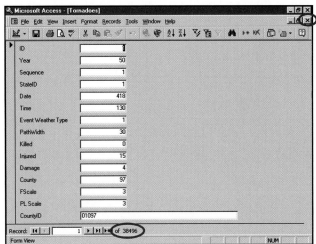

Pothole: A form can have one filter at a time. The Apply/Remove Filter button does not erase the filter, rather it turns the filter on and off. Once a filter is created, it persists as an invisible part of a table or form. Since you cannot erase a filter, you need to create a new one with no criteria and apply it. Also, any sorting that you do will become the default method of displaying that table or form. Therefore, the last sort you do should be on the primary key field to restore it as the default choice for displaying the records.

13 Click the **Apply Filter** button. This replaces the previous filter with a filter that has no conditions.

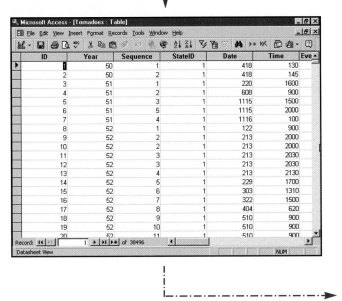

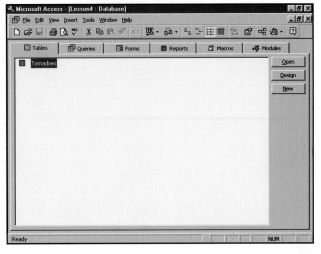

14 Click the **Close Window** button and click **No** when prompted to save the form. The **Tornadoes** table is displayed.

15 Click the **Close Window** button. The **Database** window is displayed.

Task 6

Using Select Queries to Display the Data

Why would I do this?

Filters are useful, but they are limited in what they can do. *Queries* are specifically designed to create useable subsets of the data found in large tables. After a query is designed it is run against the current information in the tables. The results of a query are known as a *dynaset*. When you save a query, Access does not save the dynaset, rather it saves the structure of the query so it can be used again. Often reports are based on queries so the information in the reports is limited to the fields and records that are needed.

In this task, you learn how to create a *select query*. Select queries may contain criteria, like a filter, but they can also limit the fields that are displayed and calculate new values based on some of the fields. In this task, you learn how to choose fields in the Tornadoes table to display, enter criteria in the Years and Fscale fields, and calculate the path width of selected tornadoes.

1 Click the **Queries** tab.

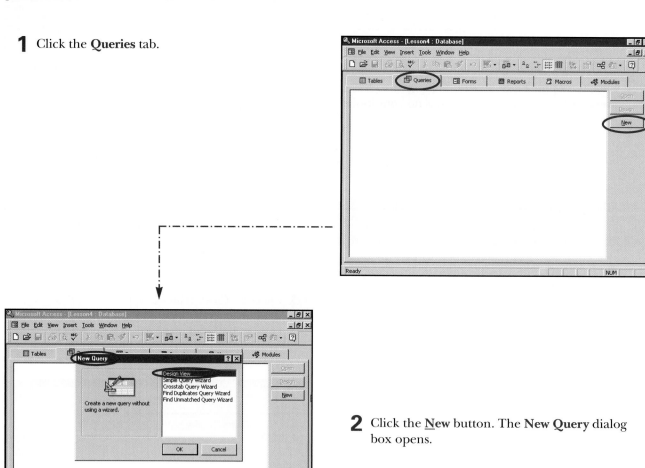

2 Click the **New** button. The **New Query** dialog box opens.

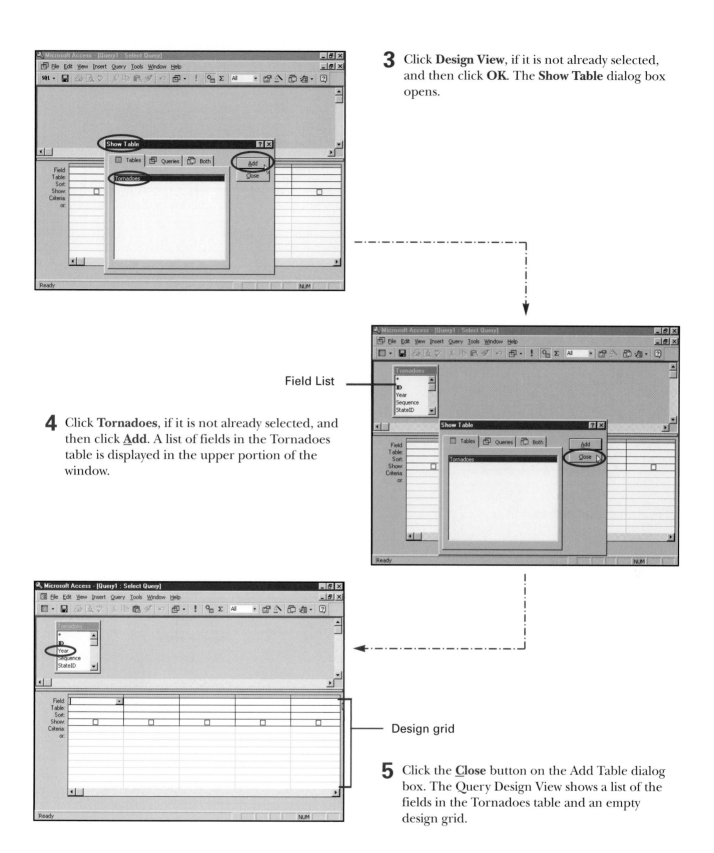

3 Click **Design View**, if it is not already selected, and then click **OK**. The **Show Table** dialog box opens.

Field List

4 Click **Tornadoes**, if it is not already selected, and then click **Add**. A list of fields in the Tornadoes table is displayed in the upper portion of the window.

Design grid

5 Click the **Close** button on the Add Table dialog box. The Query Design View shows a list of the fields in the Tornadoes table and an empty design grid.

6 Double-click the **Year** field. It is placed in the first column of the design grid along with the name of the table from which it comes.

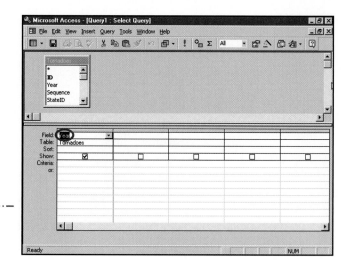

7 Scroll down the list of fields and double-click the **Killed**, **Injured**, and **PathWidth** fields. They are added to the design grid.

8 Click the **View** button and switch to **Datasheet View**. All of the records are represented, but only these four fields are displayed.

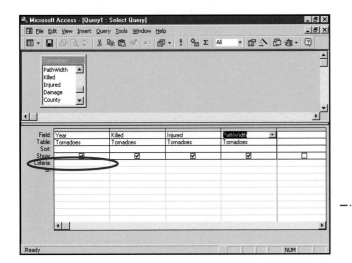

9 Click the **View** button to return to **Design View**.

10 Click the **Criteria** box in the first column under Year and type **93**.

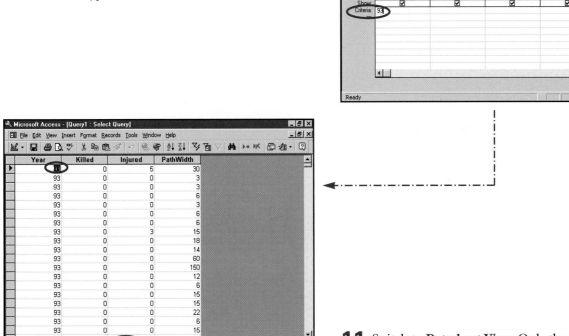

11 Switch to **Datasheet View**. Only the 1993 tornado records are displayed.

Task 7

Calculating Values for a New Column of Data

Why would I do this?

Sometimes the information you want can be derived from data in the table. For example, in a personnel database, you may need to know an employee's age for various benefits. It is better to store their birth date from which their age can be derived when needed, rather than use valuable storage space for an age field.

In the Tornado database, the tornado's path width was stored in tens of feet in the original table provided by the weather service. This could easily be misunderstood when viewed, so it would be better to display it in feet.

In this lesson, you learn how to create a new column in the table that is calculated from the PathWidth field. You also learn how to create a header for the new column and to hide unwanted columns.

1 Switch to **Design View**.

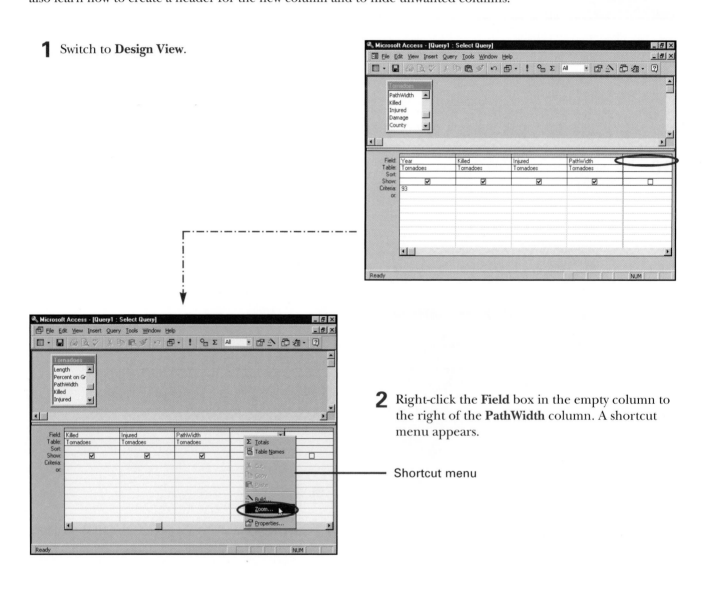

2 Right-click the **Field** box in the empty column to the right of the **PathWidth** column. A shortcut menu appears.

Shortcut menu

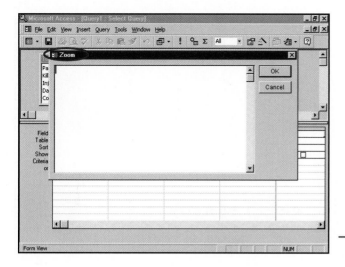

3 Click the **Zoom** option. The **Zoom** window opens. This window is useful when making longer entries in small boxes.

Field name

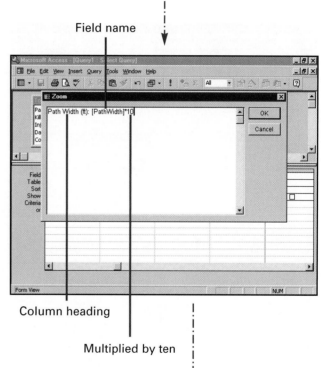

Column heading

Multiplied by ten

4 Type **Path Width (ft): [PathWidth]*10**. Make sure that the first two words are separated by a space but the fieldname is all one word. (The parentheses around **ft** have no special function, they are just used as normal parentheses in this example.)

Pothole: A calculated field uses square brackets, [] to enclose the field name, not parentheses, (), or braces, {}. It is easy to get these confused. It is also important that the field name is spelled exactly as it appears in the table field list. If it is misspelled, a parameter box will open asking for more information when you run the query. If this happens, return to the query design and fix the spelling of the field name. You will learn how to create parameter queries in the next task.

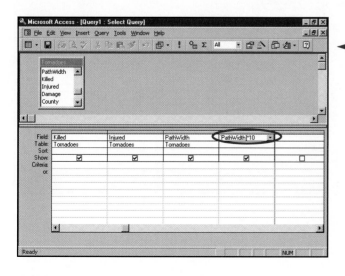

5 Click **OK**. The statement is placed in the Field box in the new column.

6 Switch to **Datasheet View**. Notice that the words that were entered to the left of the colon are used as the column header. (Widen the last column if necessary to see the entire header.) Compare the figures in the right two columns to verify the result of the calculation.

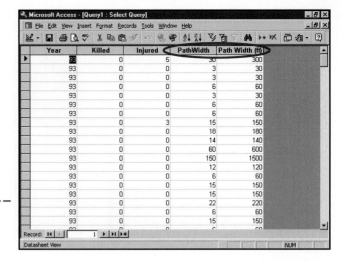

7 Switch to **Design View**.

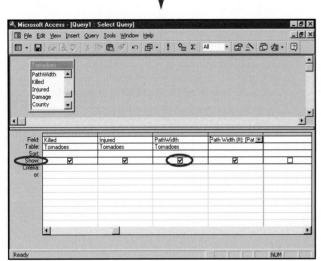

8 Click the **Show** check box in the **PathWidth** column to deselect it.

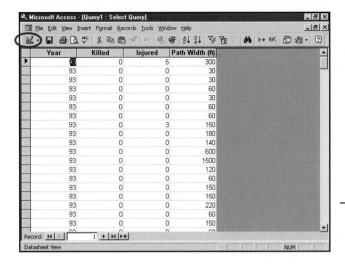

9 Switch to **Datasheet View**. Notice that the **Path-Width** column does not show.

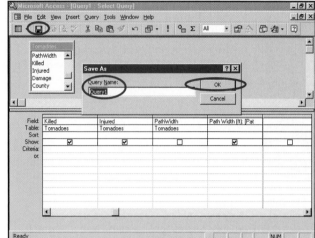

10 Switch to **Design View**. Click the **Save** button. The **Save As** dialog box opens.

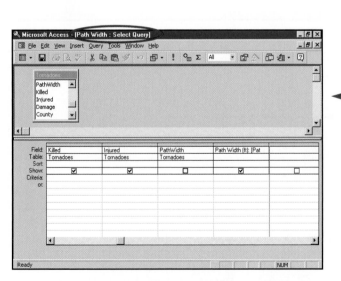

11 Type **Path Width** in the **Query Name** box and click **OK**. This saves the query for later use.

Task 8

Creating Queries that Allow the User to Change Criteria Each Time the Query is Used

Why would I do this?

The query that you created in Task 6 limits the display to the records for 1993. If you wanted to look at the path width information for several different years, it would be time consuming to change the criteria in the query design each time. Fortunately, there is a way to write the criteria so that a dialog box appears each time you go to Datasheet View which allows you to enter the value for the criteria. Values that define the output are called *parameters* and queries that use this feature are called *parameter queries*.

In this task, you learn how to set up a parameter query so that you can choose the year each time the datasheet is viewed.

1 Scroll to the left to see the **Year** column of the design grid. Delete the year value that is currently in the criteria box and type **[Enter the Year]**. Notice that square brackets are used to enclose the message.

Pothole: Square brackets are used to enclose the field names for calculated fields. If the words that are enclosed do not correspond to one of the fields, the program will assume that you intend to enter the values from the keyboard and uses the enclosed words as a prompting message. Two problems can arise from this assumption. If you use a short prompting message that happens to be the name of a field, it will not work as expected. Also, if you misspell a field name or use the name of a field that has been deleted, it will assume that it is a prompting message.

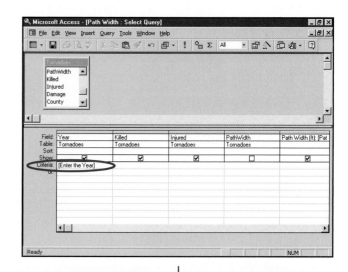

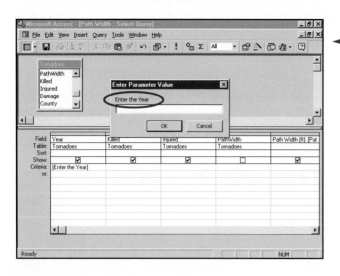

2 Switch to **Datasheet View**. A dialog box opens. Notice that the phrase you typed in step 1 between the brackets is used as a prompting message above the box.

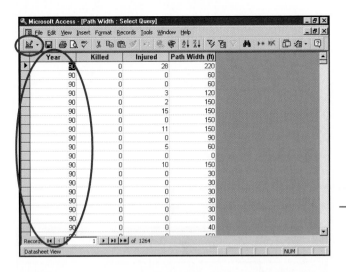

3 Type **90** and click **OK**. The **Datasheet View** opens and the records shown are limited to those from 1990.

4 Click the **View** button to switch to **Design View** and click it again to switch to **Datasheet View**. The dialog box reopens.

Quick Tip: A quick way to bring up the parameter box while still in Datasheet View is to hold down the (◆Shift) key and press **F9** on the function row of your keyboard.

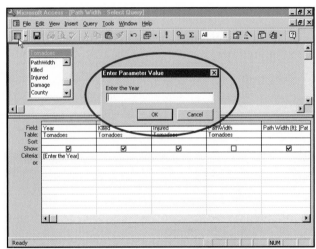

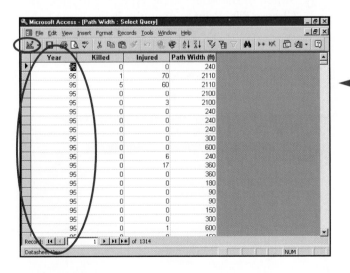

5 Type **95** and click **OK**. The display is limited to the records for 1995.

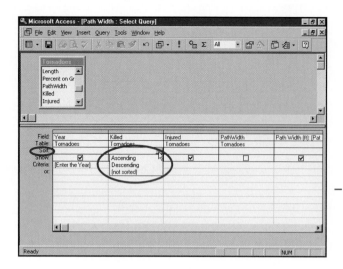

6 Switch to **Design View**. Click the **Sort** row under the **Killed** field and click the **drop-down arrow**.

7 Click **Descending** to select it. Do the same for the Injured field.

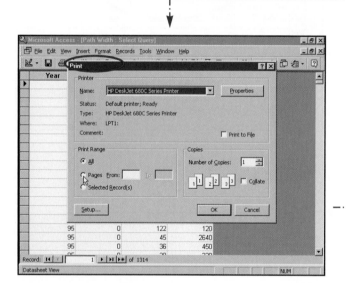

8 Switch to **Datasheet View**. Type **95** and click **Ok**. Choose **File, Print** to open the **Print** dialog box.

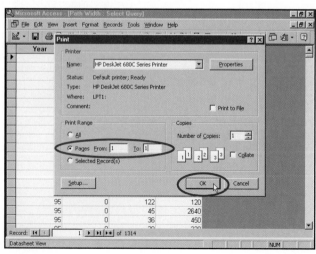

9 Type **1** in the **Pages From** and **To** boxes.

Path Width

Year	Killed	Injured	Path Width (ft)
95	5	60	2110
95	3	32	3000
95	3	24	900
95	3	6	2100
95	3	5	750
95	2	11	2640
95	2	1	300
95	1	70	2110
95	1	55	3900
95	1	20	1320
95	1	12	600
95	1	3	450
95	1	3	510
95	1	1	150
95	1	0	60
95	1	0	90
95	0	122	120
95	0	45	2640
95	0	36	450
95	0	28	220
95	0	23	2640
95	0	22	150
95	0	22	600
95	0	20	300
95	0	17	360
95	0	13	220
95	0	12	1500
95	0	12	1500
95	0	11	60
95	0	10	60
95	0	9	1200
95	0	8	210
95	0	8	300
95	0	8	300
95	0	8	600
95	0	8	90
95	0	7	600
95	0	6	980
95	0	6	2640
95	0	6	240
90	0	5	90
95	0	5	1050
95	0	5	30
95	0	5	900
95	0	5	750
95	0	5	220
95	0	4	900

Page 1

11 Click the **Close Window** button and then click **Yes** to save the changes. Leave the database open for use in the exercises.

Student Exercises

True-False

For each of the following, circle T or F to indicate whether the statement is true or false.

T   F   **1.** Within Access you can save a database file with another name using the Save <u>A</u>s command.

T   F   **2.** When you freeze a column, Access automatically moves that column to the far left position in Datasheet View.

T   F   **3.** A calculated field is a field that is derived from other information in the database.

T   F   **4.** One way to find something in a particular field is to select the field and click the Find button. Then type what you're looking for in the Find What box.

T   F   **5.** It is best to create indexes for very large databases before most of the records have been entered.

T   F   **6.** A Form Filter can be used to limit the data to specific records.

T   F   **7.** The Form Filter is limited because you can only apply one filter at a time.

T   F   **8.** To erase a Form Filter, click the Remove Filter button.

T   F   **9.** In a query, you can view selected fields, sort on one or more fields, and set criteria in one or more fields.

T   F   **10.** A parameter query can be used to quickly choose the data you want to look at because it creates a dialog box that prompts you to specify a value.

Identifying Parts of the Access Screen

Refer to the figure and identify the numbered parts of the screen. Write the letter of the correct label in the space next to the number.

1. _____
2. _____
3. _____
4. _____
5. _____
6. _____
7. _____
8. _____
9. _____
10. _____

A. Sort Descending button
B. Apply/Remove Filter button
C. Indicates a filter is applied
D. Sort Ascending button
E. Filter by Form button
F. Number of the record that is selected or highlighted
G. Last Record button
H. New Object button
I. Find button
J. Number of records filtered

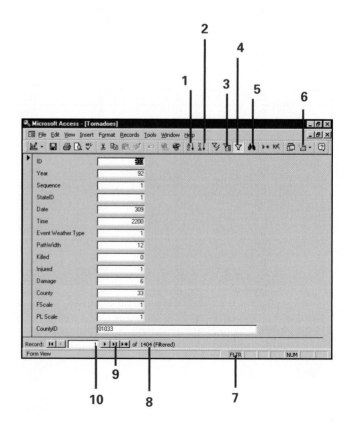

Matching

Match the statements below to the word or phrase that is the best match from the list. Write the letter of the matching word or phrase in the space provided next to the number.

1. ___ Name of the button with a picture of binoculars on it

2. ___ Sort order that sorts in alphabetical order

3. ___ Used to open the parameter box in Datasheet View of a parameter query

4. ___ Action that places a field name in the query grid

5. ___ These are used in a query to surround a field name that is being used in a calculated field

6. ___ This action brings up a shortcut menu

7. ___ Used to select fields when adding fields to a query

8. ___ A type of query that allows the user to enter a value each time the query is run

9. ___ A command in Datasheet View that moves a column to the far left and keeps it in place as you scroll

10. ___ A large box used to write expressions so you can see more than what would fit in a small query grid box

A. Field List box

B. [ ]

C. Zoom

D. Freeze columns

E. Double-click a field name

F. ⬆Shift+F9

G. Ascending

H. Find

I. Right-click

J. ↵Enter

K. Parameter query

Application Exercises

Exercise 1 – Finding Records

1. Open the **Lesson4** database, if necessary, and open the **Tornadoes** table.

2. Freeze the **Year** column. Scroll to the right until the **FScale** column is next to the **Year** column.

3. These records were grouped together from individual state tables. Even though the Year column looks like it is sorted, if you scroll down you will see that the years start at 50 again (86 if you are using the smaller database) for the next state. Sort the table in **ascending order** on the **Year** column.

4. Click anywhere in the **FScale** column and click the **Find** button.

5. Answer the following questions:
  a. What was the first year in which a tornado occurred that was rated **5** on the FScale? _____
  b. When the scale was created, it defined ratings from zero to 6. How many tornadoes have been rated a 6?

Exercise 2 – Using a Form to Define a Filter

1. Open the **Tornadoes** table and create an **AutoForm**.

2. Click the **Filter by Form** button. Enter <u>90</u> for the Year and <u>5</u> for the FScale.

3. Apply the filter and look at the number of records that match the criteria. This is the number of F5 tornadoes in 1990.

4. Use this method to answer the following questions:
  a. How many tornadoes were rated 5 on the FScale in 1990? _____
  b. How many tornadoes were rated 5 on the FScale in 1991? _____
  c. How many tornadoes were rated 5 on the FScale in 1992? _____

5. Clear the grid and use the **Or** feature to determine the number of tornadoes that occurred in 1995 that were rated 3 or 4. _____

6. Clear the grid. Determine the number of tornadoes that have killed more than 20 people. (Hint: in the **Killed** box, enter <u>>20</u>.) _____

7. Close the form. Do not save the form.

Exercise 3 – Creating a Select Query

1. Create a new query that contains the **Year**, **StateID, Killed**, and **Injured** fields.

2. You are going to determine how many tornadoes killed more people than it injured. Create a calculated field that has the header, **Killed to Injured Ratio,** and divides the number **Killed** by the number **Injured**.

3. Use a criteria of **>0** in the **Killed** and **Injured** fields to eliminate tornadoes where no one was killed or injured. Use a criteria of **>1** in the newly created column to show only those tornadoes where the ratio will be greater than 1, indicating that the number killed was greater than the number injured.

4. Sort in descending order on the new **Killed to Injured Ratio** field.

5. View the datasheet. How many recorded tornadoes killed more people than it injured? _____

6. In Datasheet View, resort the query on the **StateID** field. From visual examination, which state ID occurs most frequently? ____ How many times has this state had more people killed than injured from a tornado? ____

7. In the Datasheet View of the query, click the **Print** button to print the results of your query. It should print on one page.

8. Close the query and save it as **More Deaths than Injuries**.

Exercise 4 – Using a Parameter Query

1. Create a new query based on the **Tornadoes Table** that contains the **Year**, **Killed**, **Injured**, and **FScale** fields.

2. Sort the query in descending order on the **Killed** field.

3. In the criteria box for the **Year** field, enter this prompting message: **[Enter the Year]**.

4. Enter a similar prompting message in the criteria box for the **FScale** field.

5. To limit the records displayed to only those tornadoes that resulted in fatalities, type **>0** in the criteria box for the **Killed** field.

6. Use this parameter query to answer the following questions:
   a. How many F5 tornadoes caused fatalities in 1990? _____
   b. How many F4 tornadoes caused fatalities in 1987? _____

7. What does the query show when there are no matches? Search for the following:
   a. How many F5 tornadoes caused fatalities in 1973?____ What does the record number show at the bottom? ____
   b. How many F5 tornadoes caused fatalities in 1975?____ What does the record number show at the bottom? ____

8. Close the query and name it **Fatalities by Year**.

9. Close the database and exit Access.

Lesson 5
Using Two or More Tables In Combination

Task 1 Importing or Linking to a Table

Task 2 Creating a Relationship between Tables

Task 3 Creating a Union Query that Uses Fields from Both Tables

Task 4 Using Advanced Parameter Query Methods with a Union Query

Task 5 Creating a Form that Displays Data from Two or More Tables

Task 6 Creating a Report that Uses the Union Query

Introduction

There are several techniques that are used to reduce the size of databases. One way is to limit the field size by using two- or three-digit codes for fields that are repeated frequently. For example, if a an entry, such as the name of a state, is repeated many times, it is more efficient to represent that state or county with a number. Then a separate table can be created that contains the number and the corresponding name of the state. When the data is entered, a two-digit number may be entered rather than the full name, thus reducing the overall size of the database. When the data is reported, the name can be recalled from the second table and displayed instead of the number. The two tables are related to each other through a common field such as the state's identifying number. Databases that use related tables are called *relational databases*.

In this lesson, you learn how to import or link a table that contains state names and how to link a table that contains county names to the Tornado data table. You also learn how to create a relationship between the tables and how to create queries, forms, and reports that utilize that relationship.

Visual Summary

When you have completed Task 6, you will have created a report that looks like this:

Tornadoes by State

State Name	Oklahoma			

County Name	Love			
	Year	**Killed**	**Injured**	**FSale**
	95	3	6	3

County Name	Pawnee			
	Year	**Killed**	**Injured**	**FSale**
	91	1	5	4

County Name	Payne			
	Year	**Killed**	**Injured**	**FSale**
	90	1	12	3

County Name	Rogers			
	Year	**Killed**	**Injured**	**FSale**
	93	7	100	4

County Name	Washington			
	Year	**Killed**	**Injured**	**FSale**
	91	1	10	2

Task 1

Importing or Linking to a Table

Why would I do this?

In many cases, a large database table is provided by your employer or a government archive. It is unnecessary to recreate the table in every database that uses it. Rather, you can import the table from its original source and use the information in a your own database. In some cases, the company's computer will only allow you to read the data and not to copy or change it. In these instances, it is better to create a link from your database to the database that contains the large table.

In this task, you open a database that contains the names of the counties in the U.S. Then you import a small table of state names into the database that contains the county information. Finally, you learn how to link this database to the large table of tornado data that was used in the previous lesson.

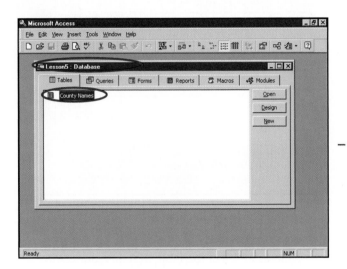

1 Use Windows Explorer to find the **Less0501** file that was provided with your book and rename it **Lesson5**. Launch Access and open **Lesson5**. Notice that this file contains the table **County Names**.

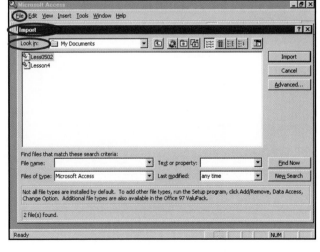

2 Choose **File**, **Get External Data**, **Import**. The **Import** dialog box opens.

> **In Depth:** When you look for files, the list of files in the import dialog box on your screen will be different from those that appear in the figure. Your files may also be located in a different folder on your computer. Click the drop-down arrow at the right end of the **Look-in** box and follow your instructor's direction to locate the correct files.

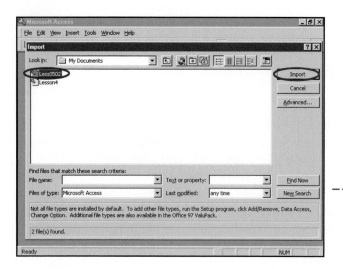

3 Find the **Less0502** file that was provided with the book.

4 Click the **Import** button. The **Import Objects** dialog box opens. The dialog box resembles the Database window with tabs for the same six database objects.

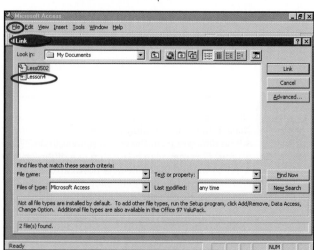

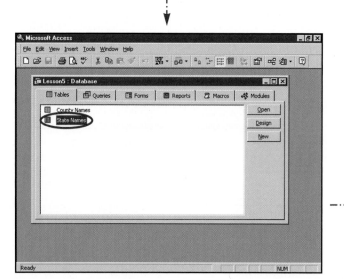

5 Click the **Tables** tab, if necessary, click **State Names** to select the table of state names, and click **OK**. The table is imported into the Lesson5 database.

6 Choose **File**, **Get External Data**, **Link Tables**. The **Link** dialog box opens.

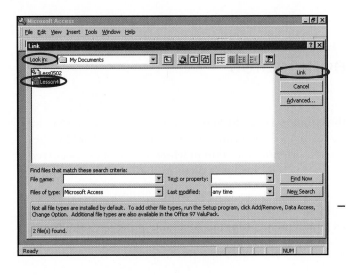

7 Find the **Lesson4** file that was used in the previous lesson. (If you have not done that lesson, find **Less0401**.)

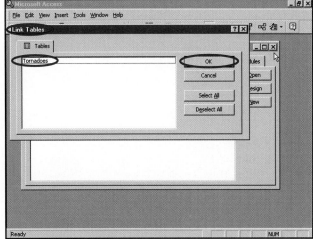

8 Click **Lesson4** and then click **Link**. The **Link Tables** dialog box opens.

Arrow indicating
a linked table

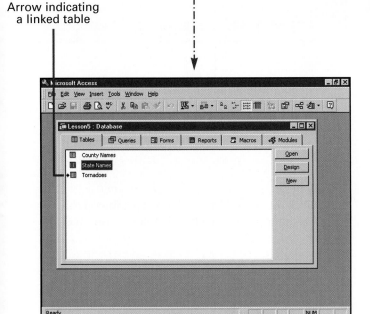

9 Click **Tornadoes** and then click **OK**. The Tornadoes table is linked to the Lesson5 database. Notice the small arrow next to the table's name, indicating a linked table.

In Depth: Before you move on to the next task, take a moment to open the tables and examine the fields in each one. Notice that the County Names table contains 3038 records of county names and a corresponding ID number. The State Names table is similarly structured. You worked in Lesson 4 with the Tornadoes table and know that it contains fields for State ID and County ID numbers.

Task 2

Creating a Relationship between Tables

Why would I do this?

The most common way to relate two tables is to connect the primary key field in one table to the same field in another table. In this example, the State Names table has one record for each state and the primary key field is the StateID field. The Tornadoes table also has a field that is used to identify the state in which the tornado occurred. Each state will have numerous tornadoes, so the same state code will occur many times in the Tornadoes table. This type of relationship is called a *one-to-many relationship*.

In this task, you learn how to create one-to-many relationships between the State Names table and the Tornadoes table and between the County Names table and Tornadoes table. In each case the first table represents the "one" side of the one-to-many relationship that will be created.

1 Choose **Tools**, **Relationships**. The **Relationships** window opens.

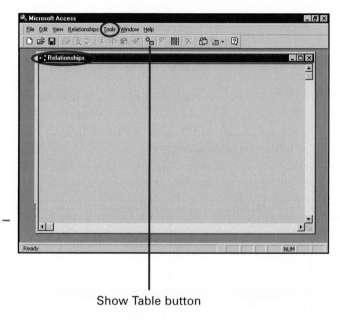

Show Table button

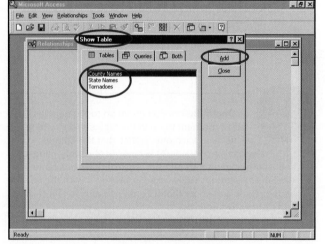

2 Click the **Show Table** button. The **Show Table** window opens and a list of tables is displayed.

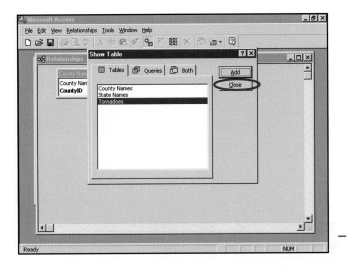

3 Click **Add** to add the **County Names** table. Click **State Names**, click **Add**, click **Tornadoes**, and click **Add** again. All three tables are added to the **Relationships** window.

Pothole: You may successfully add a table to the Relationships window, but it could be hidden behind the Show Table window. If you are not sure, move the Show Table window aside. If you have accidentally added a table twice, click on the extra table field list and press Del to remove it.

Title bar

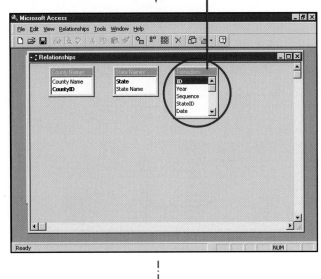

4 Click **Close** to close the **Show Table** window. The three tables are displayed in the **Relationships** window.

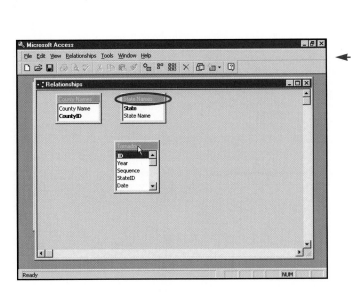

5 The relationship lines will be easier to see if you rearrange the tables so that the **Tornadoes** table is between the other two. Point to the **title** bar of the **Tornadoes** table. Click and drag the table to a spot below the other two tables, as shown in the figure.

6 Point to the **title** bar of the **State Names** table. Click and drag the table to the right. Use the same method to move the **Tornadoes** table up between the other two tables, as shown in the figure.

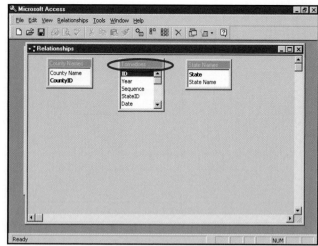

Pointer changes to a two-headed arrow when used to drag the edge.

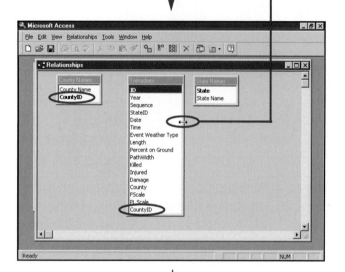

7 Click and drag the bottom edge of the **Tornadoes** table downward until all of the fields are displayed. Click and drag the right side of the **Tornadoes** table until the full field names are visible.

In Depth: It is not necessary to enlarge the table but, if you have room on the screen, it is recommended to reduce the likelihood of mistaking one field for another.

8 Point at the **CountyID** field in the **County Names** table and hold down the left mouse button. Move the pointer to the **CountyID** field in the **Tornadoes** table and release the mouse. The **Relationships** dialog box opens. Notice the relationship type is one-to-many.

In Depth: Notice that the pointer is the shape of a small rectangle while on top of one of the fields in a table. In the open space between the tables, the pointer looks like a universal symbol for "no," or Ø.

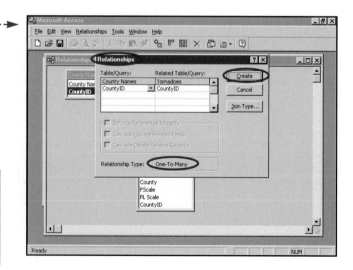

9 Click the **Create** button. A line connects the two fields to indicate that the tables are related.

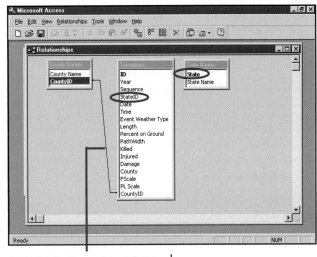

> **In Depth:** The two fields do not have to have the exact same name, but they do have to be the same field type and have the same properties. For example, the CountyID fields in both tables are text fields and the State and StateID fields in both tables are number fields. Also, the field in the "one" side of a one-to-many relationship must be the primary key field.

Line indicates related fields

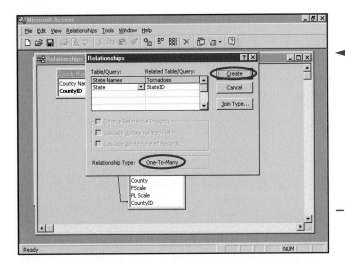

10 Click and drag from the **State** field in the **State Names** table to the **StateID** field in the **Tornadoes** table. The **Relationships** dialog box opens.

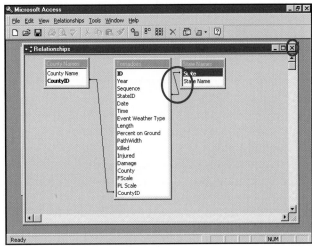

11 Click **Create**. A second line indicates a relationship between the **State Names** table and the **Tornadoes** table.

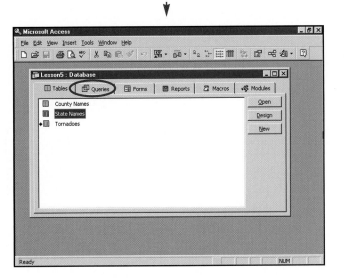

12 Click the **Close Window** button and click **Yes** to save the changes. The **Relationships** window closes and the Database window is displayed.

Task 3

Creating a Union Query that Uses Fields from Both Tables

Why would I do this?

The power of a relational database is the ability to bring together data from a number of different tables. In this lesson, we opened a database with the County Names table, imported the State Names table, and then linked to the Tornadoes table. Then a relationship was established between the tables. Now that the tables are related, a union query can be used so information from the different tables can be included in the query. A *union query* has the same properties as a select query, plus the ability to use fields from more than one table, if the tables are related.

In this task, you use the actual state and county names from the State Names and County Names tables in combination with the fields from the Tornadoes table. You then learn how to add criteria and use parameters to create a powerful tool for analyzing this data.

1 Click the **Queries** tab and click **New**. The **New Query** dialog box opens.

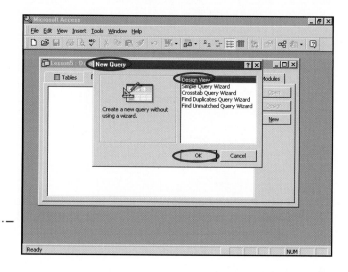

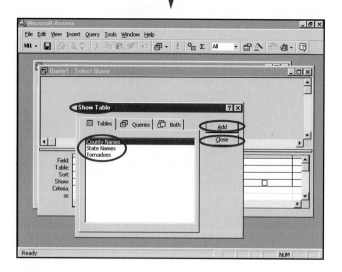

2 Click **Design View** and click **OK**. The **Show Table** dialog box opens.

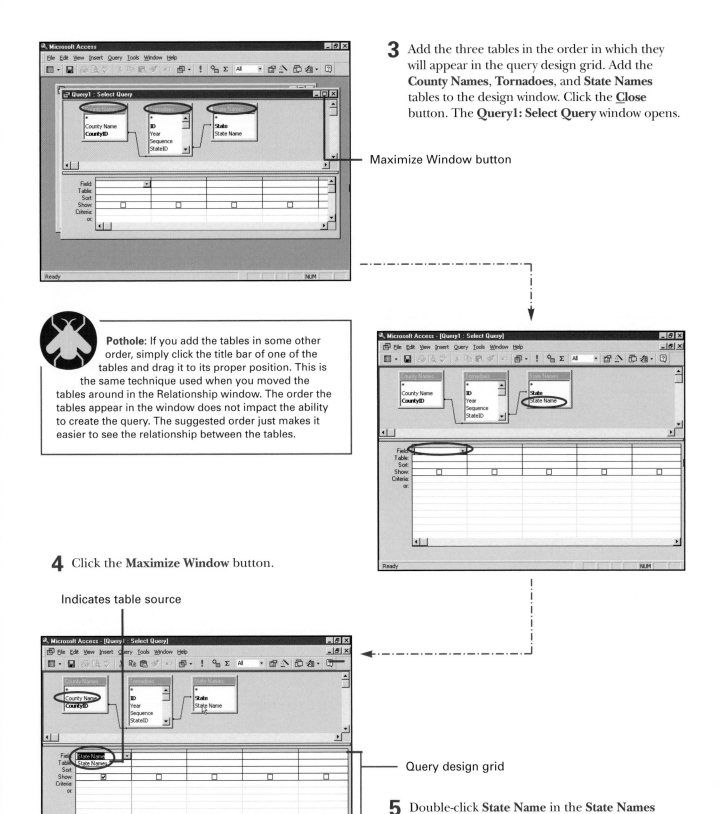

3 Add the three tables in the order in which they will appear in the query design grid. Add the **County Names**, **Tornadoes**, and **State Names** tables to the design window. Click the **Close** button. The **Query1: Select Query** window opens.

Maximize Window button

Pothole: If you add the tables in some other order, simply click the title bar of one of the tables and drag it to its proper position. This is the same technique used when you moved the tables around in the Relationship window. The order the tables appear in the window does not impact the ability to create the query. The suggested order just makes it easier to see the relationship between the tables.

4 Click the **Maximize Window** button.

Indicates table source

Query design grid

5 Double-click **State Name** in the **State Names** table field list box. The State Name field is placed in the first Field text box of the query design grid and the name of the table from which it comes is identified in the Table text box below it.

6 Double-click **County Name** in the **County Names** table field list box. The County Name field is placed in the second Field text box of the query design grid, along with the name of its table in the Table text box below it.

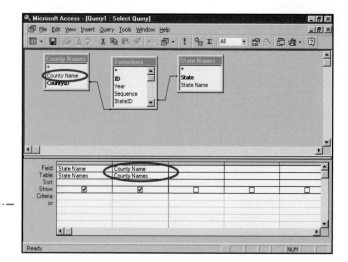

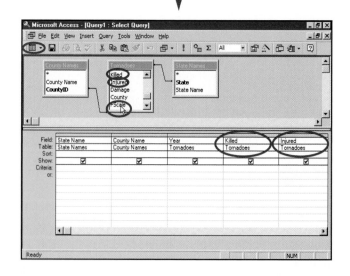

7 Double-click **Year** in the **Tornadoes** table field list box. Year is added to the query design grid. The source table is Tornadoes.

Quick Tip: You can select several noncontiguous fields from a table at one time by using the Ctrl key on your keyboard. Click the first field to be selected, then hold down the Ctrl key and click each additional field you want to include from that table. When all fields are selected, point to any one of the selected fields and click and drag it to the first open field box in the query design grid. Each of the selected fields will be added to the grid in the same order that they appear in the field list box.

8 Scroll down the list of fields in the **Tornadoes** table field list box and double click the **Killed**, **Injured**, and **FScale** fields. They are added to the query design grid. (The **FScale** field may be off the screen to the right. Scroll to the right to view the field.) The source table is Tornadoes.

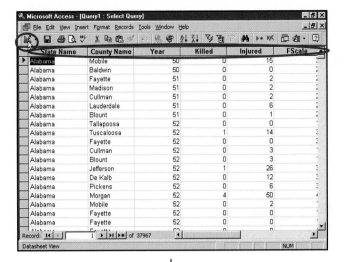

9 Click the **View** button to switch to **Datasheet View**. The query displays the names of the states and counties instead of just their numbers.

In Depth: The number of records shown at the bottom of the screen is less than the total number of records in the Tornadoes table. That is because there are some tornado records that do not have a county name listed or the county code that they have does not match any of the current county names.

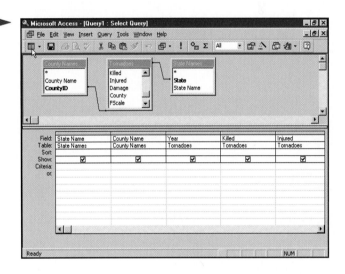

10 Click the **View** button again to switch to **Design View**.

Task 4

Using Advanced Parameter Query Methods with a Union Query

Why would I do this?

In Lesson 4 you were introduced to parameter queries. As you saw, a parameter query can be used to control the results of a query each time it is run. There are a few extra techniques that can be added to the use of parameters that make them very powerful analysis tools. Parameters can be written in a way that allows you to extract a range of data. For example, in a personnel database you may need to know who will turn 62 in January. You can write a parameter query that allows you to enter a beginning date and an ending date which will give you all of the people who fit the criteria in that range. The use of these techniques makes parameter queries even more flexible, which helps you to create queries that can be tailored to your specific needs each time they are run.

In this task, you learn how to use two different *comparison operators*. These operators, as the name suggests, allow you to compare data in a particular way. The Like operator is used so that the entry made in a parameter box does not have to match all of the letters in the field or so you can see any value in the field. You will also learn how to use the Between . . . And operator to specify a range of dates or numbers.

1 In the query design grid, click the Criteria text box below the **State Name** field and type **[Enter State]**.

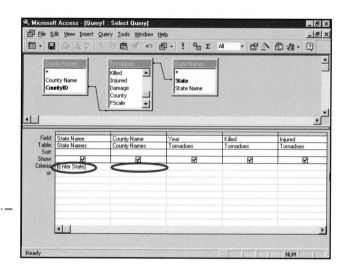

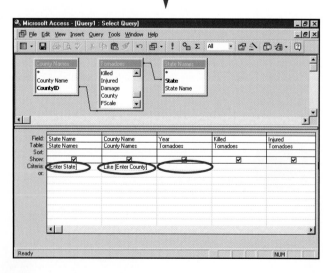

2 Click the Criteria text box below the **County Name** field and type **Like [Enter County]**. This is a useful variation of the parameter query that allows the use of asterisks to replace all or part of the entry.

3 Click the Criteria text box below the **Year** field and type **Between [From] And [Through]**. This type of criteria lets you specify a range of years. If you wanted just one year, you would enter the specific year in both the From and Through parameter boxes.

 In Depth: To see the entire entry for the previous step, right click on it and choose Zoom from the shortcut menu.

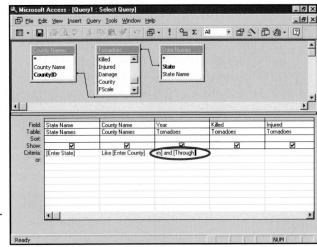

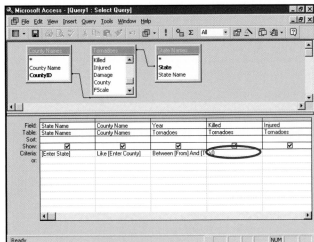

5 Click the **View** button. The **Enter Parameter Value** dialog box opens. Type **Michigan**.

4 Click the **Criteria** text box below the **Killed** field and type **>0**. This will limit the records to just those tornadoes that caused fatalities.

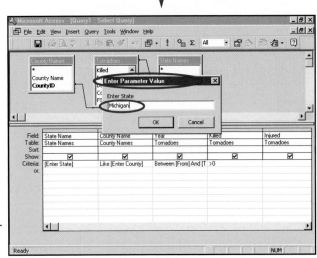

6 Click **OK**. The **Enter Paramater Value** dialog box for the County opens. Type an asterisk, *****, in the box. The use of an asterisk will display all of the county names.

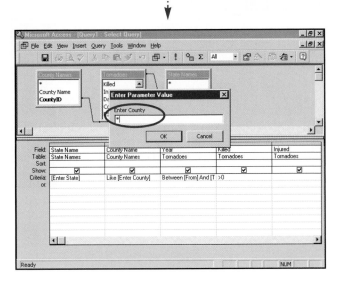

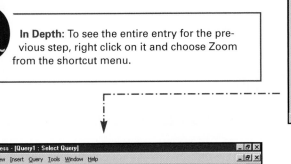 **In Depth:** An asterisk is known as a *wildcard* and can be used to search for any number of characters. It can be used as the first or last character in a string of characters. In this example, the asterisk may be used with part of the county name. For example, if you had typed W*, you would have gotten all of the county names that begin with a W.

7 Click **OK**. Type <u>**50**</u> in the **Enter Parameter Value** dialog box to indicate 1950 and click **OK**. Type **95** in the next parameter box to indicate 1995 and click **OK** again. The query will display the forty tornadoes that have killed people in Michigan between 1950 and 1995.

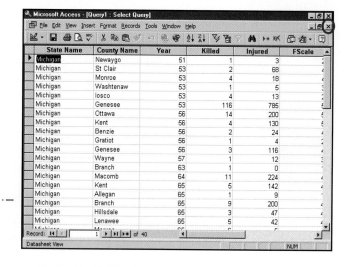

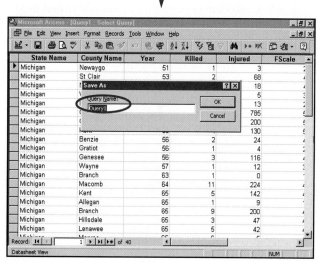

8 Click the **Close Window** button and click **Yes** to save the query. The **Save As** dialog box opens.

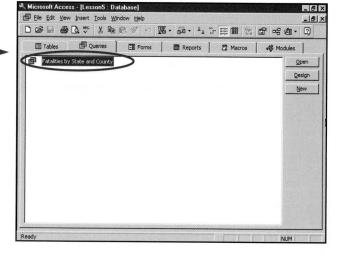

9 Type <u>**Fatalities by State and County**</u> and click **OK**. The query is saved as part of the database for future use.

Task 5

Creating a Form that Displays Data from Two or More Tables

Why would I do this?

Just like a union query is used to include information from more than one table, forms are also capable of showing data from two tables at once, if the tables are related. A special type of form that can be used for this purpose is known as a form with subform. With this type of form you can scroll through records for one table and find the related records from a second table. For example, in a personnel database, you might have one table of departments and another table of personnel information. By using a subform, you can scroll through the department table and see the employees that are assigned to that department. A form with subform is like a form within a form.

In this task, you learn how to create a form that allows you to scroll through the records by state and within that form create a subform that allows you to scroll through the tornadoes that have occurred in that state.

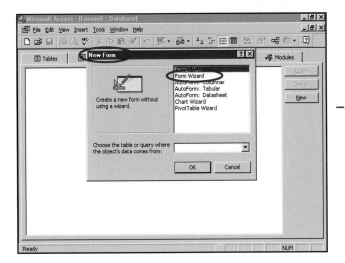

1 Click the **Forms** tab and click **New**. The **New Form** dialog box opens.

List arrow

2 Click **Form Wizard** and click **OK**. The **Form Wizard** dialog box opens.

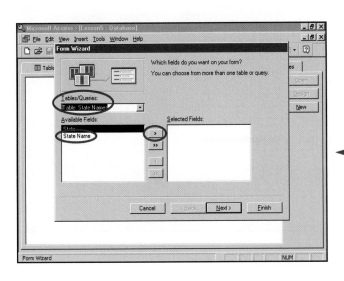

3 Click the list arrow next to the **Tables/Queries** box and click **Table: State Names**. A list of the fields in that table is displayed in the **Available Fields** box.

4 Click **State Name** to select it and then click the **Add** button next to the Available Fields box (single arrow pointing to the right). State Name moves to the **Selected Fields** box.

Quick Tip: If you double-click the name of a field in the Available Fields box, it will move to the Selected Fields box automatically. This works faster than selecting a field and clicking the arrow button.

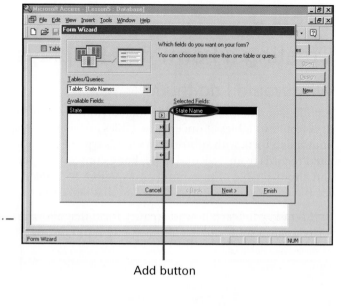

Add button

5 Click the list arrow next to the **Tables/Queries** box and select **Table: Tornadoes**. A list of the fields in the Tornadoes table is displayed in the **Available Fields** box.

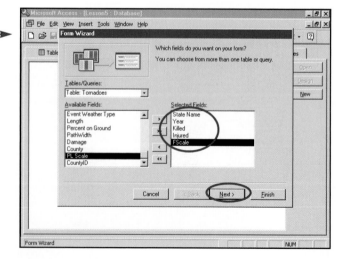

6 Click **Year** and then the **Add** button to add this field to the Selected Fields box. Scroll down the list and select and add the **Killed**, **Injured**, and **Fscale** fields. The form will use the five fields selected from the two tables.

7 Click **Next**. The next **Form Wizard** dialog box opens. This dialog box asks you how you want to view your data. The field selected determines which table is used for the main part of the form. In this case, make sure the State Names table is selected. Also notice that the **Form with subform(s)** option is selected.

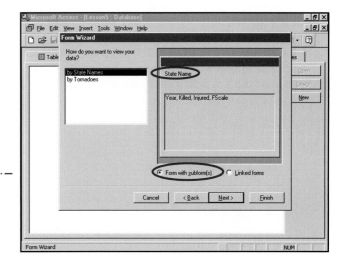

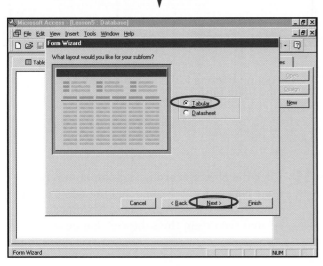

8 Click **Next**. Click the **Tabular** option button to select a tabular layout for your subform.

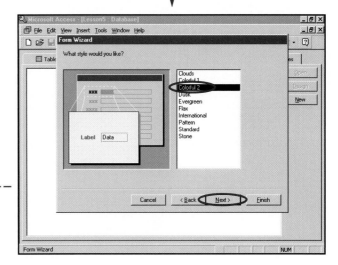

9 Click **Next**. Click the different layout options and select one that you like. (The following figures use Colorful 2.)

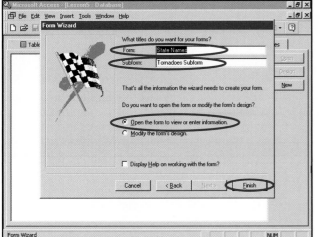

10 Click **Next**. Leave the suggested titles for the form and subform based on the table names from which the data is drawn as shown. Make sure the **Open the form to view or enter information** option is selected.

11 Click **Finish**. You have designed a main form based on the State Names table and a subform based on the Tornadoes table. The two forms are related so that when you scroll through the state names, the tornado records shown in the subform are just for that state.

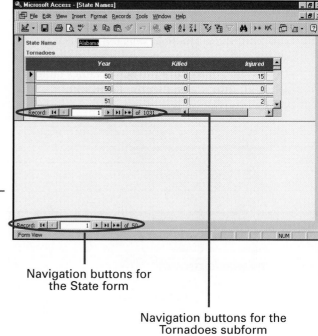

Navigation buttons for the State form

Navigation buttons for the Tornadoes subform

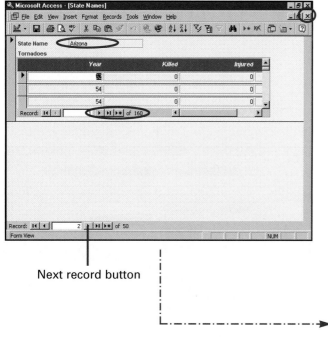

Next record button

12 Click the **Next Record** navigation button on the **State Names** form. Notice that the name of the state changes from Alabama to Arizona and the related records in the subform change as well.

13 Click the **Close Window** button. The form closes and the Database window shows the names of the two forms.

Task 6

Creating a Report that Uses the Union Query

Why would I do this?

Using the Report Wizard, you can produce a report that contains fields from more than one related table. As you have seen with queries and forms, it is useful to be able to include data from more than one table. To limit the records that are included in a report, you create a union query and set criteria to extract the data you need. When dealing with a large database, such as the Tornadoes table, it is helpful to limit the records so the report is smaller and includes only those records that are needed. Reports that are very large often contain too much information, which results in the reports not being used effectively.

In this task, you learn how to use the Report Wizard to create a report based on the Fatalities by State and County query you created in Tasks 3 and 4.

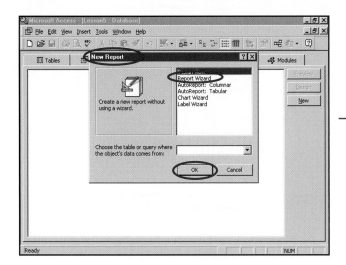

1 Click the **Reports** tab and click **New**. The **New Report** dialog box opens.

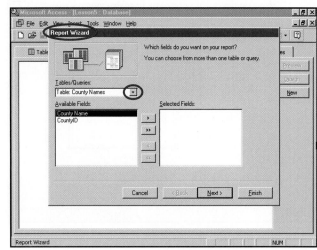

2 Click **Report Wizard** and click **OK**. The **Report Wizard** dialog box opens.

All button

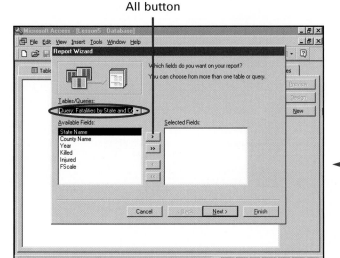

3 Click the list arrow on the **Tables/Queries** box and click **Query: Fatalities by State and County.**

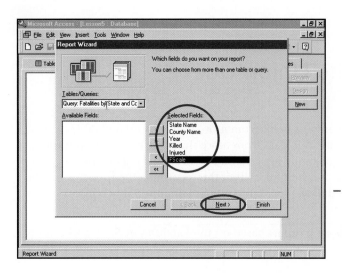

4 Click the **Add All** button to move all of the fields into the **Selected Fields** box.

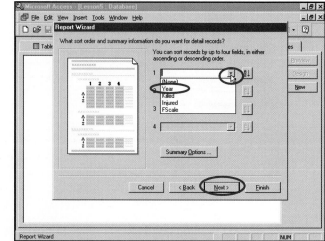

5 Click **Next**. Leave the suggested grouping of records by the State Name field as shown.

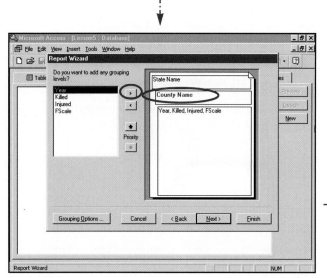

6 Click **Next**. Additional suggestions for grouping the records are provided. In this case, it makes sense to group the records by the County Name field. Click **County Name** in the field list box and then the **Add** button. The example report changes to show how the records are grouped.

7 Click **Next**. You can now sort the records on up to four of the remaining fields. Click the list arrow next to the first sort order text box to display a list of appropriate fields.

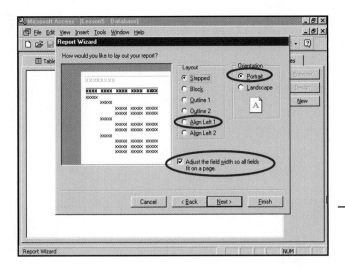

8 Click **Year**. This is the only field that will be sorted. Click **Next**. Several report layout options are provided.

9 Click the **Align Left 1** and **Portrait** orientation option buttons. If necessary, click the **Adjust the field width so all fields fit on a page** check box to select it.

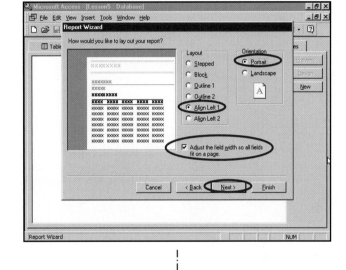

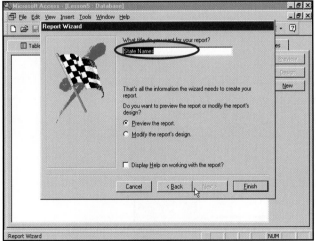

10 Click **Next**. Several style options are displayed. Choose **Bold** and click **Next**.

11 Type **Tornadoes by State** as the title for your report.

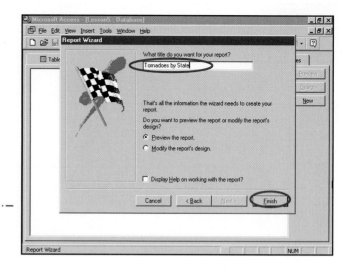

12 Click **Finish**. The **Enter Parameter Value** dialog box opens.

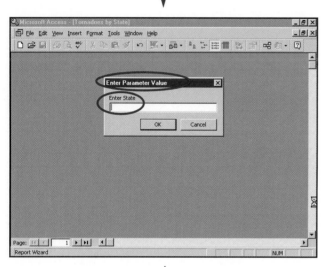

> **In Depth:** This report is based on a parameter query. Therefore, before the report will open you need to respond to each of the Enter Parameter Value dialog boxes. This will be true each time the report is printed or opened to preview. This report allows you to control the records that are included in the report based on the parameters that were established in the query.

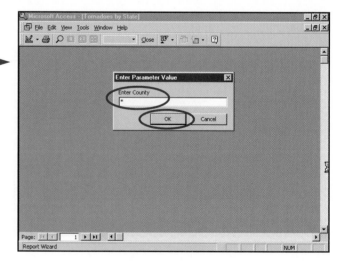

13 Type **Oklahoma** in the **Enter State** parameter box and click **OK**. In the next dialog box, type *, to indicate all counties.

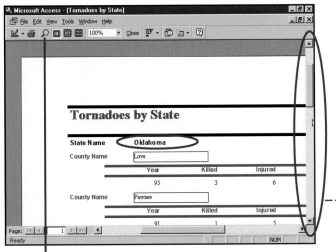

Zoom button

14 Click <u>OK</u>. Type <u>90</u>, click **OK**, type <u>95</u>, and click **OK**. This limits the report to all the counties in Oklahoma that had a tornado which killed at least one person between 1990 and 1995. (Remember: the query has a criteria of >0 in the Killed column). A preview of the report is displayed.

15 Scroll through the report and use Zoom to get a look at the layout of the report. Notice that the page navigation buttons are dimmed because this report is only one page long. Click the **Print** button to print the report.

Pothole: Be careful to check the page length before you print a report that is based on a large table. You can use the navigation buttons to determine how long a report is: Click the Last Record button, ⬜, to move to the last page of the report.

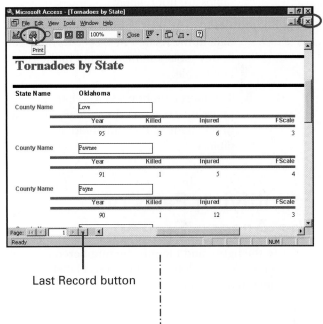

Last Record button

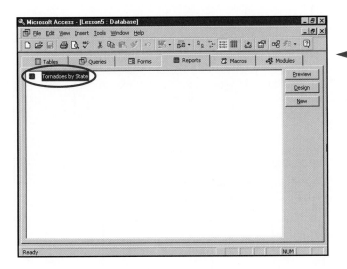

16 Click the **Close Window** button. The report closes and its name is displayed in the **Database** window. Close the database and exit Access.

Student Exercises

True-False

For each of the following, circle T or F to indicate whether the statement is true or false.

T F **1.** To create a relationship between two tables, both tables must include a field with exactly the same name.

T F **2.** The link tables option is best used for large databases or databases that you cannot copy or change.

T F **3.** If you use the Form Wizard to create a form, you will be able to view fields from two tables at the same time, even if the tables are not related.

T F **4.** A one-to-many relationship occurs when data in the related fields occurs one time in one table and many times in the related table.

T F **5.** The most common way to relate two tables is to connect the primary key field in one table to the same field in another table.

T F **6.** A union query has different properties than a select query.

T F **7.** Using "Like" as part of a parameter query criteria allows the user to use a wildcard when searching the database.

T F **8.** In a parameter query, the "Between. . . And" operator allows the user to specify a range of dates or numbers.

T F **9.** For large databases, it is best to create a report based on a union query in order to see all of the records in the database displayed in the report.

T F **10.** In a report, you can group records on only one field.

Identifying Parts of the Access Screen

Refer to the figure and identify the numbered parts of the screen. Write the letter of the correct label in the space next to the number.

1. _____
2. _____
3. _____
4. _____
5. _____
6. _____
7. _____
8. _____

A. Join line
B. Simple parameter criteria
C. "Like" parameter criteria
D. Field source row
E. Parameter criteria that allows a range of data
F. View button
G. Field list title bar
H. Criteria that restricts data to a positive number in this field

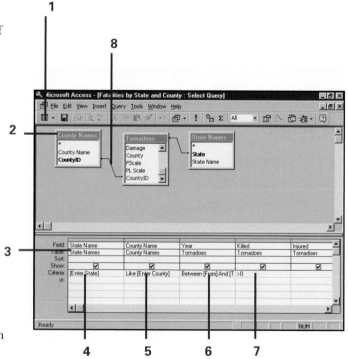

Matching

Match the statements below to the word or phrase that is the best match from the list. Write the letter of the matching word or phrase in the space provided next to the number.

1. ___ Button used to establish a relationship between tables in the Relationship dialog box

2. ___ Indicates a linked table

3. ___ An example of a wildcard symbol

4. ___ A type of relationship where data occurs one time in one table and several times in another table

5. ___ Show Table button

6. ___ Symbol for the Add button which moves a single field from the Available Fields box to the Selected Fields box in Form Wizard

7. ___ Moves to the last record in a database form or report

8. ___ View button

9. ___ Symbol for the Add All button which moves all fields from the Available Fields box to the Selected Fields box in Form Wizard

10. ___ A way to use information from another table without having the table reside in your database

A. One-to-many relationship

B. >

C.

D.

E. Create

F. >>

G.

H.

I. Relate

J. *

K. Link

Application Exercises

The following exercises use the **Lesson5** database. The first three exercises are meant to be done together.

Exercise 1 – Creating a Table of FScale Descriptions

1. Launch Access and open the **Lesson5** database.

2. Create a new table that has two fields: **FScale** and **Description**. The FScale field is a number field and the Description field is a text field. Make the **FScale** field the primary key field. Name the table **Description of the FScale**.

3. Enter the following data into the table:

F Scale	Description
0	Light Damage (40-72 mph)
1	Moderate Damage (73-112 mph)
2	Significant Damage (113-157 mph)
3	Severe Damage (158-206 mph)
4	Devastating Damage (207-260 mph)
5	Incredible Damage (261-318 mph)

Exercise 2 – Creating a Relationship between the Tornadoes Table and the Description of the FScale Table

1. Choose **Tools** and **Relationships** from the menu to open the **Relationships** window.

2. Click the **Show Table** button and then add the new table.

3. Drag a relationship between the **FScale** field in the **Description of the FScale** table and the **FScale** field in the **Tornadoes** table.

4. Close the **Relationships** window and save the changes.

Exercise 3 – Creating a Union Query that Uses the Description of the FScale

1. Create a new query and add the **Tornadoes**, **State Names**, and **Description of the FScale** tables.

2. Double-click the **State Name** field in the **State Names** table, the **Year** and the **FScale** fields in the **Tornadoes** table, and the **Description** field in the **Description of the FScale** table to add them to the query design grid.

3. Click the **Save** button to save the query and name it **Exercise Three**.

4. Type **89** in the Criteria box below the the Year field and type **≥2** in the Criteria box below the FScale field.

5. Click the **View** button to switch to **Datasheet View** to view the results. There were 36 tornadoes with an FScale rating greater than 2 in 1989.

6. Click the **Print Preview** button to preview the query and then print the query. (Hint: Adjust the column widths as needed to print the full FScale description.) Write your name on the printout to hand in.

7. Close the query and save the changes.

Exercise 4 – Creating a Report Based on a Query

1. Create a report, using Report Wizard, based on the **Exercise Three** query.

2. Include in the report all of the fields that are in the query. View by **State Name**. Do not use any grouping levels. Sort on **Year**. Choose **Align Left 2** and **Portrait** orientation. Choose any style. Title the report **Exercise Four**.

3. If needed, adjust the **Description** text box size so the entire description shows in the report.

4. **Print** the report. Write your name on it.

Exercise 5 – Creating a Form with Subform Based on Related Tables

1. Use the Form Wizard to create a new form based on the **Tornadoes** table, **State Names** table, and the **Description of the FScale** table.

2. Use the **Year** and **FScale** fields from the **Tornadoes** table, the **State Name** field from the **State Names** table, and the **Description** field from the **Description of the FScale** table.

3. View the data by **Description of the FScale**. This selection will determine the main form and will change the option in the Form Wizard from Single Form to Form with Subform.

4. Finish the form. Scroll the main form to show the tornadoes with a rating of **4**.

5. Look at the navigation bar on the subform. How many tornadoes were rated a 4? _____

Exercise 6 – Adding a Table to Describe the Event Weather Type

1. Create a new table named **Weather Type** in the **Lesson5** database to hold the following data. The **Event** field is a number field. Designate it as the primary key field. The **Description** field is a memo field.

Event	Description
1	Tornado
2	Funnel cloud
3	Water spout
4	Water spout moving ashore
5	Tornado moving over large body of water
6	Hail, average size of hailstones are greater than $3/4$ inches in diameter
7	Non-tornadic winds greater than 50 knots (57+ miles per hour)
8	Hail aloft, average size of hailstones are greater than $3/4$ inches in diameter
9	Extreme turbulence

2. Create a relationship between the **Weather Type** table and the **Tornadoes** table using the **Event** and **Event Weather Type** fields.

3. Create a union query that contains the **State Name** field in the **State Names** table, the **Year** and the **Event Weather Type** fields in the **Tornadoes** table, and the **Description** field in the **Weather Type** table.

4. In the **Criteria** box below the **Event Weather Type** field, type **[Enter Weather Type code 1-9]**.

5. Save the query and name it **Type of Weather**.

6. View the query and adjust the columns as needed so all of the information prints on one page. **Print** a list of tornadoes that were seen moving over a large body of water (event 5).

7. Close the database and exit Access.

Lesson 6
Using Queries and Reports to Analyze Data

Task 1 Creating a Simple Crosstab Query

Task 2 Creating a Multilevel Crosstab Query

Task 3 Editing a Query

Task 4 Adding the Totals Function to a Query

Task 5 Creating a Pivot Table in a Form

Task 6 Creating a Report that Groups Data and Displays Subtotals and Totals

Introduction

Databases traditionally have been used to store large lists of related information so that information can be extracted as needed. Data analysis was often done by sending the database information to a spreadsheet. Access has a number of features that allow you to perform data analysis right in the database. These include various ways to count, add, summarize, and group information. There are data analysis features included in the table, query, form, and report functions of Access.

In previous lessons you used business and scientific databases as examples. In this lesson you will use a social science database, a transcription of the Alcona County Michigan 1900 Federal Census. You will learn how to analyze a large amount of historical census data to gain an understanding about what life was like in a rural county in Michigan at the turn of the century.

Visual Summary

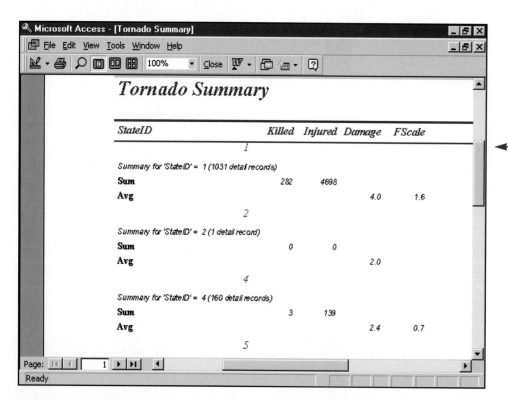

When you have completed this lesson, you will have created several data summaries, one of which will look like this:

Task 1

Creating a Simple Crosstab Query

Why would I do this?

Creating a *crosstab query* is particularly useful when you need to see the relationship among several categories of numeric data. A crosstab query displays summarized values (sums, counts, and averages) from one field in a table and groups them based on at least two other fields. It displays data in a spreadsheet format with data from one field displayed on the vertical axis in the left column and data from another field displayed on the horizontal axis across the top. The intersection of the two fields is used for the summary data of a third numeric field. For example, a crosstab query might display school districts names on the vertical axis down the left column, and the students' gender across the top, and with average SAT scores in the data area. Crosstab queries help group and summarize several fields at a time.

In this task, you learn how to use a crosstab query to display the types of occupations that the men and women of the county had in 1900.

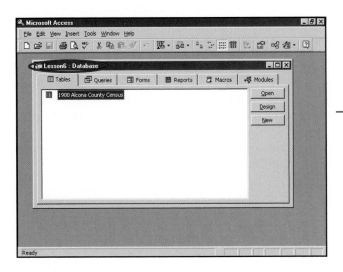

1 Using Windows Explorer, make a copy of **Less0601** and rename the copy **Lesson6**. Launch Microsoft Access. Choose **Open an Existing Database**, find the file **Lesson6**, and open the file.

2 Select the **Queries** tab. Several queries have already been created for this database.

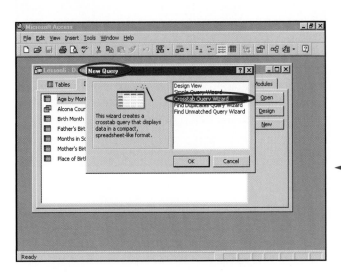

3 Click the **New** button to create a new query. The **New Query** dialog box opens. Select the **Crosstab Query Wizard** option.

4 Click **OK**. The first **Crosstab Query Wizard** dialog box opens, asking which table or query should be used as a data source. You will be using information from the **1900 Alcona County Census** table, which is the default selection.

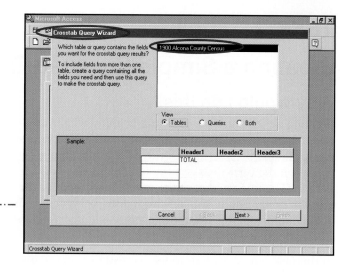

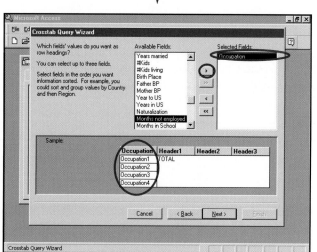

5 Click **Next** to move to the second **Crosstab Query Wizard** dialog box, which allows you to select the row heading(s) for the crosstab. Scroll down the field list, select **Occupation**, and click the **Add** button to add the field to the **Selected Fields** box.

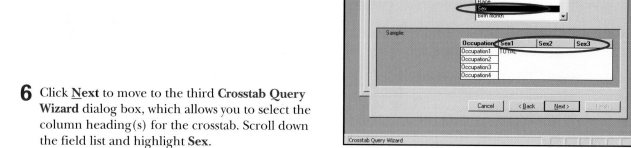

6 Click **Next** to move to the third **Crosstab Query Wizard** dialog box, which allows you to select the column heading(s) for the crosstab. Scroll down the field list and highlight **Sex**.

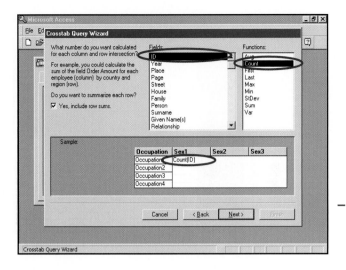

7 Click **Next** to move to the fourth **Crosstab Query Wizard** dialog box, which allows you to choose the method of summarizing your data. Leave **ID** selected in the **Fields** box, then select **Count** from the **Functions** box. This will count the number of men and women in each of the occupational categories.

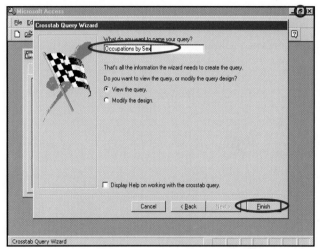

8 Click **Next** to move to the fifth **Crosstab Query Wizard** dialog box. Change the name of the crosstab to **Occupations by Sex**.

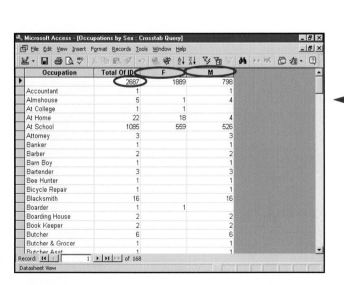

9 Click **Finish**, then click the **Maximize** button to maximize the window. A list of occupations is displayed (note that 2,687 people, mostly women and small children, do not have occupations listed).

10 Click in the *field selector* area at the top of the **Total of ID** column. The whole column is selected.

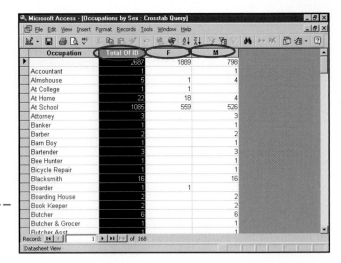

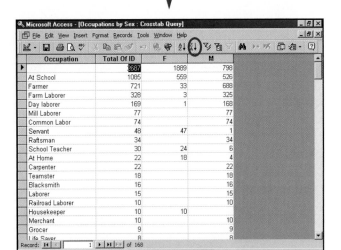

11 Click the **Sort Descending** button to look at the most common occupations.

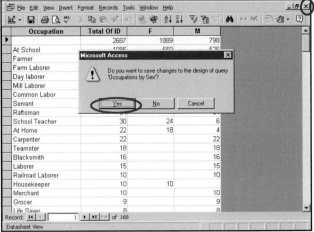

12 Click the **Close Window** button to close the crosstab query. When prompted to save your changes, click **Yes**.

Task 2

Creating a Multilevel Crosstab Query

Why would I do this?

A simple crosstab creates a tabular display showing how one field is summarized based on two other fields that are used to create the row heading and the column heading. The cells are filled with summary data that relies on those fields. Sometimes you may want to further subdivide the analysis by using more than two fields. A multilevel crosstab can summarize one field based on more than two other fields. The additional fields are added to the row headings, subdividing the row headings, while only one field is used for column headings.

In this task, you learn how to create a crosstab query that counts the number of people according to sex, location, and marital status. The columns will be based on the Marital Status field and the rows will be based on the Place and Sex fields. The resulting crosstab allows the user to see how many people of each sex and marital status lived in each location.

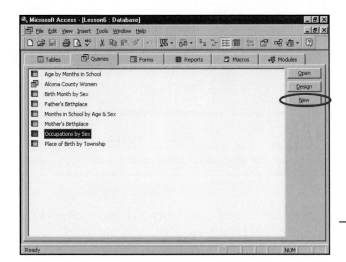

1 In the **Database Window**, select the **Queries** tab, if necessary.

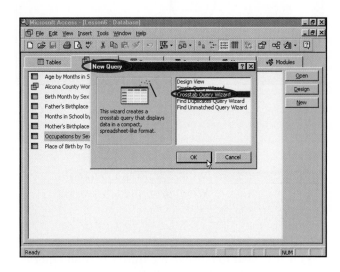

2 Click the **New** button to create a new query. The **New Query** dialog box opens. Highlight the **Crosstab Query Wizard** option.

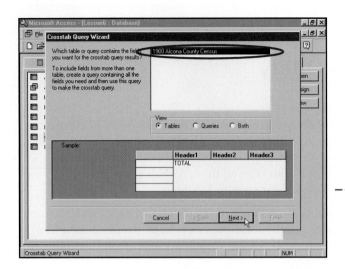

3 Click **OK**. The first **Crosstab Query Wizard** dialog box opens, asking where you want the data to be taken from. You will be using information from the **1900 Alcona County Census** table, which is the default selection.

4 Click **Next** to move to the second **Crosstab Query Wizard** dialog box. Highlight **Place** in the **Available Fields** box and click the **Add** button to move the field into the **Selected Fields** box.

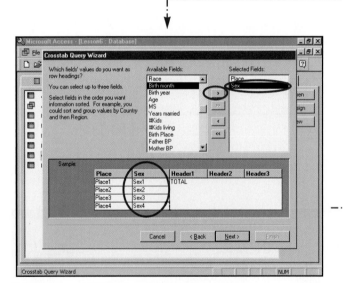

5 Scroll down the field list and highlight **Sex** in the **Available Fields** box. Click the **Add** button to move the field into the **Selected Fields** box. Notice that a second set of row headings is displayed in the preview area.

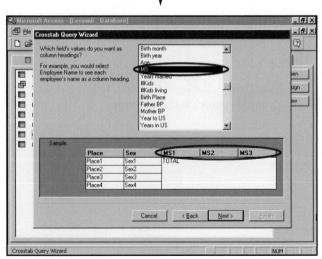

6 Click **Next** to move to the third **Crosstab Query Wizard** dialog box. Scroll down the field list and highlight the marital status (**MS**) field.

7 Click **Next** to move to the fourth **Crosstab Query Wizard** dialog box. Leave **ID** selected in the **Fields** box, then select **Count** from the **Functions** box.

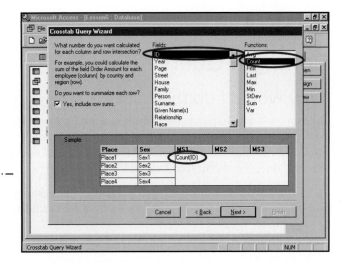

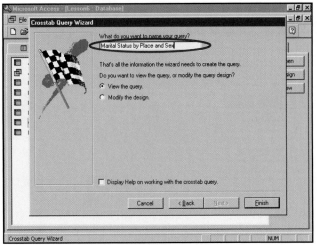

8 Click **Next** to move to the fifth **Crosstab Query Wizard** dialog box. Change the name of the crosstab to <u>**Marital Status by Place and Sex**</u>.

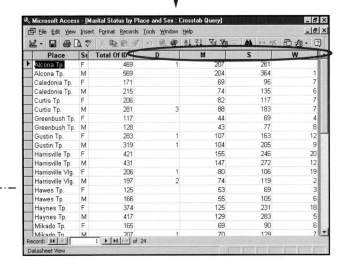

9 Click **Finish**. A list of males and females in each place is summarized by the number who are divorced, married, single, and widowed. This crosstab also gives you the total number of males and females in each location. Notice that in most locations there are more males than females.

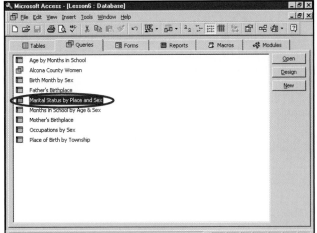

10 Click the **Close Window** button to close the crosstab query. If prompted to save your changes, click **Yes**.

Task 3

Editing a Query

Why would I do this?

When you create a query using the **Crosstab Query Wizard**, you are allowed to choose the fields to be used for the row and column headings, but that is about all. In order to analyze only certain data that meets special conditions, you have two choices—create a separate query that restricts the data and base the new query on the old query, or create a query and edit it in **Design View**.

In this task, you learn how to use Design View to edit a query of all women in Alcona County to show only those women living in Haynes Township who have had children. You will also edit the query to sort the data.

1 In the **Queries** tab, select the **Alcona County Women** query.

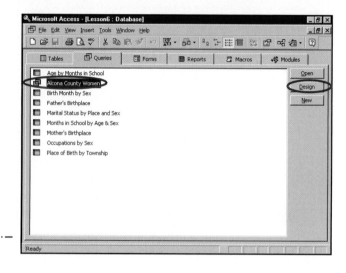

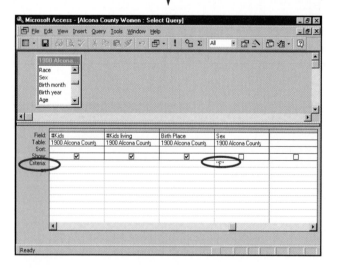

2 Click the **Design** button. The **Design View** is displayed. Scroll to the right until the last four fields are shown. Notice that the **Criteria** text box for the **Sex** field contains an **"F"**, which restricts the query to only females.

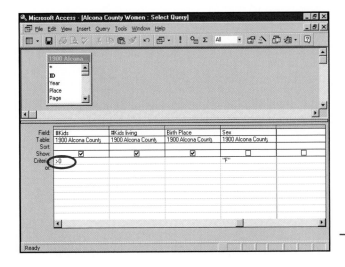

3 In the **Criteria** text box below the **#Kids** field, type **≥0**. This will restrict the output to women who have had at least one child.

> **In Depth:** If you place two criteria on the same row, both criteria must be met for a record to be displayed. This is known as an **And** condition. The row underneath the criteria row is the **Or** criteria row. If criteria is entered on both lines, the second criteria is on the **Or** line, and the record will be displayed if either condition is true. This is known as an **Or** condition.

Empty field

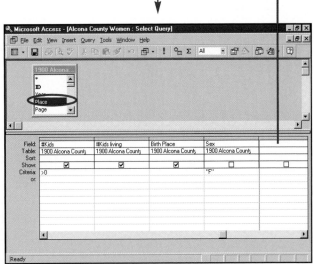

4 Select **Place** from the **Field List** box. Make sure an empty field is available on the right.

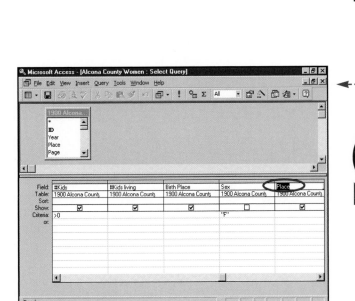

> **Quick Tip:** You can also double-click on the **Place** field and it will automatically be placed in the next open field text box.

5 Click and drag the **Place** field to the **Field** row and drop it in the empty field text box to the right of the **Sex** field text box.

6 Click the **Show** check box below the **Place** field to keep this field from being displayed when the query is run.

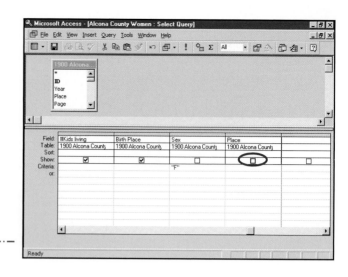

Pothole: If the new column was the last empty column showing on your screen, the first time you click anywhere in the column, the program adds another empty column to the right. In this case, the check mark in the show box does not go away, and you have to click it a second time. Make sure the check mark is not showing to ensure that the **Place** field does not show when you run the query.

7 Type **Haynes Tp.** in the **Criteria** text box below the **Place** field. When you click outside the **Criteria** text box, the program puts quotation marks around the text you typed.

Pothole: If you run your query and no records are shown, chances are you have typed a criteria incorrectly. In this example, if you leave the period off the end of *Haynes Tp.* the query will find nothing because it needs an exact match.

Run button

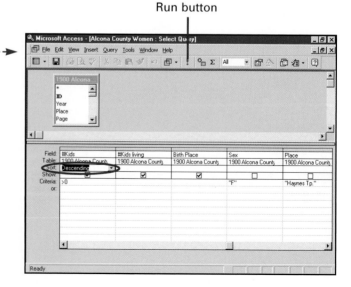

8 Scroll back so you can see the **#Kids** field. Click in the **Sort** box and choose **Descending** from the drop-down list. This will set the order of display starting with the woman with the most children.

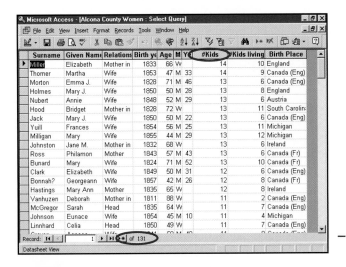

9 Click the **Run** button to see the results of your edits. Notice that **131** women in the township are mothers. Also notice that the records are sorted in descending order by the number of children each woman had.

In Depth: The Run button is another way to view the results of a query. You can use either the View button or the Run button. Some special types of queries, known as action queries, require the use of the Run button to run the query against the data to change records or make new tables. This type of query is not covered in this book.

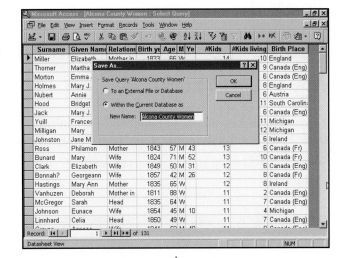

10 To save this version of the query without over-writing the original version, choose **File** and **Save As/Export** from the menu. The **Save As** dialog box opens.

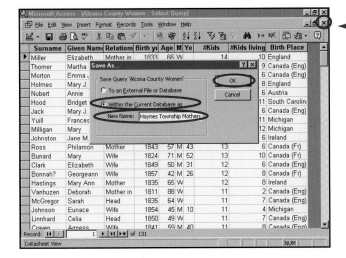

11 Make sure the **Within the Current Database as** action button is selected, then type **Haynes Township Mothers** in the **New Name** box.

12 Click **OK**. Click the **Close Window** button to close the query.

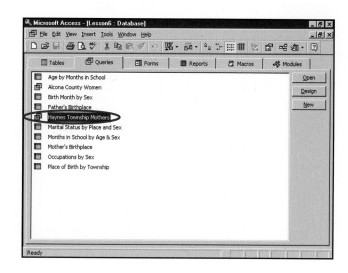

Task 4

Adding the Totals Function to a Query

Why would I do this?

Instead of showing records that match certain conditions, you will sometimes want the query to provide summary data only. Crosstab queries will do that for two or more fields, but you will often want to summarize data for a single field. The **Totals** button in the query **Design View** allows you to do a single field summary.

In this task, you learn how to create a query that counts the number of people born in each place listed in the **Birth Place** field.

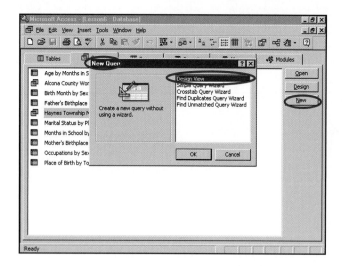

1 Click the **New** button. The **New Query** dialog box opens. Select **Design View**.

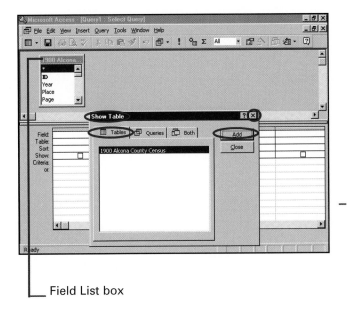

Field List box

2 Click OK. The **Show Table** dialog box opens. Select the **Tables** tab, if necessary. The **1900 Alcona County Census** is highlighted. Click the **Add** button. The table **field list** is added to **Design View**.

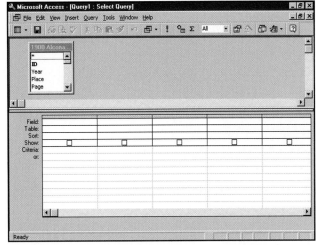

3 Click the **Close** button to close the **Show Table** dialog box. The empty **Design View** is displayed.

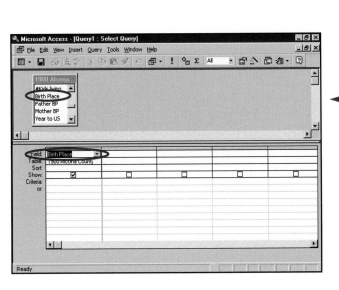

4 Scroll down the **field list** until you see the **Birth Place** field. Double-click to add this field to the first empty Field text box.

5 Scroll to the top of the **field list**. Select the **ID** field and double-click to add it to the next open Field text box.

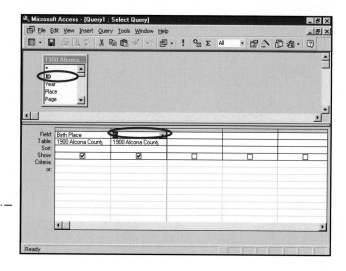

Totals button

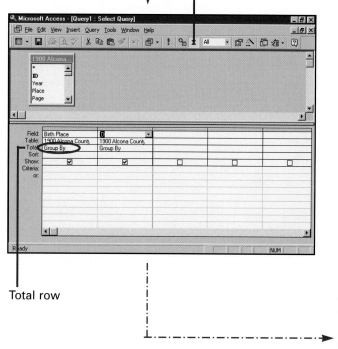

Total row

6 Click the **Totals** button. A new **Total** row is added to the search grid. Notice that the default choice in the Total row is Group By, which is correct for the Birth Place field.

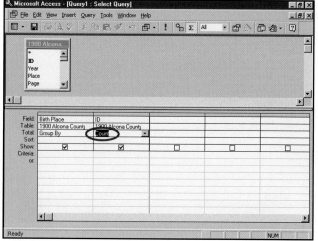

7 Place the cursor in the **Total** text box below the **ID** field. Click the drop-down arrow and select **Count** from the list. This will give you a count for the grouped birthplaces.

8 Place the cursor in the **Sort** text box below the **ID** field. Click the drop-down arrow and select **Descending** from the list. This shows the most common birthplaces first.

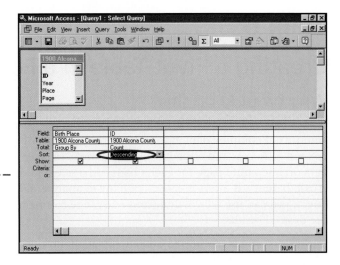

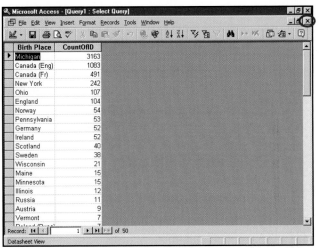

9 Click the **Run** button. A summary list of birthplaces is shown.

10 Click the **Close Window** button. When prompted to save changes, click **Yes**. The **Save As** dialog box opens.

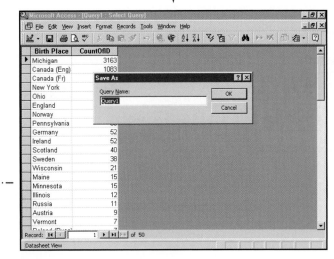

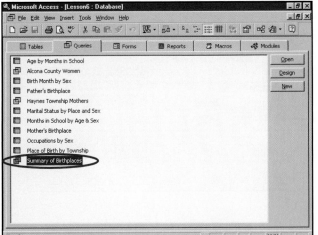

11 Type **Summary of Birthplaces** and click **OK** to return to the Database window.

Task 5

Creating a Pivot Table in a Form

Why would I do this?

A *pivot table* is an interactive table that is used to perform calculations, and it is often the best way to analyze large amounts of complex data. Pivot tables are usually associated with an Excel spreadsheet, but pivot tables can be created in Access and edited using Excel tools. In Access, a pivot table is displayed as a form allowing you to print data on a separate page for each change in a selected category. While a pivot table performs much the same as a crosstab query, it offers greater flexibility to analyze data in different ways. Rather than having to create a new query, you can use a Pivot table and rearrange row headings, column headings, and page fields until you achieve the desired results.

In this task, you learn how to quickly calculate the average age of the males and females in each township and village in Alcona County.

1 Click the **Forms** tab and then click the **New** button. The **New Form** dialog box opens.

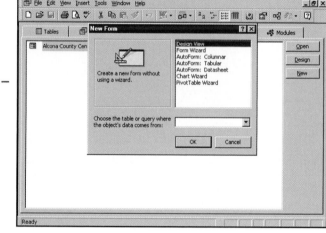

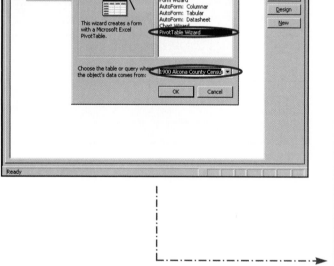

2 Click the **PivotTable Wizard** and select the **1900 Alcona County Census** from the drop-down list.

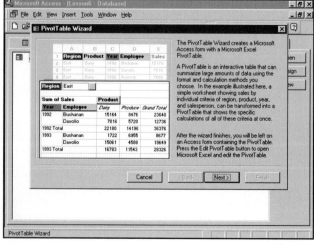

3 Click **OK**. The first **PivotTable Wizard** dialog box opens. It is an introduction to the PivotTable Wizard.

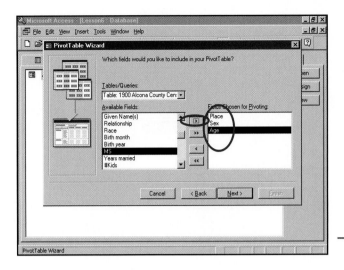

4 Click **Next**. The second **PivotTable Wizard** dialog box opens. Select the **Place** field and click the **Add** button to add it to **Fields Chosen for Pivoting**. Do the same for the **Sex** and the **Age** fields.

5 Click **Next**. After a minute or so, the third **Pivot-Table Wizard** dialog box is displayed. Excel was opened in the process and can be seen in the background. The fields you chose are shown on the right side of the dialog box.

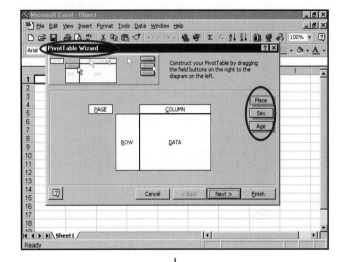

🐝 **Pothole:** You must have Excel installed on your computer for this procedure to work. If you get an error message telling you that the program can't find Excel, move to another computer or skip the rest of this task. When Excel opens, the Office Assistant may also open. Click the Close button to close it.

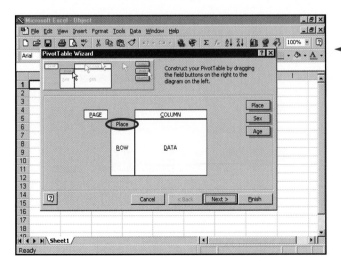

🐝 **Pothole:** For Step 6 to work properly, you must drag the field name into the box. If you try to place it outside the box, the place-holder for the field name will not move.

6 Click and drag the **Place** field into the white box labeled **ROW**. The **Place** field is positioned at the top of the row area.

7 Click and drag the **Sex** field into the **COLUMN** area and the **Age** field into the **DATA** area, as shown in the figure.

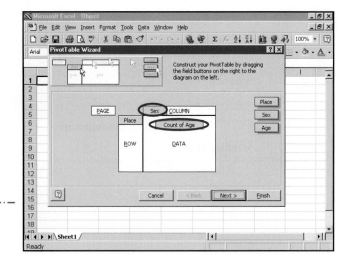

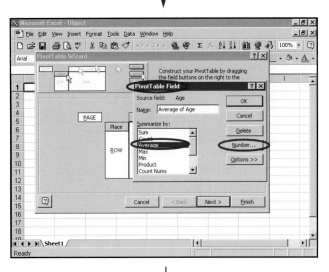

8 Double-click the **Count of Age** box in the **DATA** area. The **PivotTable Field** dialog box opens. Select **Average** from the list.

9 Click the **Number** button. The **Format Cells** dialog box opens. Click **Number** in the **Category** box, and select **1** in the **Decimal places** box.

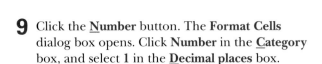

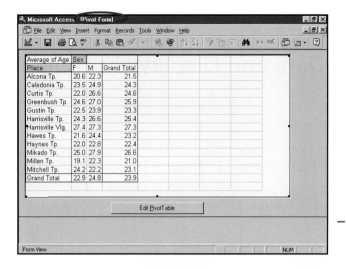

10 Click **OK** twice, then click **Finish**. Excel is closed, and the pivot table is displayed as a **Pivot Form** in Access.

> **In Depth:** You can only edit the pivot table in Excel. If you click the **Edit PivotTable** button, it will launch Excel and open a toolbar that can be used to edit your pivot table. To return to Access, close the Excel window. It is also best to print the data from Excel.

11 Click the **Close Window** button and choose **Yes** when asked if you want to save your changes. Type **Average Age by Place and Sex** in the **Save As** dialog box.

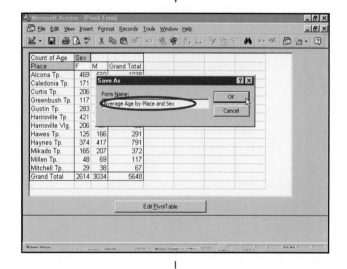

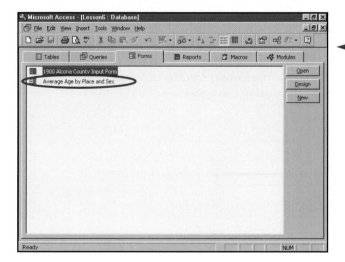

12 Click **OK** to return to the Database Window.

Task 6

Creating a Report that Groups Data and Displays Subtotals and Totals

Why would I do this?

You have learned how to analyze and specify data using tables (with filters), queries, and forms. There is also a technique for grouping and summarizing data using reports. Reports create a professional-looking layout for your data and are used to distribute information.

In this task, you learn how to look at the average age, number of children, and number of children living for the women in each location.

1 Click the **Reports** tab and click **New**. The **New Report** dialog box opens.

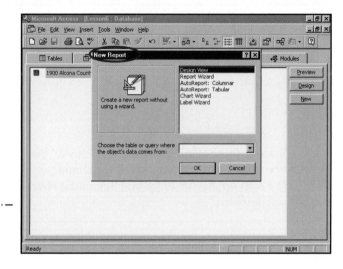

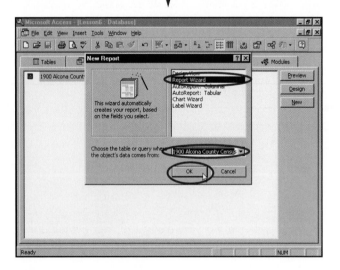

2 Select the **Report Wizard** and choose the **1900 Alcona County Census** table as a data source, as shown in the figure.

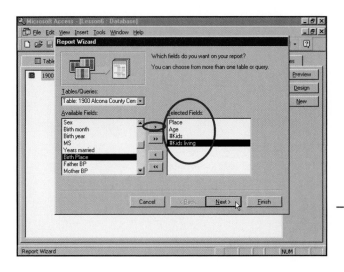

3 Click **OK**. In the first **Report Wizard** dialog box, highlight the **Place** field and click the **Add** button to add the field to the **Selected Fields** box. Follow the same procedure to select the **Age**, **#Kids**, and **#Kids living** fields.

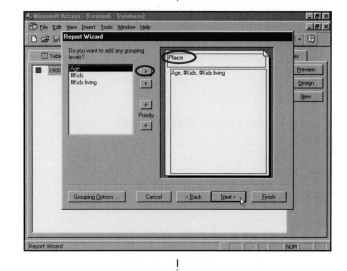

4 Click **Next**. In the second **Report Wizard** dialog box, highlight the **Place** field and click the **Add** button to add the field to the **preview box**. This will group the report by place.

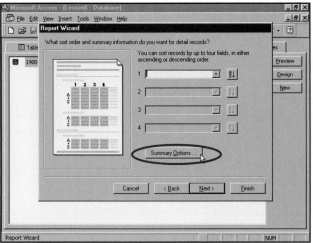

5 Click **Next**. The third **Report Wizard** dialog box opens. It allows you to sort the data (which is un-necessary in this case) and includes a **Summary Options** button.

6 Click the **Summary Options** button. The **Summary Options** dialog box opens. Select **Avg** for all three fields. In the **Show** box, select **Summary Only**.

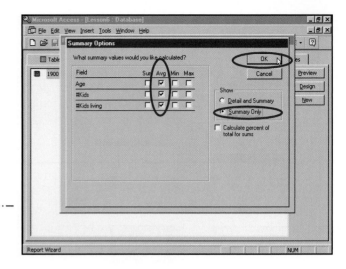

7 Click **OK** to return to the third **Report Wizard** dialog box, then click **Finish** to accept the default layout and design options. A preview of the report is displayed. Notice that the averages show more than one decimal place.

> **In Depth:** You can continue through the **Report Wizard** to customize the layout and design of your report if you choose. The layout of your report will look different from the one in the figure if the default settings on your computer are different, or if you go through the rest of the Wizard and select another layout.

1900 Alcona County Census

Place	Age	#Kids	#Kids living
Alcona Tp.			
Summary for 'Place' = Alcona Tp. (1038 detail records)			
Avg	21.523121	4.4648649	3.47567567568
Caledonia Tp.			
Summary for 'Place' = Caledonia Tp. (386 detail records)			
Avg	24.285714	5.2941176	4.02941176471
Curtis Tp.			

8 Click the **View** button to switch to **Design View**. (If necessary close the Toolbox.) In the **Place Footer** section, click the **=Avg(Age)** box, hold down the ⇧Shift key, and click **=Avg(#Kids)** and **=Avg(#Kids living)**. All three fields are currently selected.

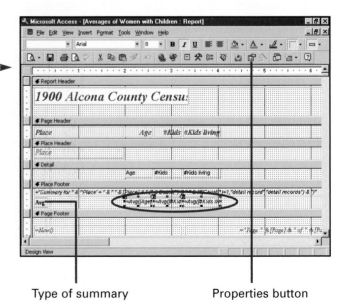

Type of summary   Properties button

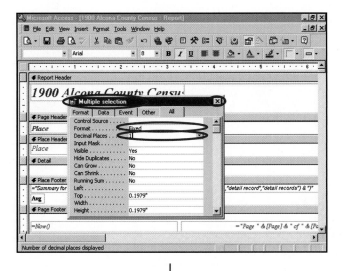

9 Click the **Properties** button to display the **Multiple selection** properties dialog box. Click in the **Format** box, and click the drop-down arrow. Select **Fixed** for the number type. In the **Decimal Places** box, select **1**, as shown in the figure.

In Depth: Each item on a report is known as a control, and can be modified by the use of a Properties box. When you select an item and then click the Properties button, the title bar of the Properties box has the name of the part of the report you have selected. In this case, you selected three controls used to calculate the averages, so the title in the Properties box is *Multiple selection*. If you had selected just one control, the name of that one control would be the title of the Properties box.

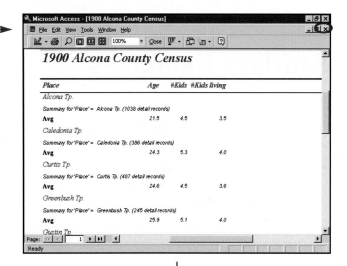

10 Click the **Close Window** button to return to **Design View**. Click the **Print Preview** button to view your changes. Use the scroll bars to show the maximum information on the screen. Notice that the average woman had five children and lost one. Click the **Print** button to print the report.

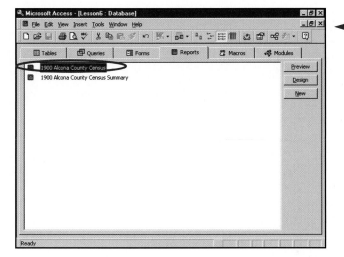

11 Click the **Close Window** button and choose **Yes** when asked if you want to save your changes.

12 Select the **1900 Alcona County Census** report that you just created. Choose **Edit**, **Rename**, then type **Averages of Women with Children**. Press Enter to record the name change.

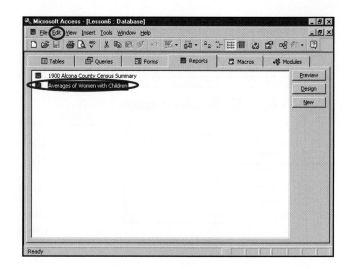

13 Close your **Lesson 6** database.

Student Exercises

True-False

For each of the following, circle T or F to indicate whether the statement is true or false.

T F **1.** Data analysis features are included in the tables, queries, forms, and reports functions of Access.

T F **2.** The summary data that shows in the intersection of a crosstab query must be numeric

T F **3.** A simple crosstab creates a tabular display that shows how one field may be summarized based on two other fields.

T F **4.** A multilevel crosstab can summarize one field based on multiple fields as column headings.

T F **5.** When editing a query, if you place two criteria in the same Criteria row, a record that meets either criteria is displayed.

T F **6.** To determine the average of data in a single field, the Totals button in the query Design View should be used rather than a pivot table.

T F **7.** Pivot tables created in Access are edited in Access.

T F **8.** When you create a pivot table using the PivotTable Wizard, Access opens Excel at the same time the first dialog box opens.

T F **9.** Pivot tables are less flexible to use than crosstab queries.

T F **10.** Reports can be used as a data analysis tool because they can group data and display subtotals and totals.

Identifying Parts of the Access Screens

Refer to the figures and identify the numbered parts of the screen. Write the letter of the correct label in the space next to the number.

1. _____
2. _____
3. _____
4. _____
5. _____

A. Decimal places
B. Number format
C. Properties button
D. Type of summary
E. Field to be summarized

6. _____
7. _____
8. _____
9. _____
10. _____

F. Field List
G. Totals button
H. Design grid
I. Run button
J. Field to be summarized

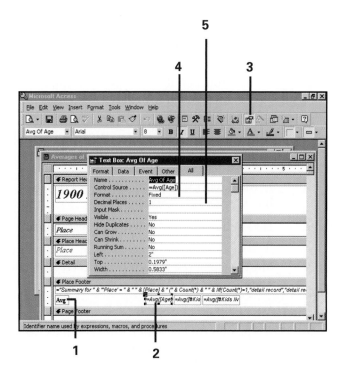

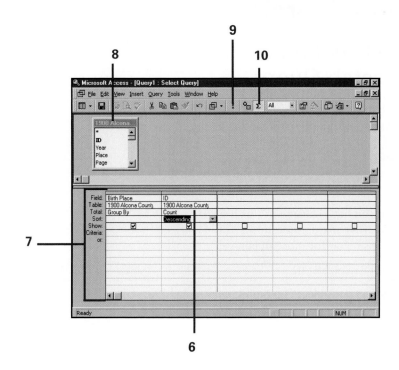

Matching

Match the statements below to the word or phrase that is the best match from the list. Write the letter of the matching word or phrase in the space provided next to the number.

1. ___ Where you set number types and decimal places in a report

2. ___ A query function that groups and summarizes data on multiple fields

3. ___ Shows the results of a query

4. ___ Accessed by choosing New from the Forms tab

5. ___ In the Report Wizard this activates a dialog box to select types of summaries

6. ___ Determines whether a field is displayed in a query

7. ___ Must be open when a pivot table is created or edited

8. ___ Where the crosstab function is found

9. ___ A type of form that summarizes complex data and performs calculations

10. ___ Allows you to summarize a single field

A. Run button

B. Show check box

C. Excel spreadsheet

D. Pivot table

E. Crosstab

F. Summary Options button

G. Maximize button

H. Query tab

I. Properties box

J. PivotTable Wizard

K. Totals button

Application Exercises

Exercise 1 – Creating a Simple Crosstab Query

1. Using Windows Explorer, make a copy of **Ex0601** and rename it **Exercise6**. Launch Microsoft Access. Choose **Open an Existing Database**, find the file **Exercise6**, and open the file. This is a smaller version of the tornado database you used in Lesson 4.

2. Use the skills that you have learned in this lesson to create a simple crosstab query as shown in the figure. See the steps below for more detail.

3. Click the **Queries** tab to select it.

4. Click the **New** button and select **Crosstab Query Wizard**.

5. Select the **Tornadoes** table.

6. Select the **StateID** field for the row heading.

StateI	Total Of ID	<>	0	1	2	3	4	5
1	1031	8	157	364	323	129	36	14
2	1	1						
4	160	31	59	57	11	2		
5	1007	16	182	298	331	149	31	
6	223	39	103	58	21	2		
8	1172	55	561	441	99	15	1	
9	65	1	8	29	20	5	2	
10	55	2	18	23	11	1		
11	1		1					
12	2148	145	1011	665	293	30	4	
13	1032	2	145	537	266	65	17	
15	28	14	8	3	3			
16	124	10	53	53	8			
17	1342	38	393	440	316	113	39	3
18	1038	40	206	336	263	108	77	8
19	1607	94	384	506	421	119	74	9
20	2363	269	842	610	404	168	54	16
21	483	1	78	168	133	65	35	3
22	1254	1	224	620	268	123	16	2
23	82	12	9	44	17			

7. Select the **FScale** (the measure of a tornado's intensity) field as the column heading.

8. Select the **Count** function to count the **ID** field.

9. Name the query Tornado Intensity by State.

10. View the query. Adjust the columns widths so you can view all of the columns on screen. (Check StateID 48 to make sure the data has not changed to scientific notation. Readjust the column width if necessary to show the full number.) The results in the column labeled <> represent tornadoes that were not rated. This a notation for not equal.

11. Choose **File**, **Print.** Close the query, saving your changes when prompted.

Exercise 2 – Creating a Multilevel Crosstab Query

1. Use the skills that you have learned in this lesson to create a multilevel Crosstab query as shown in the figure. See the steps below for more detail.

2. Make sure the **Queries** tab is selected.

3. Select the **New** option and select the **Crosstab Query Wizard**.

4. Select the **Tornadoes** table.

5. Select the **StateID** field for the row heading, then select the **FScale** field as the subheading for the StateID field.

6. Select the **Damage** field for the column heading. (The damage ratings go from minor damage at the lower end of the scale to millions of dollars of damage in the 7 and 8 categories.)

7. Select the **Count** function to count the **ID** field.

8. Name the query Tornado Damage by State and Intensity.

9. View the query. For each **StateID** the intensity scale is listed in the second column. Notice that not all states had tornadoes at all levels of intensity. The third column is the total of each category of intensity by state. The data under the columns labeled <> (not equal) through **8** is the number of tornadoes in each range of monetary damage. For example, in State #1 (Alabama), Fscale 4, there were a total of 36 tornadoes, and all of them had a monetary damage rating of 4 or higher.

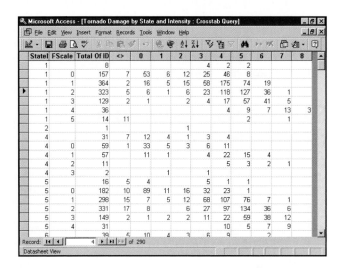

StateI	FScale	Total Of ID	<>	0	1	2	3	4	5	6	7	8
1		8						4	2	2		
1	0	157	7	53	6	12	25	46	8			
1	1	364	2	16	5	15	58	175	74	19		
1	2	323	5	6	1	6	23	118	127	36	1	
1	3	129	2	1		2	4	17	57	41	5	
1	4	36						4	9	7	13	3
1	5	14	11						2		1	
2		1				1						
4		31	7	12	4	1	3	4				
4	0	59	1	33	5	3	6	11				
4	1	57		11	1		4	22	15	4		
4	2	11						5	3	2	1	
4	3	2			1		1					
5		16	5	4			5	1	1			
5	0	182	10	89	11	16	32	23	1			
5	1	298	15	7	5	12	68	107	76	7	1	
5	2	331	17	8		6	27	97	134	36	6	
5	3	149	2	1	2	2	11	22	59	38	12	
5	4	31						10	5	7	9	
6		39	5	10	4	3	6	9		2		

Record: ◄ ◄ 4 ► ►I ►* of 290

Datasheet View

The amount of monetary damage for each tornado is a code representing a range of damage as follows:

0	No damage
1	Less than $50
2	$50 to $500
3	$500 to $5,000
4	$5,000 to $50,000
5	$50,000 to $500,000
6	$500,000 to $5 million
7	$5 million to $50 million
8	$50 million to $500 million
9	$500 million to $5 billion

10. Adjust the columns widths so you can view all of the columns on the screen. Scroll through the query to make sure figures have not changed to scientific notation. Readjust the column width as necessary.

11. Choose **File**, **Print**. Print one page of the query. Save the query and leave it open to use in the next exercise.

Exercise 3 – Editing a Crosstab Query

1. Use the skills that you have learned in this lesson to edit a multilevel crosstab query as shown in the figure. See the steps below for more detail.

2. Click the **View** button to change to Design View of the **Tornado Damage by State and Intensity** query.

3. Sort the **FScale** field in **descending** order.

4. Run the crosstab query to view the results of your edits.

5. Choose **File**, **Print**. Print the first page of the query. Close the query, saving your changes when prompted.

Exercise 4 – Using the Totals Function in a Query

1. Use the skills that you have learned in this lesson to create a query that uses the **Totals** function.

2. If necessary, click the **Queries** tab to select it.

3. Click the **New** button and select **Design View**.

4. **Add** the **Tornadoes** table.

5. Add the **Year**, **Killed**, and **Injured** fields into the design grid.

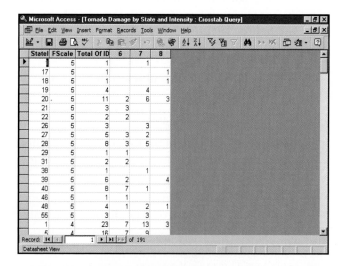

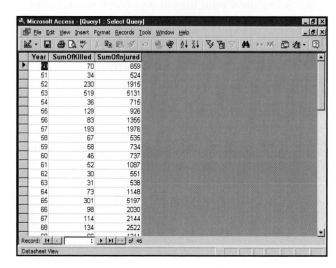

6. Click the **Totals** button to add a Totals row.

7. Select the **Sum** function in the **Totals** row for the **Killed** and the **Injured** fields.

8. Run the query to see the number of people killed and injured by tornadoes in the U.S. by year.

9. Choose **File**, **Print**.

10. Close the query and name it **Tornado Casualties by Year**.

Exercise 5 – Grouping Data and Displaying Totals in a Report

1. Use the skills that you have learned in this lesson to group and summarize data using the report summary.

2. Click the **Reports** tab to select it.

3. Click the **New** button. Choose Report Wizard and select the Tornadoes table as the source of data for this report.

4. Select the **StateID**, **Killed**, **Injured**, **Damage**, and **FScale** fields.

5. Group on the **StateID** field.

6. Click the **Summary Options** button.

7. Select the **Sum** function for the **Killed** and the **Injured** fields.

8. Select the **Avg** function for the **Damage** and the **FScale** fields.

9. Select the **Summary Only** option. Click **OK**. (Sorting is unnecessary.)

10. Accept the default layout, orientation, and style options.

11. Name the report **Tornado Summary** and preview the report.

12. Move to Design View and select both the =**Avg(Damage)** and =**Avg(FScale)** fields.

13. Click the **Properties** button and change the **Format** to a **Fixed** number and the **Decimal Places** to 1.

14. Preview the report.

15. Choose **File**, **Print**. Print the first page of the report.

16. Close the report and save your changes. Exit Access.

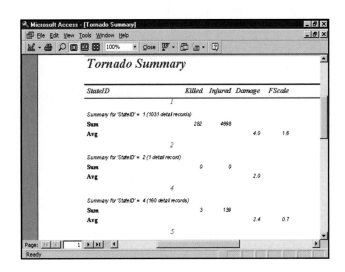

Lesson 7
Connecting to Other Types of Files and Getting Help

Task 1 Linking an Access Table to a Word Document

Task 2 Merging an Access Table with a Word Document

Task 3 Importing a Table from Excel

Task 4 Importing Tables from Other Database Programs

Task 5 Adding Hyperlinks to the Database

Task 6 Getting Help Using the Office Assistant

Task 7 Getting Help On the Internet

Task 8 Finding Reference Books and Self-Help Textbooks

Introduction

Your database does not exist by itself. As you have seen, the data may come from somewhere else, as in the case of the Tornado database which was obtained over the Internet from the U.S. Weather Bureau. Likewise, the reports, queries, and forms you create may need to be seen by others. In Lesson 5 you saw that you can import other Access tables or link to other Access tables. Access also has several powerful tools that you can use to share your database by importing information from a spreadsheet or document. The files you link to may be on your computer or on a computer anywhere in the world over the Internet. You can also use this ability to connect to other files to get help. There is help available from the files stored in your computer as well as from Microsoft's Internet site.

In this lesson, you learn how to use this connectivity to share the results of your work, and to get help when you need it.

Visual Summary

When you have completed this lesson, you will have created a document that merges data from a table of addresses, imported a table of data from a non-Access source, and found help on the Internet. The merged document and the imported table look like this:

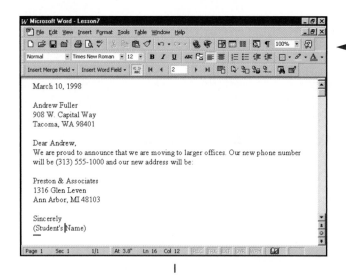

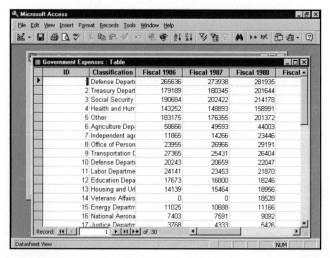

Task 1

Linking an Access Table to a Word Document

Why would I do this?

Databases that contain names and addresses can be merged with Microsoft Word documents to create a series of documents where each document contains data that is unique to that individual. We have all received mail that has a label attached with our names and addresses on it, and most of us have received letters that have our names, birthdays, addresses, or phone numbers imbedded in the text. These are examples of how an organization can communicate with its members. Such mailings are not limited to the postal service; you can also create mailings that use FAX or e-mail.

In this task, you learn how to create a letter to notify your business associates that you are moving and will have a new address and phone number.

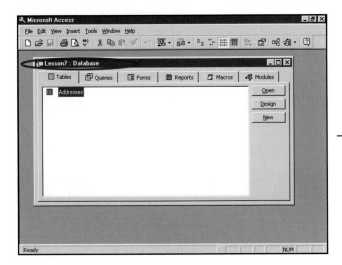

1 Find the **Less0701** database and rename it **Lesson7**. Launch Access and open **Lesson7**. The Addresses database table contains five records and is similar to the table you created in **Lesson 1**.

Office Links button

2 If it is not already highlighted, select the **Addresses** table and click the list arrow to the right of the **Office Links** button on the Standard toolbar.

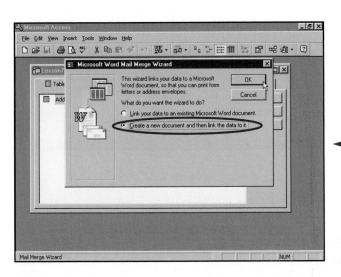

3 Click **Merge It with MS Word**. The **Microsoft Word Mail Merge Wizard** window opens.

4 Click **Create a new document and then link the data to it**. Click **OK**. Microsoft Word launches and a new document opens. Notice that the Mail Merge toolbar is displayed.

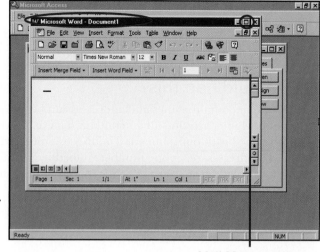

Mail Merge toolbar

5 Maximize the **Word** window, change the Zoom to **100%**, and set the Font Size to **12**, as shown.

Pothole: The Mail Merge toolbar should open. It may be above or below the Formatting or Standard toolbar. If it does not open, you can open it by choosing **View**, **Toolbars** from the menu and then clicking **Mail Merge**.

Quick Tip: Notice that when you begin typing the date, Word automatically suggests the month, then the date. If you press ⏎Enter twice, once to accept the month and the next time to accept the rest of the date, the date will be completed for you.

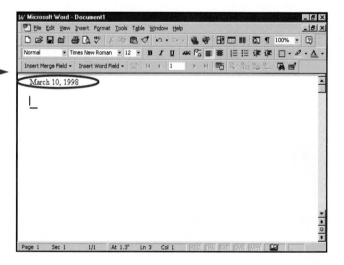

6 Type today's date in the first line and press ⏎Enter twice.

7 Click the **Insert Merge Field** button on the **Mail Merge** toolbar. A list of fields from the **Addresses** table in the **Lesson7** database is displayed.

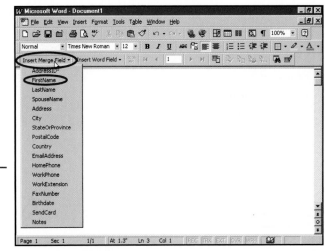

8 Click **FirstName**. The name of the field is placed in the document.

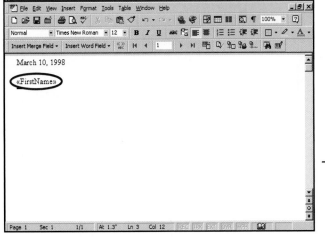

9 Press (Spacebar) to enter a blank space after the first name. Click the **Insert Merge Field** button again and click **LastName**.

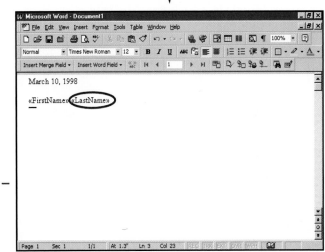

10 Press (↵Enter) to move to the next line of the address. Refer to the figure to create the rest of the document. Insert the fields as shown. (If the Office Assistant pops up during this process, click **Cancel** to close it.)

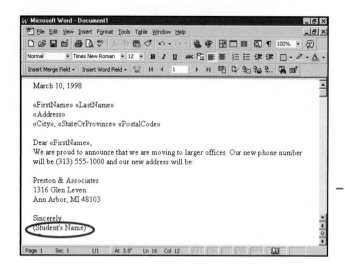

11 Type your name in the last line.

Pothole: The font size on your letter may revert to 10 or whatever default font is set for your computer. If this happens, don't worry about it. The goal of this task is to show you how to merge a database file with a word document and the formatting of the letter is not critical to this purpose.

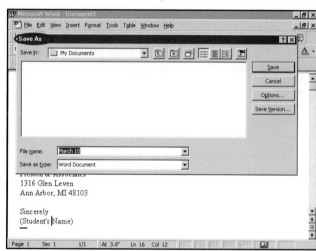

12 Click the **Save** button. The **Save As** window opens.

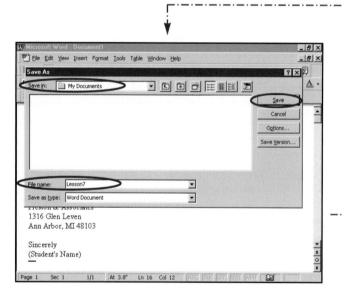

13 Type **Lesson7** in the **File name** box and use the **Save in** box to select the folder that you are using for your files.

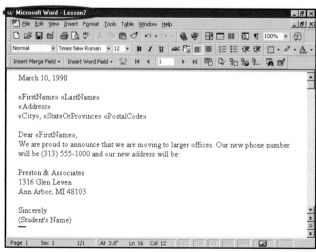

14 Click **Save**. The document is saved as **Lesson7** for later use.

Task 2

Merging an Access Table with a Word Document

Why would I do this?

Once you have linked the database field names to a Word document, you can easily create a personalized letter to each person in the database. This process creates a file of the merged, personalized letters that you can use as a record to document that the letter was mailed. It is important to test your document with the data before you try to print large quantities, to ensure that the letter looks the way you intended.

In this task, you learn how to merge the database file into the letter, then review the document on screen and print the first two letters.

View Merged Data button

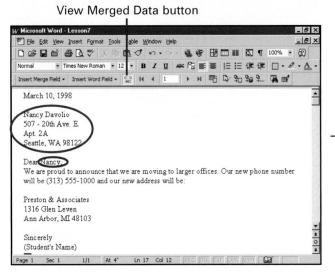

1 Click the **View Merged Data** button. The data from the first record in the **Addresses** table is inserted into the document.

Mail Merge button

Next Record button

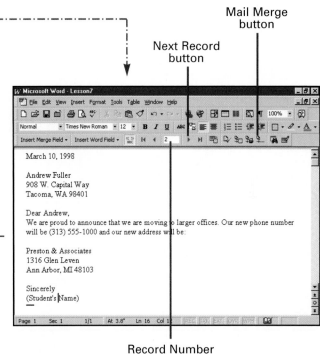

Record Number

In Depth: Notice that the address of the first person takes two lines, while the second person's address takes only one line. Word adjusts for multiple line addresses and for empty fields.

2 Click the **Next Record** button. The data from the second record is displayed.

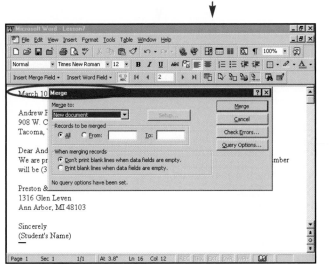

3 Click the **Mail Merge** button. The **Merge** dialog box opens.

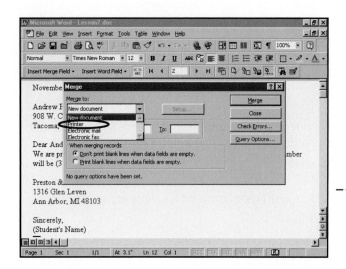

4 Click the list arrow next to the **Merge to** box. Notice that you can send this letter electronically by e-mail or FAX. Click **Printer**.

5 Click the **From:** box in the **Records to be merged** section and type **1**. Type **2** in the **To:** box.

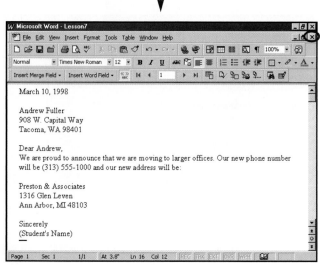

6 Click the **Merge** button to print the letters to the first two people in the **Addresses** table. The **Print** dialog box opens.

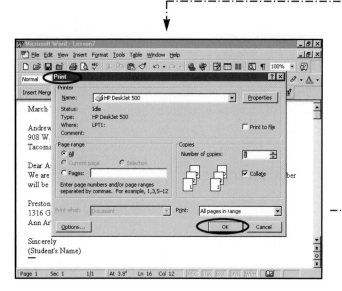

7 Click **OK** to print the first two letters.

8 Close the **Lesson7 Word** document. Save any
changes when prompted. Close **Microsoft Word**.
Leave the **Lesson7 Access** database open for use
in the next task.

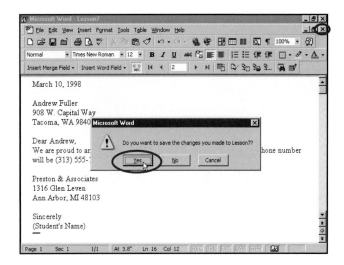

Task 3

Importing a Table from Excel

Why would I do this?

Excel has some database management features such as the ability to sort and filter data. Therefore, many people
use Excel as a crude database management program. There will be a time when you need to import data that is
stored in an Excel spreadsheet and use it with an Access database.

In this task, you learn how to import an Excel spreadsheet that contains budget information for the U.S. government into the Lesson7 Access database that is open from the previous task. The Lesson7 database is used simply
as an example of a how to import data from various sources. The information being imported in the next three
tasks is not related to the address table in the database. The open database is used for convenience to demonstrate
how to import different sources of information.

1 Use Windows Explorer to make a copy of the file
Less0702 and name the copy **Expenses**.

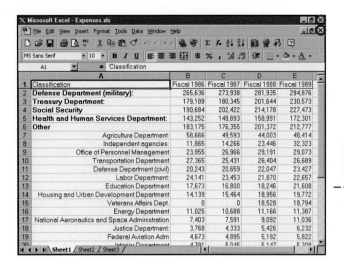

2 Double-click on the **Expenses** filename to launch Excel and open the file. Scroll the file and examine the data. Notice that each row is a record of a type of government expense. The column headings will become field names. Click the **Close** button to close the file and close Excel.

3 Switch to **Access** and the **Lesson7** database.

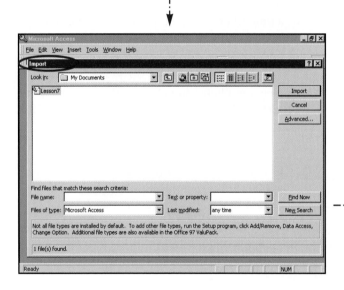

4 Choose **File**, **Get External Data**, **Import**. The **Import** dialog box opens.

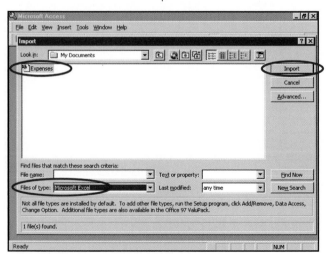

5 Click the **list arrow** next to the **Files of type** box and select **Microsoft Excel**.

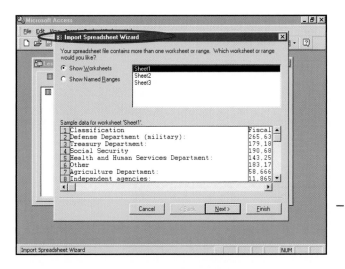

6 Click the **Expenses** file and then click the **Import** button. The **Import Spreadsheet Wizard** dialog box opens.

7 Make sure the **Show Worksheets** option is selected and that **Sheet1** is highlighted.

In Depth: A spreadsheet must be set up like a database table, if you are going to import it successfully. Check to make sure that the Excel data is arranged in rows and columns where each column is a field type and each row is a record. If necessary, copy the data to a new spreadsheet. Remove blank rows or rows that contain decorative characters such as dashes, colons, exclamation points, or other non-numeric or non-alpha characters.

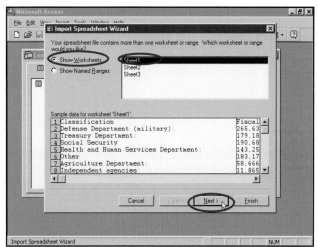

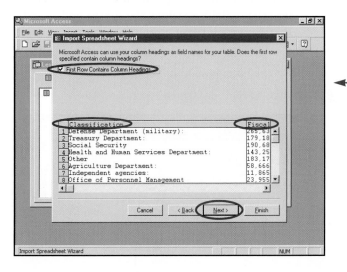

8 Click **Next**. Click the check box next to **First Row Contains Column Headings**. Notice how the row that contains the words **Classification** and **Fiscal** are converted to headers.

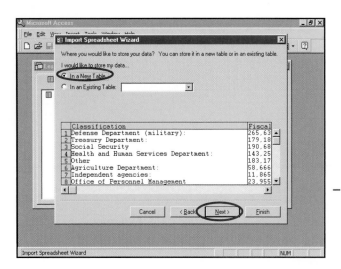

9 Click **Next**. Make sure that the **In a New Table** option is selected.

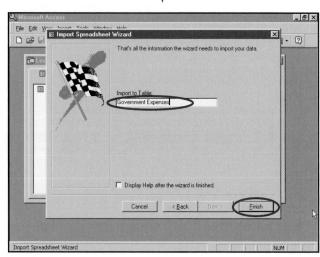

10 Click **Next**. Do not add indexes to any of the fields.

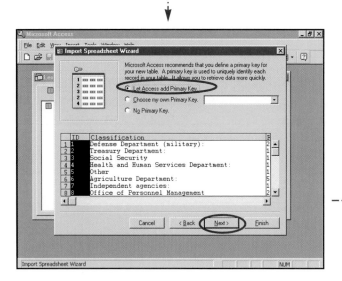

11 Click **Next**. Select **Let Access add Primary Key**, if it is not already selected. In this case, there are no unique fields so we can let Access add a field that gives each row a unique number.

12 Click **Next**. Type **Government Expenses** in the Import to Table: box.

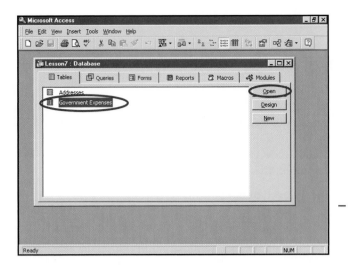

13 Click **Finish**. Click **OK** when prompted. The **Government Expenses** data is added to the database as a new table.

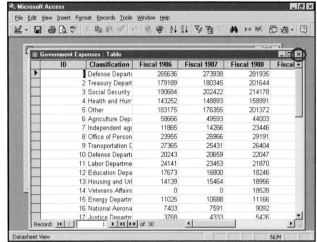

14 Click the **Open** button. The **Government Expenses** table opens.

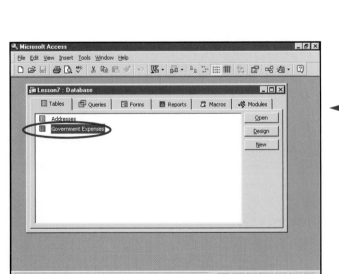

15 Click the **Close Window** button. This table is now available for use. Leave the **Lesson7** database open for the next task.

Task 4

Importing Tables from Other Database Programs

Why would I do this?

Importing a table from another personal computer database management program, such as dBASE or FoxPro, is similar to importing a spreadsheet from Excel. If the data is stored in a format that is not directly supported by Access, you can still import the table after you have saved it as a text file. Most database management programs, including most mainframe database programs, can save a table as a text file.

In this task, you learn how to import a table that has already been saved as a text file for you.

1 Make a copy of the file **Less0703** and name the copy **Parts**.

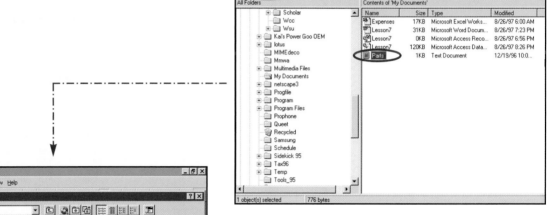

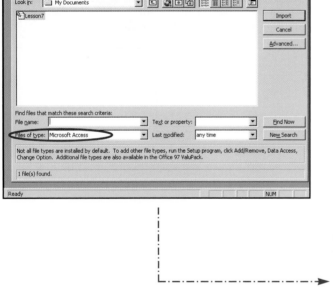

2 Switch to Access and the **Lesson7** database. Choose **File**, **Get External Data**, **Import**. The **Import** dialog box opens.

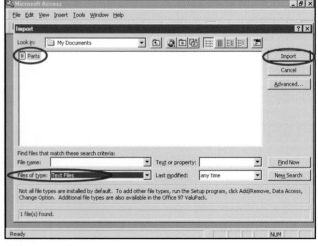

3 Click the list arrow next to the **Files of type** box and click **Text Files**.

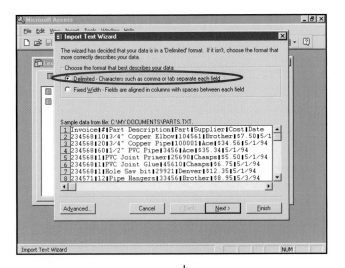

4 Select the **Parts** file and click the **Import** button. The **Import Text Wizard** dialog box opens.

In Depth: An important factor in saving the data as a text file is deciding how to separate the fields. One way is to specify that the position of a certain number of characters in each row represents data for a particular field. For example, characters in positions 3 through 18 might be reserved for the Last Name field. This method is called **Fixed width fields**. Another method is to place a particular character between the data for each field. This method is called **Delimited Fields**. The example you are using has delimited fields; that is, fields have been separated one from another by a special character.

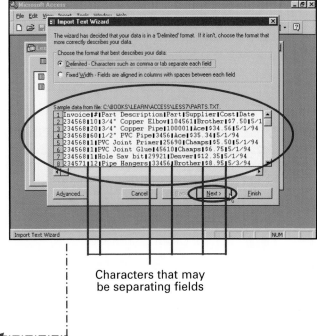

Characters that may
be separating fields

5 Examine the sample data from the **Parts** table. The small black rectangles indicate where the program thinks the separation between fields occurs. In this case, it is correct.

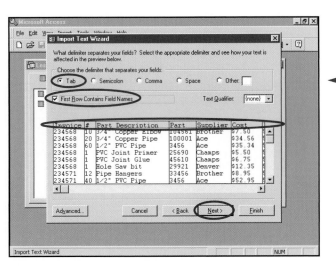

6 Click **Next**. In the next dialog box, you see that this table uses Tab characters to separate the fields. This has been correctly identified by the program. Click the **First Row Contains Field Names** check box.

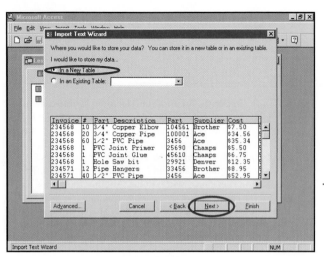

7 Click **Next**. Make sure the **In a New Table** option is selected.

8 Click **Next**. This table does not have a key field and none of the fields need to be indexed. No changes are needed.

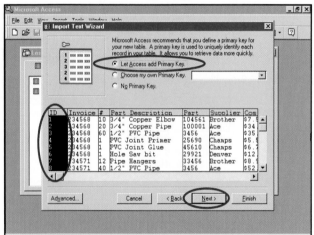

9 Click **Next**. If it is not already selected, select the **Let Access add Primary Key** option. The **ID** field is added to the table.

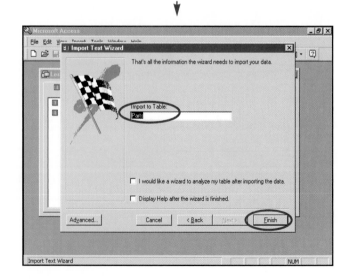

10 Click **Next**. Type **Parts** in the **Import to Table** box.

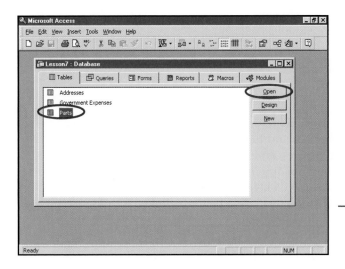

11 Click **Finish**. Click **OK** when prompted that the table has been imported successfully.

12 Click **Open** to examine the **Parts** database table. It contains records about items that have been purchased.

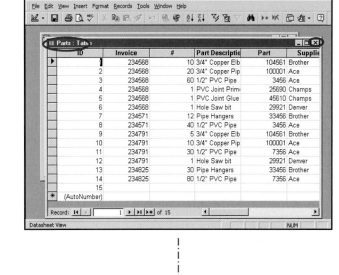

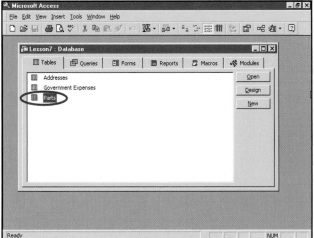

13 Click the **Close Window** button. The **Parts** table is now available for use. Leave the **Lesson7** database open for the next task.

Task 5

Adding Hyperlinks to the Database

Why would I do this?

Sometime you may need to make the data in your database available to others in your office or workgroup. Likewise, you may need to link to information that is contained in another file without making the data part of your file. Access 97 is capable of using hyperlinks in its forms, tables, and queries. A *hyperlink* links or connects a word or object in one document to a word or object in another document. This type of connection can be made between spreadsheets, documents, graphic programs, or databases. A hyperlink can be made in a table by specifying that the field is a hyperlink. Clicking a hyperlink quickly jumps you directly to the linked location so you can reference that information.

In this task, you learn how to modify the **Addresses** table to include hyperlink addresses for those individuals who have home pages.

1 Click the **Addresses** table and click **Design**. The **Addresses** table opens in Design View.

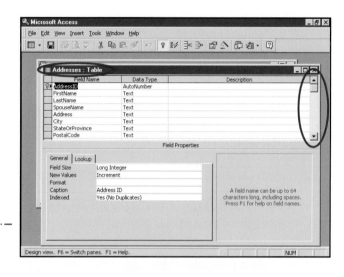

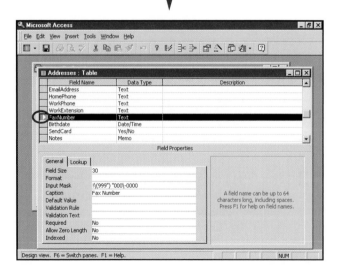

2 Scroll down the list of field names and click the row selector for the **FaxNumber** field.

3 Click the **Insert Row** button. A blank row is inserted in the design.

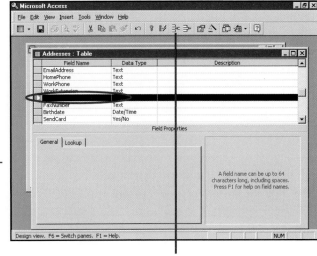

Insert Row button

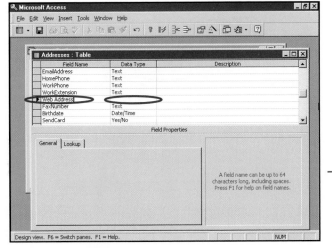

4 Click in the blank Field Name box and type **Web Address**.

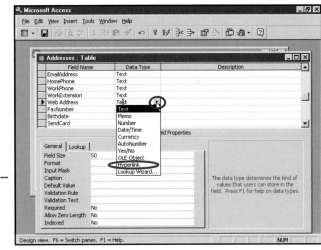

5 Tab to the **Data Type** box and click the list arrow.

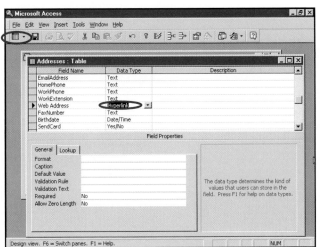

6 Click **Hyperlink**. This type of field may be used to store Internet links or links to other files.

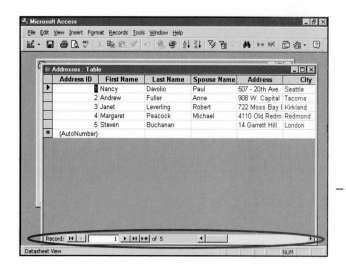

7 Click the **View** button to switch to **Datasheet View**. Click **Yes** to save the changes to the table.

8 Scroll to the right to find the **Web Address** field and click in the box for the first record.

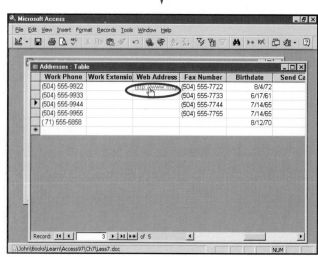

9 Type **http://www.mcp.com/queet** in the **Web Address** box for the first record. This is the web address of the Que Education and Training group of Macmillan Publishing Company.

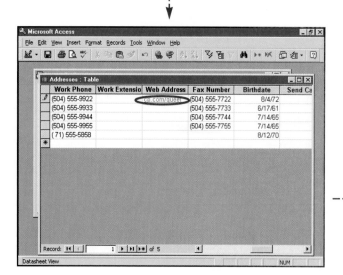

10 Click some other part of the table and then move the pointer back to the web address. The pointer changes to a small hand.

11 If you have an Internet connection, click the address. Your registered browser opens and connects to this site.

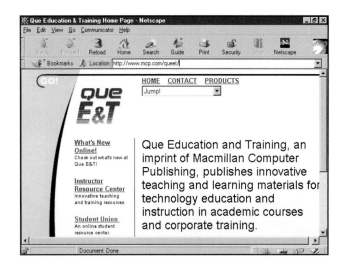

Pothole: The screen you see may look different from the one in the figure. This is a live Internet site, and the screen is subject to change by the company that owns it.

12 Close the browser. Close the **Lesson7** table.

Task 6

Getting Help Using the Office Assistant

Why would I do this?

This book provides an introduction to many Access topics. There are, however, many more Access features than have been covered here. Fortunately there are many powerful tools at your disposal to help you expand your working knowledge of Access and to answer your specific application questions. There is an entire help manual on disk that comes with Access that can be searched electronically.

In this task, you learn how to use the Office Assistant, one powerful Access help tool, to find out more about the use of the greater than (>) symbol.

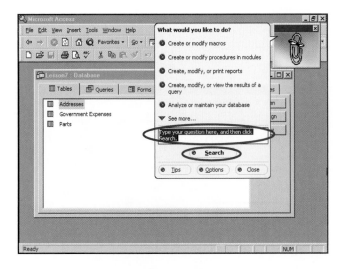

1 Select **Help**, **Microsoft Access Help**. The Office Assistant opens.

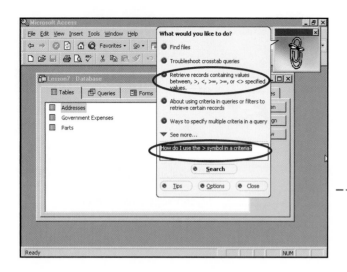

2 Type **How do I use the > symbol in a criteria?** and click the **Search** button. The Office Assistant scans your sentence for key words, looks up topics that are related to your request, and displays them.

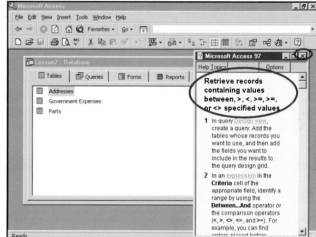

3 Click the third suggested topic that shows examples of operators used to retrieve records. Read the **Help** screen to see the different types of criteria that you can use to select records for inclusion in a query.

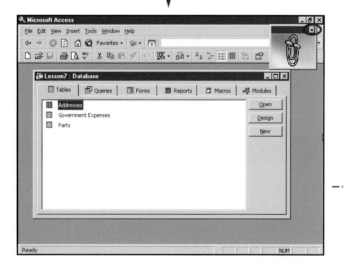

4 Close the **Help** window.

5 Close the **Office Assistant**. Close the **Lesson7** Database window, but do not exit Access.

Task 7

Getting Help On the Internet

Why would I do this?

Sometimes the program does not behave as you think it should and the help manual included with the program does not answer your question. Another place to get help is to go to Microsoft's online support on the *Internet*, an interconnection of world wide computer networks, where you can search their knowledge base. If that does not help, you can go to the newsgroups section and post your question. Other users and experts from around the world see your question and post their suggestions or share their experiences.

In this task, you learn how to go to Microsoft's support web page and use several types of help.

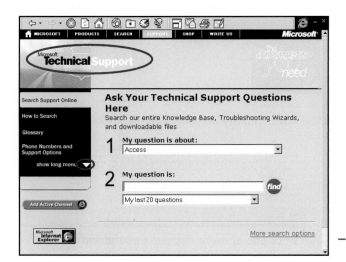

1 Choose **Help**, **Microsoft on the Web**, **Online Support**. If your computer is connected to the Internet, the **Microsoft Technical Support** page opens.

In Depth: Pages change rapidly on the Internet and it is likely that Microsoft's Technical Help page will change several times during the useful life of this book. If the pages you see are not the same as those shown in the book, you should still be able to find the same topics that are discussed. The browser that you use may also differ from the one illustrated here (Internet Explorer 4.0 using the Full Screen option).

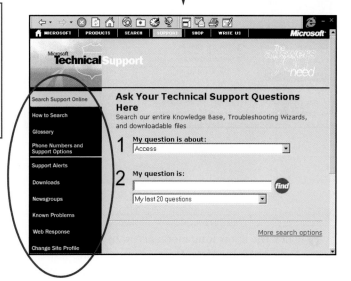

2 Examine the options at the left side of the screen. If necessary, click the show long menu arrow.

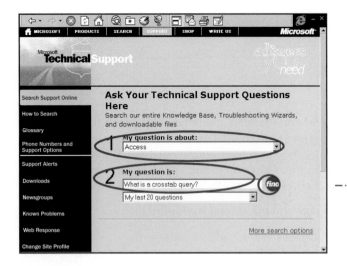

3 Make sure that **Access** is selected in box 1 and type a question about **Access** into the second box.

4 Click the **find** button next to the question. Explore the different options that are available from this window.

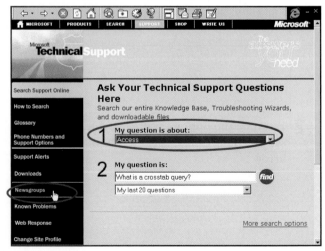

Your search for *what is a crosstab query?* found the following articles:

1. **ACC: Changing Column Headings in a Crosstab Query Using Code**
   Excerpt from this page: Moderate: Requires basic macro, coding, and interoperability skills. This article shows you how to change the column headings in a crosstab query using Visual Basic for Applications. This article assumes that you are familiar with Visual Basic fo... *(size 11,313 bytes, updated 11/10/97 9:09:54 PM GMT)*

2. **ACC: Tips for Optimizing Queries on Attached SQL Tables**
   Excerpt from this page: Advanced: Requires expert coding, interoperability, and multiuser skills. Special considerations must be made for performance optimization of queries built on attached SQL database tables. An SQL database, for this article, is defined as any clien... *(size 11,992 bytes, updated 11/11/97 2:35:24 AM GMT)*

3. ACC: Total Row Not Reset Switching from Crosstab to Make Table

Click one or more of these options and explore

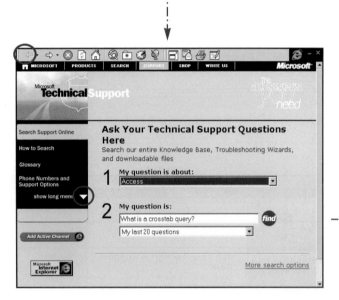

5 Click the **Back** button repeatedly until you return to the opening page, **Microsoft Technical Support**.

6 Click the **show long menu** arrow to reveal the **Newsgroups** option. Newsgroups provide the ability to read and ask questions about **Access**. The advice that is given here is from other users and is not guaranteed to be accurate, but it is often a good place to go if you cannot find the answer anywhere else.

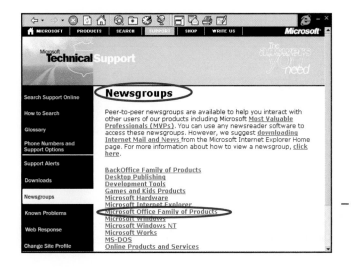

7 Click **Newsgroups**. The Newsgroup reader that is registered on your computer opens. (You may have a different newsgroup reader installed on your computer. If you do not have a newsgroup reader installed or it is not available at your location, skip the rest of this task.)

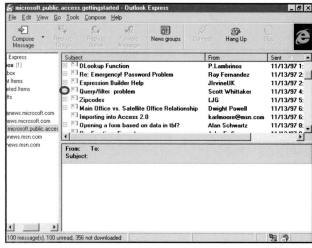

8 Click the appropriate selections to get to the newsgroups related to **Access**. (The options used change often. At the time of this writing, they were **Microsoft Office Family of Products**, **Access**, and **Access Database Getting Started**.) A list of messages is displayed.(Note: The messages on your screen will be dated with current dates.) Messages with a + sign next to them have responses.

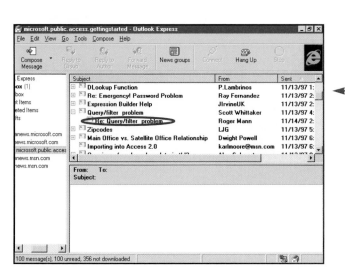

9 Click the + sign next to one of the messages. The response(s) to the message are listed. The title of a response begins with **Re:**.

10 Double-click a response to open it. The original message is repeated with each line marked with a > symbol.

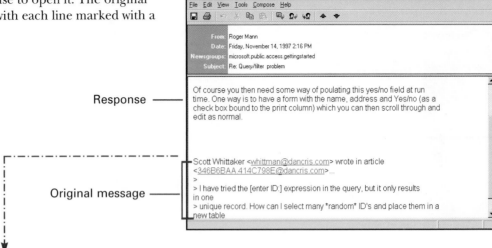

Response ———

Original message ———

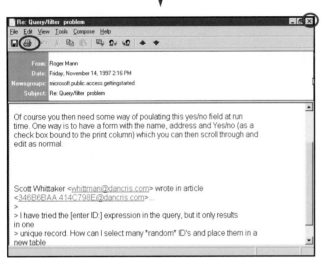

11 Click the **Print** button on your **Newsreader's** toolbar to print a copy of the message. (Your printer options will be different depending on the browser and your printer setup.)

12 If necessary, click **OK** to print. Close your Newsgroup window to return to your Internet browser.

Task 8

Finding Reference Books and Self-Help Textbooks

Why would I do this?

Computer software is constantly changing, and you will need to upgrade your skills or add new skills. You may not have time to take a class or feel that you do not need to know as much as an entire class would cover. In some cases you may have an occasional need for a very specific tool in Access that is not covered in a class. In these situations, it is valuable to have additional resources available. If you found this book to be easy to use on your own, you may want to use one of the other books in the **Learn** series to teach yourself Word, PowerPoint, Excel, Windows 95, or the Internet.

Another type of book you may consider is a reference book. These are not designed to be read from cover to cover but are used to find detailed instructions on how to perform specific tasks. Most of the large publishing houses have web sites where you can look at descriptions of their books and place orders for them.

In this task, you will take a look at Que's web site as an example. You will also see how to use the Web toolbar in Access with your browser.

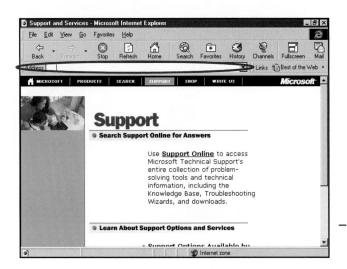

1 Click the **Address** box. Delete the address that is currently displayed.

In Depth: Access97 has a Web toolbar that can be opened and closed by clicking the Web Toolbar button. This toolbar looks like the toolbar you see on a Web page. You can use this bar to enter a URL address and press ↵Enter to activate a search on the Web where information can be accessed electronically.

2 Click the Address box to select the current address. Type **http://www.queet.com/** in the **Address** box and press ↵Enter. The program automatically launches your registered browser, if it is not already running, and opens Que Education and Training's home page.

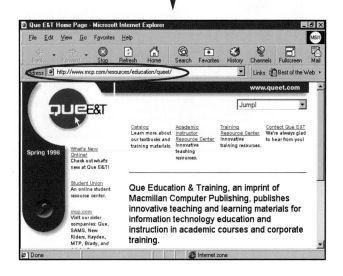

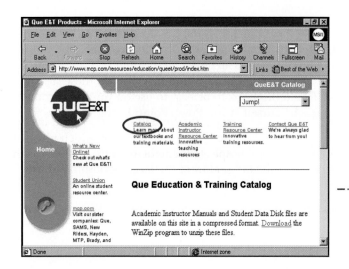

3 Click the **Catalog** hyperlink to see a list of Que's books.

4 Scroll down the page and find the list of book series that includes the **Learn** series. Click the **Learn** hyperlink.

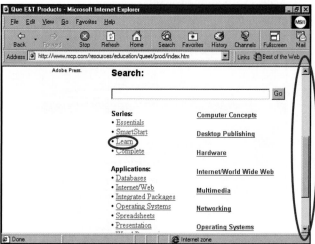

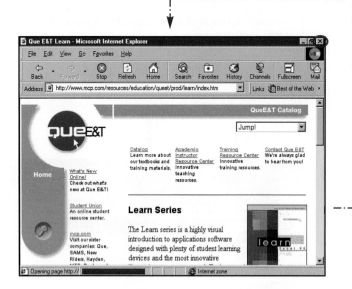

5 This page displays information about the other books in this series. It also has hyperlinks to other book series by Que that take different approaches in terms of the depth and illustration of the lessons. Close the **browser**.

6 Close **Access**, unless you plan to continue with the following exercises.

In Depth: To find other bookstores, use one of the search programs associated with your browser. Look at your browser's toolbar and click the **Search** button. Search for a key word like **Bookstore**.

Student Exercises

True-False

For each of the following, circle either T or F to indicate whether the statement is true or false.

T   F   **1.** To merge an Access database with a Word document, you must first create the document and then open the database and merge it with the document.

T   F   **2.** One reason to view your merged document before printing is to ensure that the document looks the way you intended.

T   F   **3.** When you print a merged Word/Access document, you must print all the records, rather than just a few records.

T   F   **4.** The Merge function in Access adjusts for multiple address lines and empty fields when it prints a merged document.

T   F   **5.** Text files cannot be imported into an Access database.

T   F   **6.** When importing a spreadsheet file into Access, it is important that the first row of the spreadsheet is set up with field names, and each subsequent row is a record.

T   F   **7.** An important factor when saving a database as a text file is deciding how to separate the fields. One method is the delimited fields method which places a specified character between fields as the separator.

T   F   **8.** A hyperlink connecting documents, spreadsheets, or databases is a shortcut used to link a word or object in one file to a word or object in another file.

T   F   **9.** The only help system available to Access users comes on a disk that can be searched electronically.

T   F   **10.** The Access Office Assistant allows you to ask questions; it then displays topics related to your request.

Identifying Parts of the Access Screens

Refer to the figures and identify the numbered parts of the screen. Write the letter of the correct label in the space next to the number.

1. _____
2. _____
3. _____
4. _____
5. _____
6. _____
7. _____
8. _____
9. _____

A. Button used to return to previous location
B. View Merged Data button
C. Print button
D. Box where you can indicate the Microsoft program you want help with
E. Record number
F. Mail Merge toolbar
G. Used to insert fields from the database
H. Save button
I. Mail Merge button

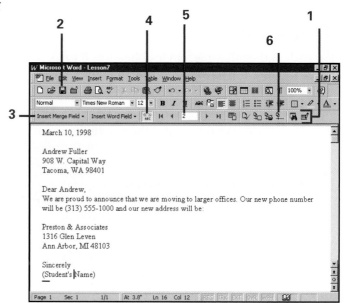

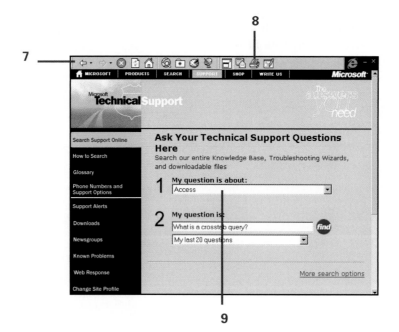

Matching

Match the statements below to the word or phrase that is the best match from the list. Write the letter of the matching word or phrase in the space provided next to the number.

1. ___ Office Assistant

2. ___ Button used to merge data from Access with a form letter or other document designed in Word

3. ___ Allows you to link an Access database with Word or Excel

4. ___ In Word, this is used to work with a merged document

5. ___ Button which opens the Merge dialog box

6. ___ An example of a web address

7. ___ Command which allows you to import files into Access

8. ___ Button used in Word to insert fields from a database into a form letter or document

9. ___ The title of a response in the on-line help found under Newsgroups starts with this

10. ___ Online support available from Microsoft

A. Insert Merge Field button

B. http://www.mcp.com/queet

C. File, Get External Data, Import

D. Microsoft Access Support Home Page

E. View Merge Data button

F. Resident Help feature of Access used to search for key words

G. Mail Merge toolbar

H. Office Links button

I. Re:

J. >

K. Mail Merge button

Application Exercises

Copy **Less0704** and rename it as **Exercise7** on your disk for use in the following exercises.

Exercise 1 – Importing a Table from Excel

1. Launch Access and open **Exercise7**.

2. Choose **File**, **Get External Data**, and **Import** from the menu.

3. Specify **Microsoft Excel** in the **Files of type** box and import the **Less0705** Excel file.

4. Import the first sheet and specify that the first row contains column headings.

5. Import both columns of the sheet into a new table.

6. Select the Year column as the primary key.

7. Name the table **Population Projection**.

8. Open the new table and review it.

9. Print the table and then close it. Leave the database open for use in the next exercise.

Exercise 2 – Importing a Table from an Old dBASE III Database

A common database for personal computers in the 1980s was dBASE III. Many database records from that period are stored in that format. In this exercise you will import data from 1987 that shows information about retail establishments and their employees in Michigan. (Sales and Payroll are in 1000s.)

1. Choose **File**, **Get External Data**, and **Import** from the menu.

2. Specify **dBASE III** in the **Files of type** box and import the **Less0706** dBASE file.

3. Open the table.

4. Click the record selector button to the left of the first record (zip code 00000).

5. Shift-click the record selector next to the tenth record (zip code 48010) to select the first ten records.

6. Choose **File**, **Print**.

7. Click **Selected Record(s)** in the **Print Range** section of the **Print** dialog box.

8. Click **OK**.

9. Close the table. Leave the database open for use in the next exercise.

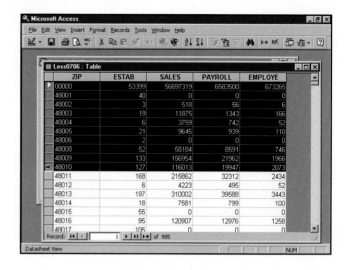

Exercise 3 – Merging a Word Document and an Access Query

You can merge documents with queries as well as with tables. In this exercise you will use a query that has been created to include only those records which have a birth date in August and have a **Yes** in the **SendCard** field. When this query is used, you combine the filtering capabilities of Access with the Word processing power of Word.

1. Click the **Queries** tab and make sure the **August Birthdays** query is selected.

2. Click the list arrow next to the **OfficeLinks** button on the Standard toolbar and select **Merge it with MS Word**.

3. Create a new document that could be used by an organization to wish someone a happy birthday. Include all of the query's fields in the document except for **AddressID**, **Expr1**, and **SendCard**.

4. Include your name in the document.

5. Save the document as **Birthday**.

6. Print the two letters.

7. Close the document and the database.

Exercise 4—Getting Help Using the Office Assistant

The **August Birthdays** query in the preceding exercise used the **DatePart** function. In this exercise, you will find out more about this function using the **Office Assistant**.

1. Click the **Office Assistant** button on the Standard toolbar. It is the far right button with the question mark.

2. Type **Tell me more about DatePart** and click **Search**.

3. Select **Extract part of existing date values using a calculated field** and read the description.

4. Click **Options**, **Print Topic**.

5. Close the **Office Assistant**.

Exercise 5—Getting Help on the Internet

If you cannot find the help you need in the Office Assistant you can try the online help over the Internet. In this exercise you will connect to Microsoft's support site and get more help on the DatePart function.

1. Click **Help**, **Microsoft on the Web**, and **Online Support**.

2. Make sure that **Access** is in box 1 and type **DatePart** in box 2 on the **Technical Support** page.

3. Click **Find**.

4. Scroll through the list of articles and look for an article named **ACC2: DatePart(), DateDiff() Functions Ignore Global Settings**. (If this article is no longer available when you use this site, return to the previous page and enter another feature of Access that you would like to look up.)

5. Use your browser's Print button to print this two-page description.

6. Close your **browser**.

Glossary

Autoform   a form that will list all of the fields in a table.

Columnar report   a type of report that prints the fields of each record in a single column.

Combo box   on a form, a text box that presents a drop-down list of options for data that can be selected for a field. With a combo box you also have the option to enter data manually if the options presented do not contain the correct information.

Comparison operators   used in queries to compare data to a specific condition. Equal is assumed in a criteria unless modified by a comparison operator. Comparison operators include (less than) <, (greater than) >, (equal) =, (less than or equal) <=, (greater than or equal) >=, (not equal) <>, Between . . . And, Like, In.

Concatenated field   a field that combines two fields or expressions to form a new field.

Control   a graphical object on a form or report that is used to display data, perform an action, or make a form or report easier to read.

Criteria   used in a query to restrict data to those records that meets certain conditions.

Crosstab query   displays summarized values (sums, counts, and averages) from one field in a table and groups them based on at least two other fields.

Data type   used in a table to specify the kind of information that will be entered in a field. The most common data type is text.

Database   a management system that allows the user to store, retrieve, analyze, and print large amounts of data.

Database Wizard   a program that creates a database by guiding you through a series of options.

Datasheet View   displays the data in rows and columns.

Date   a data type used to store and display dates.

Default Values   values that are pre-set. Default values will automatically be filled in when a new record is added unless overwritten.

Design View   a view of a database object that is used to examine or modify the object.

Detail section   the area of a form or report where records from the form or report source are displayed.

Dynaset   the results of running a query.

Field   a single category of data or information that makes up a record.

Field selector   the column label at the top of each column in Table view, used to select the whole column.

Filter   a method used on a form to limit the data to records that meet certain conditions.

Form   a database object used to display or edit one record at a time.

Hyperlinks   a connection to other documents, spreadsheets, or databases on your computer or on the Internet.

Input Mask   a filed property applied in a table, that creates a format so data containing dashes or parentheses is entered in a consistent way. Common examples include social security numbers, zip codes, and phone numbers.

Internet   an interconnection of worldwide computer networks.

Label   text in a form or report that is not data, usually the field name.

Label box   a control on a form or report that contains descriptive text such as a title or caption.

List box   on a form, a text box that presents a list of options from which to choose data. With a list box, the list always shows on the screen and you can only select from the options that are presented.

Macros   one of the six objects in a database. Macors are used to automate existing Access commands. Sometimes macros consist of a series of commands that may be attached to buttons on forms, tables, or queries.

Memo   a data type that is used for unstructured comments.

Modules   one of the six objects in a database. Modules are programs in the Visual Basic programming language used to customize the database for special needs.

Navigation buttons   allow you to move through the records by moving to the next record, previous record, to the end, or the beginning of the records.

Objects   a general term for the six parts of an Access database: tables, queries, forms, reports, macros and modules.

One-to-many relationship   a relationship where data in a field occurs one time on the first table and many times in the related table.

Page Footer   the area at the bottom of a form or report that will show the same information on each page when the object is printed.

Parameter queries   queries that use values to define output as part of the query structure.

Parameters   values that define output.

Pivot table   an interactive table that performs calculations; most often used to analyze large amounts of complex data.

Placeholder   a rectangle that shows the position of an object that is being moved.

Primary key   used to designate a field that contains a unique value for each record.

Primary Key fields   a field that has unique values for each record and that are used to speed up sorting and finding data in a large table and to link tables together.

Query   one of the six objects in a database. Queries are used to sort, search, and limit the data to just those records that you need to see.

RAM   a type of computer memory that is fast enough to keep up with the processor but requires constant power to function.

Record   a group of data pertaining to one event, transaction, or person. The categories of information in a record are called fields.

Record selector   the small box to the left of each record on the table's Datasheet View that allows you to select all of the fields in a record.

Relational databases   Datablases that use related tables.

Reports   one of the six objects in a database. Reports are sued to summarize information for printing and presentation of the data.

Select query   a query that can be used to filter records, sort, and limit the fields included.

Tab order   the order the cursor follows in moving from field to field in a form.

Tables   one of the six objects in a database. Tables store data and are the foundation of the database.

Template   a pre-designed form or format that can be used instead of creating one of your own.

Text   a data type in a table that is readable content. May be used to store short phrases or words, or numbers that will not be used in calculations such as phone numbers or social security numbers.

Text box   a box on a form that show data from a field or calculation.

Union query   a union query has the same properties as a select query plus the ability to use fields from more than one table if the tables are related.

Wildcard   a symbol that is used to search for unspecified characters. An asterisk (*) can be used as the first or last character in a string of characters to match any number of characters.

Yes/No   a data type in a table used to store data that can only have two logical states.

Index